A Souvenir
for Howard & Karin
from Mary - Australia 200

EXTREME
SOUTH

First published in 1999 by Australian Geographic Pty Ltd
PO Box 321, Terrey Hills NSW 2084, Australia
Phone: (02) 9450 2344, fax (02) 9450 2990
email: books@ausgeo.com.au

Managing Director: Paul Gregory
Publisher: Howard Whelan
Production/Creative Director: Tony Gordon
Managing Editor, Books: Averil Moffat

Editor: Peter Meredith
Design and Photographic Edit: Mark Thacker, Big Cat Design
Director of Cartography: Will Pringle
Production Manager: Jozica Crncec
Picture Research: Chrissie Goldrick
Cartographer: Wendy Boyce-Davies
Proofreading: Laraine Newberry
Editorial Assistant: Sandy Richardson

Text © Ian Brown
Photography © Ian Brown

Printed in Australia by InPrint

Acknowledgements
For their assistance with the book, Australian Geographic would like to thank: Colin Monteath;
Børge Ousland; David Matthews and Alec Waugh, Arnott's; Margaret Picariello, News Limited;
Peter Boyer, Australian Antarctic Division; Charles Swithinbank; Doug Woods, Anne Kershaw,
Joan Elms, Adventure Network International.

National Library of Australia Cataloguing-in-Publication Data:

Brown, Ian, 1954-,
Extreme South

Includes index.
ISBN 1 86276 031 4.

1. Explorers – Australia – History. 2. South Pole – Discovery and exploration – Australian. I. Title.
919.8904

*Page 1: On the Sallee Snowfield; pages 2–3: Sastrugi on the Polar Plateau;
pages 4–5: Climbing Wujek Ridge; this page: Blizzard on the Ronne Ice Shelf;
pages 8–9: Passing the Forrestal Range; page 10: Camp on Berkner Island*

EXTREME
SOUTH

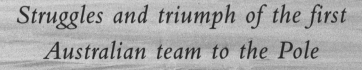

*Struggles and triumph of the first
Australian team to the Pole*

Ian Brown

CONTENTS

DEDICATION

To my family, especially Marianne, Cale, Holly and my mother Doris: who put up with so much and then waited some more. To John Leece: without whose faith and untiring efforts we never would have left. To Keith and Peter: because we not only left, we finished. And to our sponsors, supporters and everyone else who helped and trusted us.

ACKNOWLEDGEMENTS

This book has involved the labour of many people, but remaining imperfections and oversights are my responsibility alone. Expeditioners Peter Treseder, Keith Williams and John Leece trusted me with their diaries and notes and granted me the freedom to include their thoughts. Each of them provided valuable comment on the manuscript, the first chapter was written with extensive input from John and Keith was the main contributor to the food appendix. My editors Peter Meredith, Ian Connellan and Averil Moffat supplied the necessary rigour when I could no longer see the blizzard for the snowflakes, and saved the reader from an excess of adjectives.

The book could never have been written without the support of my wife, Marianne Bate. She and our children put up with too much time when I just wasn't there. The assistance of the New South Wales National Parks and Wildlife Service is gratefully acknowledged.

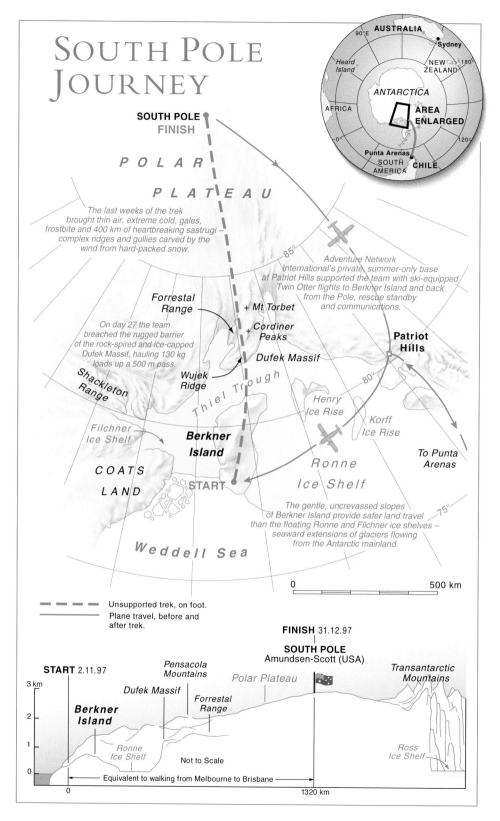

SOUTH POLE JOURNEY

AUSTRALIA
Sydney
90°E
Heard Island
NEW ZEALAND
180°
ANTARCTICA
AFRICA
AREA ENLARGED
0°
120°
Punta Arenas
SOUTH AMERICA
CHILE

SOUTH POLE
FINISH

P O L A R

P L A T E A U

The last weeks of the trek brought thin air, extreme cold, gales, frostbite and 400 km of heartbreaking sastrugi – complex ridges and gullies carved by the wind from hard-packed snow.

85°

Adventure Network International's private, summer-only base at Patriot Hills supported the team with ski-equipped Twin Otter flights to Berkner Island and back from the Pole, rescue standby and communications.

Forrestal Range

+ *Mt Torbet*

+ *Cordiner Peaks*

On day 27 the team breached the rugged barrier of the rock-spired and ice-capped Dufek Massif, hauling 130 kg loads up a 500 m pass.

Dufek Massif

Patriot Hills

Wujek Ridge

Shackleton Range

Thiel Trough

80°

Henry Ice Rise

Korff Ice Rise

Filchner Ice Shelf

Berkner Island

R o n n e

To Punta Arenas

C O A T S

L A N D

START

Ice Shelf

75°

The gentle, uncrevassed slopes of Berkner Island provide safer land travel than the floating Ronne and Filchner ice shelves – seaward extensions of glaciers flowing from the Antarctic mainland.

W e d d e l l   S e a

0   500 km

- - - - - Unsupported trek, on foot.
───── Plane travel, before and after trek.

FINISH 31.12.97

SOUTH POLE
Amundsen-Scott (USA)

Transantarctic Mountains

START 2.11.97

Pensacola Mountains

3 km

Dufek Massif

Polar Plateau

Forrestal Range

2

Berkner Island

1

Ronne Ice Shelf

Ross Ice Shelf

0

Not to Scale

Equivalent to walking from Melbourne to Brisbane

0   1320 km

FOREWORD

Harsh yet magnificent, Antarctica has intrigued humans ever since the first explorers discovered its existence. Australia has long been involved in Antarctic research and protection. But no Australian team had ever walked to the South Pole, until Keith Williams, Peter Treseder and Ian Brown set out on their journey. I was honoured to be the patron-in-chief for the expedition.

Ian Brown describes how these men face the astonishing physical and mental challenge of walking unassisted to the South Pole. Even before they set out on their trek, they show great belief in themselves, and they set about fund-raising and planning with determination, backed by their great supporter John Leece and a team of helpers. The journey itself, however, stretches them almost beyond the edge of their endurance.

On the way to the Pole, the adventurers face some of the harshest conditions on the planet. Perhaps inevitably, extreme fatigue weakens them and they suffer injuries. The weather worsens their precarious situation. Yet their absolute determination to finish their adventure pushes them on to success.

But determination alone would not have sufficed. This compelling story is also a testament to the importance of cooperation and teamwork. The team's supporters anxiously monitor their progress and send messages of encouragement. And the three men never give up on each other. Each man's health is vitally important. When one man is sick, the others shoulder the burden. They perform their chores and choose their route as a team.

The Australian adventurers shed more light on the discoveries of Antarctic explorers who went before them. These modern men draw inspiration from those of the heroic age, knowing that they too will inspire future generations. Most of us will never face the challenge of walking to the South Pole. However, this story can help us all face the challenges in our own lives. In reading this book, we can each find new courage to persevere through adversity.

As the first team of Australians to walk to the South Pole, these men have added to our knowledge of a unique continent. This inspiring book and the magnificent photographs are a legacy of their journey, reminding us that we all share the responsibility to preserve the rare beauty of Antarctica.

John Howard

JOHN HOWARD, PRIME MINISTER OF AUSTRALIA

INTRODUCTION

My conclusions have cost me some labour from the want of coincidence between accounts of the same occurrences by different eyewitnesses, arising sometimes from imperfect memory, sometimes from undue partiality for one side or the other.

THUCYDIDES (C.460-400 BC), THE HISTORY OF THE PELOPONNESIAN WAR

Thucydides realised that there are as many versions of history as there are participants and observers. My experience with this story has been no different.

Preparing this book has been a journey of rediscovery. I knew mostly what to expect when I began delving into the archaeological relics – the diaries, maps and videotapes – and reliving each day of the expedition, but there were some surprises. The passing of a year can bring new perspectives, fresh under-standings, even if the remembered emotions remain strong.

There are a thousand ways to tell a story. This story is different from the one I expected to write before the walk, and it is not the same one I thought I was writing when I began.

Antarctica is a harsh mentor that may not respect the hopes and wishes of those who go there. Some have found nobility and glory, perhaps a kind of immortality. Others have found strength and power and rejoicing, even spiri-tual renewal. Many find nothing but desolation, the pain and horror of an indifferent, unknowable land. We found all of these things, and more.

Walking to the South Pole is an extremely physical undertaking, but the account of our trek is as much about psychology as physicality. Our venture was a journey into ourselves as well as into a mysterious physical realm. I do not know if, in telling this tale, I have done justice to all who took part. I do not even know if that is possible. The bare facts are beyond dispute, but the reasons that caused events to unfold as they did remain uncertain. A partici-pant who would record events assumes a great responsibility: to avoid always championing his or her own view. Although I hauled a physical burden to the Pole, I may yet have failed to deliver this even more unwieldy moral load.

I have tried to draw most of this narrative not from the smoothed version of later recollection or from the way we might like things to have been, but as much as possible from our pungent personal observations, thoughts and feelings at the time. In this I have had to depend heavily on our diaries, as well as statements we all delivered to the video camera from time to time.

Our diaries varied greatly in the detail they recorded and in the degree of intimacy with which they were written. Keith's was the most succinct, being generally brief and factual, and so this story is most deficient in his perspective. My own journal was the most detailed of all – since I knew I would be writing the book! Peter's, although mainly factual, also included illuminating personal observations. John kept notes and later wrote down his recollections.

Although leavened with input from the journals and recollections of Peter, Keith and John wherever possible, this story is mainly my own. It could only ever be so. In order to preserve the reality and intensity of the experience, I have tried to avoid colouring my record of events with understandings developed later. I may not have always succeeded; it was difficult when I was confronted with records of feelings and thoughts I later found regrettable or wondered how I could have harboured.

I have aimed to convey something of what the journey involved, what it meant to strive for ideals that reached beyond the Pole, to confront not only the whirling forces on that far white continent, but also the turmoil within oneself. In this, at least, I hope I have succeeded.

IAN BROWN, APRIL 1999

PROLOGUE

The telephone rang at my home one evening in August 1995. It was Peter Treseder. "Are you sitting down?" he asked.

"Why?"

"I've got a proposition for you."

I could hear the smile in his voice. I'd had this kind of call from Peter before.

"What is it?" I asked carefully.

"How would you like to ski to the South Pole?"

I began to tremble and sat down, my mind spinning. The proposition was outrageous and scary. I was familiar with the tales of the Heroic Age of Antarctic exploration. I knew that Reinhold Messner, the world's most accomplished mountaineer, had become the first (with Arved Fuchs) to ski most of the way across the continent in 1990. So I understood the significance of Peter's question.

Antarctica! A horrifying place and an awesome prospect, a land alien to human existence, a place of epic struggles, failure and death, but also the greatest wilderness on Earth. Many who had been there had said it was the most beautiful. Any adventurer with breath in their bodies would want to go there. I knew I was going to say yes, and that filled me with apprehension.

"I've just been to see Keith in hospital," Peter said. "He's keen to go but thought we should have a party of three. He suggested you, and I agreed." Our mutual friend Keith Williams was recovering in Sydney's Westmead Hospital from a bout of multiple sclerosis, a disease of the central nervous system.

"Why me?" I asked.

Peter insisted I was a good choice, but I wasn't so sure. I knew he was an elite athlete and Keith wasn't far behind. How would an outdoorsman of average physical ability fare against such a pair in the harshest environment on Earth? It occurred to me that Keith might want a triangle to temper Peter's bent for forced marching. Perhaps Peter had also considered the mix of personalities and needed the photography and writing skills that I could offer.

Peter gave me only sketchy details of his plan and left me to think about it. He knew I could not reject the offer.

I thought back to our first expedition together, in Far North Queensland in 1991. Keith, Peter and I, together with Greg Randall, were standing in waist-high scrub contemplating the next stage of the mountainous skyline of Hinchinbrook Island that we hoped to traverse. It was a magnificent but disheartening sight. It had taken us the whole of the previous day to cover just 2 km, clawing our way up a ridge of scrub-tangled boulders and cliffs. From the top we could either continue the high traverse or escape to the left over Mount Bowen.

"It looks impossible. Let's toss it in," Peter said.

Peter's lack of enthusiasm surprised me. I knew he had just spent two weeks tearing all over Cape York Peninsula by himself, completing 1400 km of river paddling and running, adding to his tally of hundreds of wilderness endurance records. Previously he had run the length of eastern Australia from Cape York to Wilsons Promontory – a distance of 5650 km – in a total of 41 days in three stages and had made the first complete descent of the mighty Jardine River on Cape York Peninsula. He had set records in the Blue Mountains, the Australian Alps, Tasmania, New Zealand, and on the high seas in a sea-kayak.

Distance never bothered him, nor did tough going, but I wondered if enforced slowness was too hard to take.

Soaked and tired, we discussed our preferences. Keith seemed to be cruising, as usual, and was keen to complete what we set out to do, but would go along with whatever we decided.

Although I longed to see what lay ahead, I also feared the appalling scrub was going to continue. Greg Randall was still amazed at what he had got himself into. I suggested a compromise: "Let's go on a bit further. I reckon it might get easier and we can always pike down the creek if we have to."

Without a lot of enthusiasm, we agreed to push on and moved down towards the saddle. After collecting water, we dragged ourselves up the other side. Five exhausting days later, having completed the 50 km traverse, we had taken our first steps as a team towards the South Pole.

Keith is a lover of mountains and mountain torrents, a climber, skier and kayaker of great skill. He combines faith in himself with great determination and a sometimes fatalistic approach to the vagaries of life, reflecting his strong religious convictions and perhaps in response to the health difficulties he confronts as a mild haemophiliac and multiple sclerosis sufferer. Keith has applied his many skills to a career as an outdoor teacher and program director.

He, too, has a taste for endurance challenges and has completed many runs and fast traverses in the Blue Mountains and Australian Alps. But the high glaciated peaks hold a special fascination for him. In 1990 he skied and climbed throughout the western mountains of the United States and Canada, reaching the summit of Alaska's Mount McKinley (6194 m), or Denali, the highest peak in North America.

I first met Keith at Macquarie University, where I studied during 1973–76. One weekend in 1978, he and I walked 20 km to a remote part of the Colo River, in the northern Blue Mountains, carrying rockclimbing gear. We slept where we stopped and descended into the gorge the next morning. Then we climbed a long route on the wall of the gorge, got down by sunset and walked out next day.

I would study late into the night at the university so I could spend weekends exploring the Blue Mountains. Those blue-tinged deeps directed my life's course. I decided to seek a career connected with the environment and became involved in wilderness conservation. I began to photograph the bush and write of my experiences.

Long trips in wild places, whether by land, river, sea or on vertical walls, are what I love most. It is the journey that enthrals me. Melding with the rhythms of nature, using my body to reach a goal, experiencing a sense of exploration and anticipation – these are what drive my wanderings.

Through happy domestic years, I squeezed in a few major journeys on foot and by ski and sea-kayak – in California's Sierra Nevada and on Cape York Peninsula. It was my first trip to Cape York, in 1987, that brought Peter and me together. During an eight-week exploratory walk, I'd paddled part of the Jardine River with three others. On his run from Cape York to Wilsons Promontory the following year, Peter had been taken by the mystery of the river and its remote headwaters and had decided to attempt its first complete descent. He approached me for information.

As we sat in my Blue Mountains lounge room with a map of the Jardine before us, Peter began firing questions. I was already in awe of his achievements, but as we yarned, other aspects of his personality emerged. This was no hit-and-miss adventurer; this was someone who sought the best information on any project and carefully considered all the pitfalls and how they could be avoided. His job as an investment banker reflected his prudent assessment of risks. He had succeeded on many outrageous outings by combining this methodical approach with determination and focus, both in planning and in execution. When he walked out of my front door, I had no doubt he would succeed on the Jardine.

Peter usually attempted his major challenges alone but on the Jardine he took a team. This was the first time he had done so. "When I'm going into a new environment, I don't like to go alone because it's too unfamiliar and risky," he said. "I like to dip into it with companions and then, if I feel more confident, do something by myself."

In 1992, Keith, Peter and two other bushwalkers completed a four-week journey in Western Australia's remote Kimberley, covering 650 km on foot and by raft. Next, in 1993, the three of us, with three other climbers, scaled Batu Lawi, a dagger-like peak in Borneo.

Peter claims it was his marriage to Beth Ferguson, a teacher, that awoke in him a fascination with Antarctica. While honeymooning in Victoria's Grampians in 1984, he bought a copy of *This Accursed Land*, Lennard Bickel's epic account of Douglas Mawson's 1911–14 Antarctic expedition. He was smitten by the drama and nobility it portrayed.

If the sweep of a life's experiences culminates pyramid-like at the apex of the present moment, one could argue that we had, in some sense, been preparing all our lives for this Antarctic expedition. Although some of those experiences, like walking in the tropics, might seem of little relevance to polar sledging, in fact many of the demands are identical: research, detailed planning, risk management, navigation, strenuous and sustained physical effort, hard living in wilderness for long periods, self-reliance, teamwork, determination. We certainly lacked polar sledging experience, but our combined expertise, generated by dozens of diverse journeys, was an important strength.

Still I was consumed with doubts. Was I up to the longest and toughest journey I had ever contemplated?

CHAPTER 1

GETTING *off*
the GROUND

Scott used to say that the worst part of an expedition
was over when the preparation was finished.

APSLEY CHERRY-GARRARD, THE WORST JOURNEY IN THE WORLD (1922)

I put down the phone, still shaking, and joined my wife Marianne in the kitchen. She knew something was afoot, so I came straight out with it. "That was Peter." I paused, uncertain. "He offered me a place on an expedition to Antarctica."

Her reply was immediate and enthusiastic: "That's fantastic. What an opportunity! Take it!"

Marianne knew as well as I did that I could not let this chance pass, and it is in her generous nature to be enthusiastic and supportive of my outings, at least initially. I could not have contemplated going without her approval. I knew the Antarctic trip would take many weeks, and it was bound to happen during the summer school holidays. Our children, Cale, 9, and Holly, 6, were still a handful and it would be hard on her.

Peter's invitation was no simple ticket to ride. The planning would require a mammoth group effort. Other Australian teams had tried to organise similar Antarctic journeys but had failed to raise enough money. Peter had been discussing his South Pole idea for more than a year with two other adventurers, but at a pivotal meeting they both pulled out. Peter drove straight from the meeting to Keith's bedside.

After Peter's call I rang Keith and discussed the project. Skiing from the edge of Antarctica to the South Pole, anything up to 1400 km, dragging sleds loaded

Just two weeks before we leave for Antarctica, Peter Treseder tests one of our sleds loaded with fellow expeditioner Keith Williams and Cale Brown (my son).

with all our supplies and equipment and weighing 150 kg – it was almost too big a concept to grasp. It would be like spending two months in a kitchen freezer, walking from Melbourne to Brisbane dragging a small wardrobe – and climbing higher than Mt Kosciuszko along the way. There would be no supply depots, no dog teams, no assistance from machines or the wind, no help at all. However, we would have radio contact and rescue backup.

It would have seemed impossible but for the fact that others had done it, though not Australians. I was glad we would be able to learn from them. Our lack of polar experience was a concern but also part of the challenge.

"It's going to be hell," Peter said later, meaning just the trek. He also warned that the budget would be a whopping $600,000, mainly to cover flights to and around Antarctica. We faced a huge struggle to raise this sum, but I knew that Peter, with his reputation, diligence, networking skills and extensive contacts, had a better chance than anybody of getting the necessary support together.

We felt that to justify spending so much on an adventure we should also raise funds for a worthy cause. The expedition seemed an ideal vehicle for this. We also agreed to promote the protection of Antarctica in any way we could. This was particularly important to me as conservation of wilderness had been a common element in my earlier journeys.

I studied books on modern Antarctic sledging expeditions. Even though the expeditioners had been experienced in icy environments, the books were full of the grinding drudgery of hauling in grim conditions. Some of those adventurers were supermen but others weren't. If these less-than-superhuman beings could do it, maybe Keith and I could too. I had no doubts about Peter.

We aimed for the summer of 1996–97. Tasks were identified and allocated. Keith would research food and equipment; I would investigate the route and logistics, refine the budget, devise a name and letterhead and draft a prospectus on the expedition for potential supporters. Peter would do one of the things he excels at: use his network to get support.

If we were going to be the first Australians to walk to the South Pole, we wanted to do it in the best style possible. Apart from having no external support, this meant starting from the true coast of Antarctica, where the permanent ice shelves give way to the open sea in late summer, rather than some way inland. We knew if we failed, or succeeded in a lesser way, we might cruel the chances of other Australian teams to improve on our performance. It would be very difficult to raise finance for a second attempt.

It was a hard slog in those early days. We put together what we thought was a compelling submission. In the last weeks of 1995 we began to hawk it around large firms that we thought might benefit from the imagery of trekking to the

South Pole, of taking on a mighty objective and succeeding against the odds. We received nothing but polite rejections.

We had many barriers to overcome – doubt that these nobodies could make the distance, shock at the money we needed and fear that one of us might die. We must have seemed like fools with a hopeless dream.

We tried to remain undaunted. We knew our goal was reasonable and that, given a fair chance, we could succeed. The universal willingness of those we approached to contribute not money but other kinds of support buoyed us.

Seeking the endorsement of well-known public figures was a key strategy. This would lend our scheme respectability. We pursued support across the political spectrum and soon had NSW Premier Bob Carr and several other political leaders on board as patrons. But the Prime Minister was a harder nut to crack. Not long after Peter had asked Paul Keating to be our patron-in-chief a federal election was announced. It was likely that Keating's Labor government would be defeated. So Peter wrote to Opposition Leader John Howard.

At this stage an acquaintance of Peter's, Dr John Sutton, entered the scene. John was a mountaineer, Australia's foremost expert on high-altitude medicine, a professor at Sydney University and a strong believer in the value of adventure. His connections, energy and commitment boosted our fortunes. John won the support of more political leaders and began putting together a physiological research programme for us to conduct on our journey.

Early in 1996 John and Peter drove home together from another meeting. Next morning John was dead. Just 54 years old, he had died in his sleep of an undiagnosed heart defect. In memory of his passionate belief in adventuring, we agreed to continue the expedition in his honour. We regrouped and pressed on but were forced to abandon hope of an expedition that summer. We would aim for the summer of 1997–98.

Once we'd decided to postpone, Peter quickly activated a plan to cross the Simpson Desert. He reckoned pulling heavy carts loaded with water across this sandy wilderness would be useful training for a South Pole trek.

In the winter of 1996, Peter and Keith successfully made the journey, the first unsupported crossing of the Simpson Desert by its longest axis. The arduous south–north cart-haul of some 550 km took 21 days. Keith told me horror stories of the relentless effort and Peter's determination to keep going all out. Peter's stories, of Keith's body nearly giving out, were nearly as alarming. However, the success of this expedition was fuel for our polar campaign.

John Leece, a partner in a Sydney firm of chartered accountants, rarely takes the time to relax with a newspaper. On the morning of Sunday 1 September 1996 he did. By such chance events are our lives changed.

"Among many depressing stories, I was stopped by a photograph of a fellow pulling a cart through spinifex and desert," John recalled later. "The article really captured my imagination. It was about positive attitudes and achievement against adversity and revealed the adventurer's next ambition was to walk to the South Pole."

John phoned Peter next morning and offered some dollars towards the Antarctic expedition. Peter was less interested in money than in the contacts John might provide, and he pressed him for a meeting. Though reluctant, John was intrigued and agreed to get together. At the meeting his strategic mind quickly grasped the problem we faced: writing to politicians and corporations would not get us to the Pole; phone calls and networking would. John admired Peter's aims, especially those to raise funds for charity and to inspire fellow Australians about setting goals and working to achieve them. These aims were to become the driving focus of John's involvement.

John did not realise it then, but he was hooked. Like John Sutton before him, and many more after, he was seduced by the excitement of adventure and the prospect of being part of something grand.

We agreed that John should approach the Victor Chang Cardiac Research Institute (VCCRI) with an offer to raise money for them. He was initially slow to act but relented before Peter's persistence.

"I decided the only way to get Peter off my back was to make the few phone calls I had promised," he said. "How wrong I was! The guy is tenacious."

In fact they were equally tenacious and gradually solidified into the formidable team needed to achieve the first phase of the expedition – getting it off the ground. John soon joined the expedition as our manager.

The cheapest way for us to get to Antarctica was on one of the US or New Zealand Hercules C-130 planes that service US and New Zealand Antarctic operations from Christchurch. The alternative was to use Adventure Network International (ANI), a company that had been supporting private Antarctic expeditions for 10 years. Using ANI was logistically simple but expensive: the company valued a 200-litre drum of aviation fuel delivered to the South Pole at US$16,000. It charged US$2000 to fly out each empty drum.

An important part of our plan was to involve News Limited, publishers of *The Australian* newspaper. We needed money and we needed media coverage to support the charity aims. With only eight months till our planned departure in October 1997, we had nothing but debts in the bank and little to convince sponsors we were a going concern.

After a long day on regular business, Peter arrived home to find an envelope bearing the words "Office of the Prime Minister". Peter knew that the PM's advisers considered patronage too risky. What if we died during the trek? Opening the envelope, Peter was amazed to find it said the Prime Minister would be delighted to be our patron-in-chief. John Howard must have personally believed in what we were trying to do. Coming the night before the scheduled meeting with News Limited, this was a real shot in the arm.

When Peter and John, together with representatives of the VCCRI, went to see Paul Kelly, at that time *The Australian's* editor-in-chief, they were able to announce that the Spirit of Australia South Pole Expedition had the support of the nation's leader. Paul agreed to incorporate the expedition into the paper's schools program and to approach Lachlan Murdoch, the newspaper's publisher (and later News Limited's chairman and chief executive). John also asked for sponsorship and fundraising promotions through the paper.

While all this was happening in Sydney, Keith and I were working on the nuts and bolts of the expedition from the bush – by fax, telephone and mail. Because of his interest in nutrition, Keith was looking after the critical issue of food, making sure we wouldn't starve like Scott and his men in 1912. Scott ate 18,600 kJ a day; however, based on modern Antarctic expedition experience, Keith figured we needed nearly 25,000 kJ, about three times what a normal diet provides, to prevent us from losing too much weight.

More than just a fuel, food is a key to good morale on any wilderness trek, but more so on sledging journeys, which can be a bit light on pleasure. Keith faced the challenge of making such a large diet both palatable and lightweight. He recorded:

Peter wanted sausages, gravy and mashed potatoes for dinner and plenty of chocolate and sweets for the rest of the day. Ian's preferences included salami, fruit bars and minimal muesli. I don't have a sweet tooth and as a vegetarian I like plenty of vegetables, muesli, nuts, olive oil and cookies.

From these tongue-in-cheek suggestions he developed a basic menu acceptable to all of us and then worked out the quantities and ratio of carbohydrate, protein and fat with the help of nutritionist friend Andrew Howe. Weight was a critical factor. Fats and oils would form a large proportion of the rations because they yield the most energy (kilojoules) per gram. Keith chose olive oil as a healthy source of this energy. He chased potential sponsors and devised packaging for daily portions.

Keith did some work on equipment before handing over that role to me. I researched gear and looked for suppliers and sponsors. We secured Paddy Pallin Adventure Equipment as our major equipment sponsor and adviser, working closely with them on key items like custom-made sleeping bags and parkas.

Boots were a critical issue, especially for Peter. Bony protuberances on his heels had always caused him problems. Previous British sledging teams had used inflexible plastic mountaineering boots and suffered terribly, so we chose softer Norwegian boots developed by polar trekking gurus Børge Ousland and Sjur Mørdre according to a traditional Lapp design. I sent our foot outlines to Oslo where our boots would be specially made.

There was still not a cent in the expedition coffers, not even the promise of a cent (except John's). It was not until March 1997 that persistence paid off in an audience with Lachlan Murdoch. Describing the meeting later, John wrote:

> After Peter laid out a map of Antarctica on his coffee table, Lachlan knelt on the floor and scoured it intensely, talking about the revered Antarctic adventurers of the Heroic Age …
>
> We stated our claims and made our request. As Lachlan traced the routes of Amundsen, Scott and Shackleton, he asked Peter who was his favourite Antarctic explorer. For a moment my heart sank into the depths of my stomach. Come on Peter, I prayed.
>
> "Shackleton," Peter replied.
>
> There was a pause, then Lachlan said, "He's mine too."

Lachlan offered newspaper support as well as funds, perhaps enough to cover our costs if we could get on a US or NZ government plane. However, we soon came to a dead end in our requests for support with transport from either country.

After much negotiation, the Commonwealth Bank became our second major sponsor. The bank also provided legal assistance to draw up all the sponsor contracts. Its insurance arm, Commonwealth Connect, put together a package to cover a rescue during the journey.

Despite these successes, we still did not have enough money for an all-ANI option. Time was running out for a 1997-98 expedition. Peter would not countenance further postponement, fearing another team might beat us to the Pole.

Peter came up with another idea to make our venture fit the available funding, based on a growing perception that Keith and I were perhaps losing our enthusiasm. Calculating that we might have enough money to take just two of us to Berkner Island, he suggested we all draw straws. Keith and I said Peter should definitely go, and since I thought I was the least physically capable, I suggested Keith should go with him.

The notion that I could put in all that effort and still not end up going on the trek sapped my resolve to continue. Keith, on the other hand, accepted the possibility of missing out with equanimity. He was also concerned about going without me because he was familiar with Peter's demanding style. I felt the same, so we both wanted the three of us to go.

With all these emotional cross-currents at work, we met at Peter's Wahroonga home in early June to discuss the possibility of cutting the team to two. It was the first time John had met Keith. Peter asked Keith and me if we were committed to the expedition. He was actually asking if we would commit ourselves even if at the end of the day one of us might not go. I was not afraid of going, but of NOT going, especially if I had to continue the effort of preparation. Keith must have been thinking likewise, because we were both reluctant to take a stand either way. John saw this as a lack of enthusiasm. He reported later:

> Peter clearly was committed and was going. The question did not have to be asked of him. After a while, Keith said almost half-heartedly he would be in it. I wondered if Keith and Ian were waiting to see who would commit first. There was an air of reluctance, I thought, when Ian finally said, "I need to speak to Marianne."

I drove back to the Blue Mountains late that night. Subtle signals had suggested that the commitment to getting us all to the Pole was actually quite strong, especially in John. I assessed that the risk of missing out was low and, after discussing it with Marianne, I decided to take the chance. There was never again any serious discussion that we would not be a team of three.

John decided to try another angle to get us all to Antarctica. As the new national treasurer of Scouts Australia, he was able to win the organisation's support for the charity campaign. It would provide the campaign's foot soldiers, be recognised as a major expedition partner and use the expedition to promote scouting. Its retail arm, Snowgum, would provide some of our equipment.

Thanks to John's determination and altruism, this symbiosis with Scouts Australia was to prove a vital component of the expedition's success. The strategy succeeded because of the commitment of the energetic Chief Commissioner of NSW, David Kitchin, and NSW Chief Executive Hilton Bloomfield, who recognised the potential for raising the profile of scouting among the youth of Australia and threw everything into it.

John had also taken on the task of finding a sponsor for a proposed scout television series. He arranged a meeting with Brian Paterson of the event management consultancy firm, Paterson & Associates, to discuss sponsorship for both the expedition and the television series.

Peter and John made their pitch in June 1997, when Brian was working on behalf of the biscuit giant Arnott's. He had put to them the idea of an adventure store at Sydney's Darling Harbour to be known as Arnott's Adventures and was looking for a "big adventure" to help promote the idea. Arnott's quickly agreed to become our largest financial sponsor. Through Brian Paterson, they would spend big dollars promoting our cause, the expedition and scouting; they would produce a television documentary before the expedition, print material and provide major prizes for the charity fundraising. They also provided a publicity agent to give the expedition and all our sponsors exposure.

By the middle of 1997 we were becoming a small industry, with tentacles everywhere. It was time to officially launch the expedition and on 24 July more than 30 sponsor representatives and other key players crammed into a stuffy room at the NSW scout headquarters in Sydney's suburban Haberfield. Peter explained the journey and John described the organisation needed to achieve it. Keith was not there, unable to take leave from his managerial job at the Lake Burrendong Sport and Recreation Centre. John was concerned at Keith's apparent stubbornness.

We still had no money in the bank and no signed contracts in our hands, but we had plenty of promises. The behemoth was on its way. From the launch it was only 11 weeks to D-Day, our expected departure day late in October.

Immediately after the launch I made our first major financial commitment by ordering custom-made sleds from Snowsled in England. I was also dealing with equipment suppliers in Australia and around the world to put together our kit, and working to get smaller product sponsors to provide us with navigation equipment, batteries, photographic equipment, film and other essentials. Another of my responsibilities was sorting out the route, maps and navigation techniques. I made many phone calls in the middle of the night to Norway, the US, the UK and other countries.

With a team of about 35 volunteers, John was busy coordinating the major sponsors, scouts, fundraisers and promotions. The network spawned by our journey had developed a life of its own.

Arnott's had already agreed to custom-make high-energy, low-moisture biscuits for the walk according to a recipe developed by Keith and his wife, Leanne, and refined in the Arnott's lab. An attempt to base the fundraising scheme around these biscuits failed, but a new plan was quickly adopted. Scouts Australia embraced the Trekathon concept, whereby 140 groups from around Australia would walk 10 km each, roughly equivalent to the total distance of our polar trek, with each participant being sponsored for the charities. Owing to the Christmas break, the Trekathon would have to take place on 30 November. Although the Scouts rose to the demand, some schedules cracked under pressure of time.

By this time we had enough promises of money to fund a trek either from the ANI summer base at Patriot Hills, at the southern end of the Ellsworth Mountains, or nearby Hercules Inlet. Although both sites were at least close to the geological coast of Antarctica, they were some distance "inland" from the true Antarctic coast, and more than 300 km closer to the Pole than our preferred starting point on Berkner Island, in the Weddell Sea. There was no other major sponsor on the horizon who could make up the shortfall. Would we have to settle for the shorter route which would be second best?

We originally hoped to practise sled-hauling on Australia's winter snowfields, but the late commitment forced a compressed preparation. We finally made two trips to Kosciuszko National Park in the spring. The first was to take promotional shots. On the second trip, less than three weeks before D-Day, we hastily tested our equipment – much of it only just arrived from overseas – performed for the documentary and received rudimentary instruction on using the video cameras.

On a small patch of wet snow near a road, we piled three people into the one sled we'd received from England and began dragging it. It slid beautifully; one person could pull it even with 200 kg aboard. This boosted our confidence, even if it was later to prove misleading.

Back home we tried to squeeze in some physical training. It was only in the last weeks before our departure that we began in earnest the traditional preparation for polar sledging – dragging tyres along the street. I had been running for nearly two years, trying to reach the fitness level that Peter and Keith seemed to maintain with much less effort. I ran all over the Blue Mountains, up to 40 km at a time. On the coldest morning of the 1997 winter, I ran down into the Hartley Valley and developed sore, itchy spots inside my arms and on my belly. It was −12°C that morning, but I didn't realise until later, in Antarctica, that I'd suffered frostnip, superficial freezing of the first layer of skin.

D-Day was 20 October 1997. Flights were booked from Sydney to Punta Arenas in southern Chile, the site of ANI's main operational base. With John and his team struggling to raise the last funds for the Berkner Island option, we still had not decided where we would start our trek. Promises were received from KPMG, Roche, Boerhinger Mannheim and Coles Myer. ANI were clamouring for their money and signed contracts. The commercial air fares and freight to southern Chile were another unresolved expense.

Australian Geographic and Dick Smith entered the fray. They were understandably a little miffed that they'd had to approach us so late in the piece to see if they could be involved, but we did have reasons. Because Australian Geographic was then owned by Fairfax, a rival of News Limited, we thought sponsorship from both groups might cause too many problems.

Still, it was perhaps inevitable that they would get involved. Dick and Australian Geographic had supported many of Peter's previous exploits, including those involving Keith and me; our philosophies were similar; founding editor Howard Whelan had given us valuable early advice; and both Dick and Howard had a long-standing interest in Antarctica and polar adventuring. Just before we departed, Australian Geographic offered sponsorship, but we could not accept it until News Limited approved. This meant more ticklish negotiations for John, but he emerged with a tight agreement on media rights.

Two days before our departure, we still did not have enough promises banked. What to do? John was seriously considering pulling the plug while at the same time grappling with a long-held concern: "What if one or all of them die? How could I live with myself if something happened to any of them ... It's too far, it's too cold, they're not experienced in those conditions for such duration. Give up now. Don't risk their lives."

Then, in a magnificent gesture, a benefactor who wished to remain anonymous offered to underwrite the shortfall. It would be a debt we would try to repay but could never promise to. John now had to decide: would he accept and perhaps bear the responsibility of placing our lives at risk?

He did accept, though he remained fearful that he was signing our death warrants. We would get on the 20 October plane. And we would start from Berkner Island.

The final week was a maelstrom of activity. We were trying to organise many crucial aspects of the expedition that should have been given months. It was remarkable that everything came together sufficiently for us to leave.

In a blizzard of faxes and phone calls, I'd spent the last weeks winding up issues at work and arranging the airfreighting of our gear and food to Chile. I built and modified equipment in my garage. I drove all over Sydney picking up batteries, clothes, film and other items from sponsors and suppliers. We visited a podiatrist for advice on looking after our feet. US map offices drove me to distraction because, months after I'd placed orders, maps had still not arrived. We'd had little time to familiarise ourselves with our electronic gear – our Global Positioning System (GPS) satellite-based navigation units, the Argos beacon (which would regularly transmit our position by satellite), the video cameras and the recharging equipment.

We had little sleep in those last days. We suffered bouts of flu, and our stress levels rose to new heights. The vital maps arrived with just days to spare. Keith was still chasing food packets and putting together the all-important medical kit. John and Peter were haggling with sponsors and ANI, trying to complete the financial arrangements. We put in long nights in Peter's garage sorting, modifying and packing food and equipment (including the single sled) in a large timber crate and nine cardboard removalist's cartons. It was a relief to finally see our 450 kg of freight disappear on the back of a truck only three days before our own departure.

Supplies continued to arrive and we would have to take several rucksacks of food on the plane with us. As I drove to the airport with my family I was in a daze. The sense of unreality I was experiencing would persist, in some form, for months. I said to Marianne: "I feel like spending a week in hospital!"

It was a dishevelled bunch of expeditioners that gathered at the airport. Arnott's PR company had everything ready in the VIP room. I was reluctant to have the media watch me saying goodbye to my family at what should have been a private moment. Peter was stressed but on a roll; Keith was missing and John distracted. With the press cameras blazing and still not enough dollars in the bank, we signed some of the last contracts, including the huge financial commitment to ANI. John sent the money to England after we'd arrived in Chile. Days later the Asian financial crisis erupted and the exchange rate plummeted. If that had happened earlier, the expedition would have been sunk.

Fifteen minutes after the scheduled start of the media conference, Keith still hadn't shown up. John was distraught and spoke nervously at the conference, though in fact Peter did most of the talking. I felt like a rare butterfly pinned by the jabs of the flashguns. I wore a multicoloured silk scarf around my neck, a farewell gift from my work colleagues, hand-painted with tropical images and signed with encouraging messages. I knew they would see it on television.

On the table before him, Peter displayed two precious items that we would carry on the journey: the balaclava Sir Douglas Mawson wore in Antarctica, lent by his family, and a good luck charm carved from walrus tusk and carried by Roald Amundsen to the South Pole in 1912, which came to us via Arnott's chief executive, Chris Roberts.

"How are you feeling?" one reporter asked.

Peter drew breath. "Scared," he replied, "not just for the journey but because of the huge infrastructure behind us. I'm scared of failure."

We broke for photos and individual interviews. One young reporter asked us: "Have you read the accounts of the early explorers? Do you think you might be underestimating the seriousness of the journey?"

This went right to the heart of my own fears. There was an implication that we might be naive fools. Perhaps he had sensed our own feelings of inadequacy, or we may have seemed too brash and blasé (though numb is a better description). He clearly regarded the early explorers as above the mortal plane. I knew they were ordinary mortals with determination, but whether we would be able to measure up to them we had no idea. We would soon find out.

Keith arrived an hour late, blaming the traffic. Farewells, as ever at airports, were distressing. Photographers all over us trying to get candid shots; the impossibility of intimacy. I was in a turmoil of anxiety over the journey ahead and grief at leaving my family. I felt no excitement. Marianne and Cale said little; Holly played with other kids but hugged me hugely at the end; my mother cried and my older brother, Bruce, embraced me.

"Come back with all your fingers and toes," he said.

As I walked to the departure gate, a portal to another world, I looked around and half-jokingly said: "Anyone want a ticket to the South Pole?" John stayed behind to finish the negotiations and would join us later in Chile. The rest of us were out of the maelstrom. A simpler but more threatening task lay ahead.

Somewhere over the dark Pacific, I wrote down my thoughts:

At last, we leave on the great journey ... We do not know if we will succeed or fail, whether muscle and blood, will and intellect, can overcome the rigours of the ice and our own frailty. We all have our fears, and so much can go wrong – from a blocked stove valve to a sprained ankle.

Our planning has been good, but with many shortcomings – we have tested neither our equipment nor ourselves in Antarctic conditions ... I am at the zenith of my wondering whether I am up to this journey, whether I am worthy. My concern is close to fear – there is no doubt this is the greatest challenge and most serious expedition I have ever undertaken. My mind says I can do it, but my guts want to squirm up and run away.

So it is with considerable trepidation and a great sadness that we leave our loved ones to confront the ice and ourselves. But I am uplifted by the wild magnificence we will encounter and the many, many people who have supported us, who have believed in this expedition and made it a reality.

We hope many more people will come with us to share in the journey and the difficulties and the exultations along the way. We intend to succeed, for ourselves and for everyone who has had faith in us.

Peter's concerns, put to the video during a stopover in Santiago, focused on the burden of responsibility he felt we carried:

The thing that worries me about this trip is ... there's been so much media behind it and so much money and so many people have given up their time ... that there's a hell of a lot of pressure to perform and to make this thing happen ... a lot more pressure on this trip than any other trip I've ever been involved in.

At 53°S on the afternoon of 21 October, we stepped out onto the cold and blustery tarmac at Punta Arenas airport. Steve Pinfield and Faye Somerville of ANI greeted us in the overheated terminal and took us into town by mini-bus.

The snow-capped hills behind the town sloped down to the shores of the Straits of Magellan. Beyond, Tierra del Fuego sprawled over the southern horizon, and beyond that, across 1100 km of the storm-lashed Drake Passage, lay Antarctica. As the van rattled along the potholed highway, Steve threw nearly as many questions at us as we asked of him. The wiry and energetic Englishman was to manage ANI's Antarctic base camp at Patriot Hills and provide the transport, communications and rescue backup for our expedition, so he wanted to assess these would-be South-Polers from Australia. Based on his experience in mountain and polar guiding, Steve decided then and there that we did not have the right stuff to reach the Pole. Months later he wrote:

I have seen many expeditions succeed in their quest to reach the South Pole. I have also seen just as many fail for a variety of reasons, including equipment failure, illness, injury, prolonged poor weather, difficult snow and ice conditions and mental exhaustion. I thought it unlikely the Australian expedition would succeed after my initial contact with them in Punta Arenas. Their questions, equipment, confidence, teamwork and experience appeared questionable. The last two seasons have seen periods of prolonged poor weather and I doubted their ability physically and mentally to pull their sledges for the required number of miles per day.

We were having doubts of our own. Peter was the least experienced in cold environments but the most accomplished in persevering against the odds. He claimed to be uncertain about being capable of hauling a sled to the Pole. If he had concerns about this, heaven help the rest of us! Keith was outwardly the least worried of all. The fact that others had succeeded made him quietly confident that we could too.

Tawny subalpine grasslands gave way to shanties and light industry on the city's outskirts. Soon we found ourselves in an interesting downtown mix of massive colonial stone edifices, brightly painted houses and modern architecture. We had a week here for final preparations before our scheduled departure for Patriot Hills on 29 October.

22 OCTOBER

We walked from our hotel to the ANI headquarters, a small house well positioned for radio contact with Antarctica on the city's highest hill. The house would become increasingly frenetic as ANI's summer operation got under way. Apart from our group, ANI would be supporting two Belgians on an Antarctic crossing from Queen Maud Land to the Ross Sea, a team of three Icelanders (including a father and son) making for the Pole from Patriot Hills, and New Zealand-American Helen Thayer trekking solo from Hercules Inlet.

From ANI's records I collected useful information about the 1996 sledging expeditions by Børge Ousland and Marek Kaminsky. Canadian Doug Woods, the Patriot Hills radio operator, was a fount of technical know-how and helped us with our communications gear, the solar panel and our GPS unit.

23 OCTOBER

I contacted Børge in Oslo. The Norwegian, a professional adventurer, had become our chief route adviser. The previous summer he had achieved the holy grail of polar exploration, the first unsupported crossing of the Antarctic continent from coast to coast via the Pole, and solo at that. With cunning use of a parasail, excellent equipment, great skill and perfect planning, he had completed the 2845 km journey in just 64 days. Several other parties had tried before him. He himself had made an earlier attempt but had been forced by frostbite to stop just beyond the Pole.

Børge had been generous with his knowledge of equipment, food, route and other aspects. From Punta I faxed him photocopies of our maps, which he returned annotated with succinct advice: "Wujek Ridge is much, much better than Frost Spur ... The sastrugi before the Pole you cannot avoid ... Be careful of the crevasse field at 86°S, stay east of 52° and you will miss it ... Keep west of the mountains, then straight to the Pole."

We met Helen Thayer, 59, who hoped to ski alone to the Pole and back again (after picking up a parasail) in 80 days. Her sled weighed just 115 kg and she seemed relaxed about the project. She told Peter she wanted to join the team and take care of us!

The two Twin Otters left for Patriot Hills with ANI's advance staff. They were a week late. Winter was finally releasing its grip on the frozen continent.

24 OCTOBER

Our freight had arrived – three days late. The ANI driver took us out of town to an old corrugated iron chook shed, referred to as the *parcela* (Spanish for block of land), which the company used for storage. On the crumbling concrete floor our timber crate and cartons lay beside a large cardboard package that had brought our other two sleds from England.

We set to work unpacking the two sleds first. In spite of some damaged packaging, they were in perfect order. Keith ripped the plastic wrapping from the sled accessories. "Hey, there's not enough harnesses here!" he exclaimed after a moment.

I looked. "The shoulder sections are missing … and the ropes … and shackles," I said.

We laid out all the parts and checked again, but there was no mistake. We stared at each other. I started talking first. "I can't understand it; Snowsled assured me it was all coming. It's far too late now to get the bits sent out."

Keith had a brainwave. "John's coming over tomorrow. He could bring our Simpson Desert harnesses," he said.

The phone rang for ages before John answered in Sydney, his voice croaky. It was the middle of the night. When he grasped who I was, I began to explain our predicament and where to find the gear. He was due to leave in 15 hours. "I'll go round to Peter's on the way to the airport," he said.

I phoned Snowsled and was told the missing equipment had already been sent by urgent parcel post.

When I returned to the *parcela*, I found piles of food all over the shed and our sleds heaped high with gear. Keith had his food list out and was telling Peter how to make up bags each containing a full day's food for the three of us: "One packet of muesli, one pouch of oil, one small packet of milk, one large packet of milk, six sachets of Milo, six soups, six packs of biscuits, three chocolate bars, one pack of pasta, one pack of dried vegies, one pack of parmesan cheese, three fruit biscuits … " We planned to carry equal amounts of food in each sled and consume a bag a day from each sled in turn. This meant we would each reduce our load by one bag every three days.

We weighed a few bags and found they averaged 4 kg. We had already cut the amount of food we would carry from 80 to 75 days' worth. The arithmetic of unsupported journeys is ruthless. The more you carry (or drag), the slower you go and the longer it takes to get there, so the more food you need. If you carry less food, you go slightly faster but there is the risk that you will not have enough. If you plan to eat less, your strength may fail. These iron rules were the death of Captain Scott and his men.

Peter was concerned about the weight: "Anne Kershaw reckons that, based on the experience of other manhauling teams, we should get there in about 60 days, and we need a safety margin on top of that." He suggested 70 days.

I was worried that too low a margin might encourage Peter to go fast and avoid rest days. I reckoned we were more likely to be delayed by physical problems than weather. Weight didn't bother me as much as the risk of burnout.

Keith was also keen on a few rest days but wanted to cut the weight. "We need to allow for bad weather stops, but we can go on half rations."

I took up the theme, thinking I could afford a little hunger. "Even if we have to go on short rations at the end, I reckon one way or another we can get there with 70 days' supply."

We settled on 70 days, perhaps as much out of gut feeling as logic. Keith laid out a production line and we spent most of the afternoon making up the 70 bags and packing them in our sleds. We also attended to small details like checking all the bolts on the sleds and adding pull-tabs to the tent zippers for handling with gloves. It was important to eliminate as many risks as possible, no matter how trivial. Minor problems have a habit of developing into serious ones when you're miles from nowhere.

25 OCTOBER

It was cold and windy at the *parcela*. This was the first time we had been together with all our gear in one place. Sorting and fiddling with equipment helped us function as a team. A common understanding of the workings and limitations of every piece of gear would enhance our ability to cope with the unforeseen on the ice.

We were psychologically prepared for hauling 150 kg each but soon realised it would be more like 160 kg. Later calculations revealed that we began the haul with a total of 170 kg each, including our clothes and entire kit. Again, it was just as well we never knew!

Achieving equal distribution of our cooking, camping and photographic gear was tricky. We worked with lists and a calculator, each of us taking an intense interest. Vital gear was divided between the sleds in case one was lost in a crevasse.

26 OCTOBER

We spent the morning completing the loading of our sleds and weighing them. Through dedicated eating since arriving in Punta, Keith had broken the 65 kg barrier for the first time in his life. I had added 2 kg to reach 74 kg and Peter had lost some weight to come in at 73.2 kg.

Despite a 48-hour trip, John arrived with his excitement intact and plucked banners, logos, stickers, flags and newspaper clippings from his bags. We desperately wanted to see the spare harnesses, which he produced after stringing us along for a bit. Then he sat down to write more faxes – still closing deals.

27 OCTOBER

Once we had the expedition badges on our clothing and sleds covered in stickers, we were almost looking like a real expedition. The sleds were prepared for loading onto ANI's chartered Hercules C-130 for the flight to Antarctica.

We attended an evening briefing for all the ANI customers and staff who were going on the first flight to Patriot Hills. The atmosphere was festive. Captain Roes de Villiers, leader of the South African Hercules crew, talked about landing on the legendary blue ice runway. "It is very unmodulated, it is very strange ... but it is 100 per cent safe," he said. ANI operations manager Rachel Shephard explained that a tractor was clearing windblown snow from the runway as fast as it could. The plan to load the Hercules the next day – three days later than planned – remained unchanged. The plane would then leave as soon as conditions were right, at any time of the day or night.

28 OCTOBER

We all went out to the *parcela* to help transport the sleds. A host of ANI people were on hand, including a partner in the business, lanky Australian Mike McDowell. Keith, as protective as a family dog, supervised the gentle loading of the sleds onto an old truck.

At the grey, windswept airfield, the belly of the fat-bodied C-130 hung open at the rear. The truck was unloaded and every item of cargo weighed before being carried into the cavernous interior and strapped down.

29 OCTOBER

ANI's Lesley McGee phoned us as we were having breakfast. The weather had cleared at Patriot Hills and the plane would fly later in the day as soon as the last 10 per cent of the runway's runout zone had been cleared of snow. My gut dropped in a visceral realisation that we were really going. There was no backing out now. My mind told me that everything was in order and there was little to fear. But the primitive animal in me knew this was a lie, that the unknown – most feared of all enemies – lay out there waiting for me.

Since departing from Australia we'd been interviewing each other on video. We took the camera into our confidence perhaps more than we did each other. Peter looked tense as he spoke now to the video about our feelings:

I guess when we were finally told that we were going, everybody felt a little bit apprehensive, a little nervous ... about the flight down ... about the task ahead of us because it's such a huge unknown in terms of the cold and the distances involved, and the time we'll be away from our families ... Nevertheless, the die is cast and we'll be leaving at 10 o'clock this evening.

In the evening we took what might be our last showers for months. We fretted like condemned men. By 9.30 p.m. we were falling asleep. The phone jangled; I answered. Lesley was brief and chirpy. "It's a goer for tonight. We'll pick you up in about half an hour," she said.

We dressed in our warm clothes and piled into the minibus. We travelled to the airport in silence. In the darkened terminal, all our hand baggage was weighed and added to our tally. We were paying $65 a kilo, so we took nothing not needed for the Pole trek. Departure was set for midnight. In a small room a customs officer stamped our passports.

Mike McDowell strode in: "Okay everyone, we have some bad news from the ice. The tractor has broken a steering bolt and can't finish the job. Thirteen hundred metres of runway is clear, with 200 to go, and the C-130 needs that. The flight is cancelled for the night. We've got a number of mechanics there who should be able to do something. Sorry about that. Nothing we can do."

30 OCTOBER

We took a break from fretting about gear, sponsors and planes, hired a car and drove to Fuerte Bulnes, an historic fort. Lesley phoned after dinner. "Be in the lobby at 10.30," she said

By then the edge of excitement had worn off. In the darkened terminal we waited for another midnight flight, sweltering in our fleece clothing. I thought how good it would be to get away from the smoky, overheated indoors of Punta Arenas into the cleanest air in the world.

Soon after midnight we were briskly shepherded across the black tarmac. "Come on!" Mike yelled against the wind-blast of the running engines. "We have to get to Patriot before the weather window closes!"

We hurried up the steps and the plane was taxiing down the runway almost before we'd found our seats.

On a melting snowpatch in Kosciuszko National Park, Keith checks that Peter's sledging boots, specially made in Norway, properly fit the three-pin bindings of the touring skis we would use to walk to the South Pole.

A rushed weekend trip to the Australian snowfields was our first – and last – chance to test vital equipment. Peter (top) practises pitching the small, single-skin mountaineering tent that would be our home for two months, then Showboat Entertainment cameraman Garry Maunder (above right) gives raw beginners Peter (centre) and Keith some rapid-fire hints on using our loaned video camera to make a film of the expedition. Finally, in a sunny picnic area beside the Crackenback River (left) we sort our clothing and other gear, most of it gathered from Australian suppliers and manufacturers just a few days earlier, into three piles for the coming journey.

We arrived at Punta Arenas in southern Chile – our jumping-off point for Antarctica – on 21 October 1997. After a week of final preparations, mostly in an old chook shed, our packed sleds (right) were loaded onto ANI's chartered Hercules and we began to resemble a proper expedition (top), complete with logos delivered by expedition coordinator John Leece. A typical full day's rations for the three of us (above) provided 25,000 kJ per person and weighed 4 kg in all. Olive oil, bottom left, boosted the energy content by 37 kJ per gram – twice the energy yield of protein or carbohydrate.

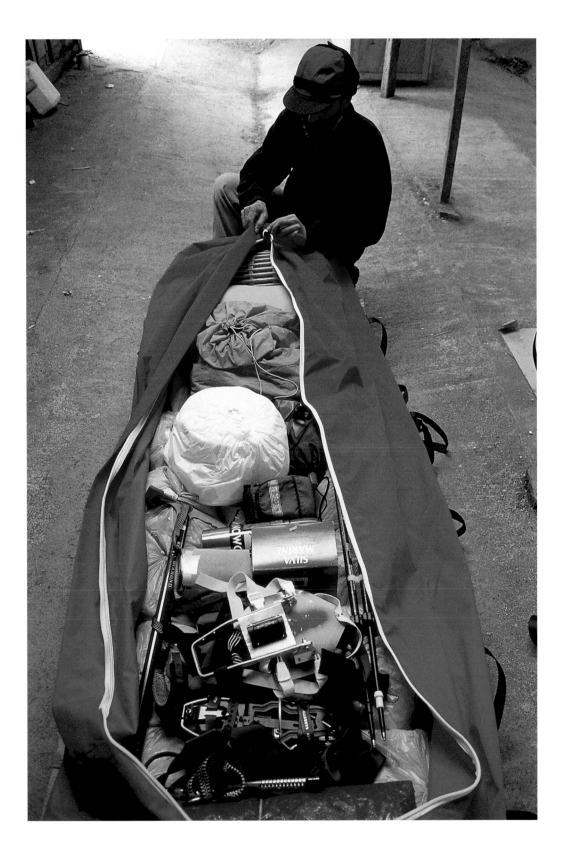

CHAPTER 2

FIRST STEPS
on the ICE

Before us lay the Antarctic with its great, white wastes
of ice; behind us nothing that could do us any good.

BØRGE OUSLAND, ALONE ACROSS ANTARCTICA (1997)

31 OCTOBER

The rear ramp of the Hercules dropped to the ground and dazzling light burst in, quickly followed by Steve Pinfield, brimming with energy. I felt as if we'd flown by spaceship to another planet and the ambassador was here to greet us.

"Welcome to Antarctica! It's about minus 20 outside with a 20-knot southerly, so make sure you're rugged up," he yelled.

We needed no further invitation and staggered out on stiff legs in full polar kit. My boots immediately skidded on the glass-hard ice and I almost fell. The cold air slapped me like a bucket of icy water. You could get frostbitten in a minute.

The waiting Patriot Hills crew attacked the back of the plane like ants whose nest had just been trodden on, rapidly unloading stores and equipment. The engines were kept running to prevent them from freezing, so the plane had to be emptied as quickly as possible before it headed back to South America. The gale and noise from the engines rattled my brain until the plane roared away in a cloud of ice-dust, leaving peace and calm just 45 minutes after landing.

Only a few hundred metres away across the flat runway, Patriot Hills rose abruptly in steep sweeps of gravel, ice and snow. Away to the west and north, rows of hard-edged mountains marched into a blue sky. The contents of the

After a smooth six-hour flight from Punta Arenas and a bone-jarring landing on the bumpy
bare-ice runway at Patriot Hills, our sleds were unloaded from the back of the Hercules.

plane were strewn all over the ice, awaiting transport to the camp a kilometre north of the runway. With some concern for their safety, I watched our heavy sleds being loaded sideways onto a large wooden sled which was then hauled away behind a skidoo.

We walked up the gentle rise to the camp. Our boots crunched and squeaked as we tried to link the patches of polystyrene-like snow and avoid the dastardly mirror-ice. The incline was partly a consequence of the camp's very existence; 10 years of blizzards have eddied around the tents and machinery, dumping their load and creating a small swell on the landscape. As I covered my first careful kilometre of Antarctica, I turned in slow circles, drinking in the glorious mountains in the invisible air. I felt I was dreaming.

The heart of the camp was the cook and dining tent. It was about the size of two rooms of a house, with a rigid curved frame of aluminium tubing covered in strong insulated fabric, and housed a gas-fired kitchen, heating stove and dining tables. A radio tent and a few robust-framed guest tents had also been erected and the staff slept in their own small mountaineering tents.

Steve assured me that by January, when we were due to return, the camp would be fully operational and have a library tent, medical tent, showers and facilities for up to 40 clients. Not far away, the two Twin Otters were lashed to long stakes in the snow, noses pointing south. A particularly windy environment is assured by the camp's location near a blue-ice strip. Beyond the Patriot Hills, the great icecap of the Polar Plateau gradually rises towards the centre of the continent, regularly sending reminders of its presence in the form of fierce gales made up of frigid, dense air that flows down the slope under the force of gravity. These are called katabatic winds.

The ANI advance party had already weathered one severe blizzard, during which they were forced to shelter in the cook tent. They'd done well to have the basic camp established in just seven days under such conditions.

The day remained mostly calm and sunny, with the temperature hovering around −25°C. When the wind blew, conditions were extremely unpleasant. We pitched our tent (expeditions must use their own gear, though John, as a standard client, slept in an insulated ANI tent), collected and packed our 45 litres of stove petrol for the traverse, fiddled with our gear, took sponsor photos and tried hauling our sleds. The snow was hard and slick, and they moved surprisingly well. This gave our confidence a boost, though we would later lump this with other subjects it was just as well we fooled ourselves with.

Our preparations were complicated by a frustrating inability to coordinate ourselves. Each was focused on what he saw as necessary and we couldn't get a consensus. When Peter and John wanted us all together for photos, Keith was fitting climbing skins (for uphill grip) to his skis; when Keith was ready, Peter had become cold and gone into the cook tent. Peter was finding the cold very difficult to cope with, compounding his dislike of waiting.

"The only way we're going to stay warm is to keep moving," he insisted, increasing my disquiet about the trek to come.

ANI cooks Fran Orio and Mike Holmes dished up a magnificent dinner of pork and vegetables followed by apple crumble and cream. Peter slept with John in the bigger tent, reckoning we would be cooped up soon enough. Keith and I took the opportunity to get into the swing of Antarctic camping and crawled into our tent. In an experiment to control condensation, we left the door wide open and suffered a little in the −30°C night. Although there had been 24-hour daylight for some weeks at this latitude of 80°S, the sun still swept behind the Patriot Hills for a few bleak hours around midnight.

In the small hours, frost settled on the sleeping bag around my face and rubbed painfully on my cold nose. My feet were cold. I reckoned that if I added warmer socks and a balaclava I'd be right. Getting undressed and dressed in the tent was a pain: with three we would have to be very organised. It was difficult trying to work out the best sequence of undressing to minimise chilling, but I hoped to have it figured out after another couple of nights. Every action takes so long in such cold that simple convenience is just as critical as whether items function well. Maybe, I thought, compared with the discomfort of camping, hauling would be the fun part.

Peter had similar thoughts. He wrote in his diary: "Fantastic to be in Antarctica. Will be difficult to get used to the cold and the discomfort. Very difficult to get the mind around how we will deal with the severity of the task at hand."

We hoped to be able to fly to Berkner Island and start on our walk the next day.

1 NOVEMBER

I was woken early by my bladder, dressed and went to the cook tent, seeking warmth and company. No-one was there, and it was freezing. I tried to read in the chill until New Zealander Max Wenden came in and set about lighting the heater. Lean and weathered, Max is a climber and an aeronautical vagabond, flying small planes in whatever interesting places he can, a man of few words who has the delightfully calm, knowledgeable air of someone who has seen a lot and doesn't let it bother him any more. He has been flying for ANI for 10 summers.

Max would probably be the one to fly us out from the Pole. With all our food gone, we would just be able to squeeze into his single-engined Cessna (known as the "Flying Pumpkin" because of its bulging, orange belly) rather than the more expensive Twin Otter. Under this plan, we could be forced to leave the sleds at the Pole for pick-up later. I looked forward to flying with one of the most experienced Antarctic pilots around.

Max left to get on with his other duties, including putting his beloved Pumpkin together. It is stored in winter, with its wings detached, in a small timber shed half-buried in the snow. I huddled over the heater, looking every inch a parody of the polar explorer, as people began to drift in from their tents.

It was going to be hard to separate ourselves from the bountiful food at Patriot Hills. For breakfast I indulged in porridge and stewed fruit, bacon, eggs and toast, fruit juice and hot chocolate. One of the great benefits of the imminent toil of an extended expedition is the freedom to eat whatever and as much as you like.

After the Hercules's visit, ANI's Patriot Hills camp crew was nearly complete. It included managers, technicians, cooks, general hands, mountain guides and crew for three planes. I sat in on the staff briefing as Steve outlined the plans for the season.

Apart from ourselves, Helen Thayer, and the Icelandic and Belgian teams, an amazing variety of other clients would pass through the camp, which is strategically located for both the Vinson Massif (at 5140 m Antarctica's highest peak) and the South Pole. The bread and butter of the business are the Vinson climbers, the tourists who go on day flights to the remote US South Pole base and those who just quarter themselves at Patriot Hills for various recreational activities. Sometimes there are "89 degree-ers", who fly to 89°S and are led on skis by ANI guides over the last 111 km to the Pole. There were also government and corporate customers, including a team from NASA testing a robot to search for meteorites on Mars.

Steve told his assembled team that the last staff plane out of Patriot Hills was scheduled for 18 January, after business had slackened and the last client plane had departed on 15 January. We had better be back by then, I thought. There was some chance that the Belgian crossing attempt would upset this timetable. The two Belgians, Alain Hubert and Didier (Dixie) Dansercoer, would be depending on ANI for emergency extraction until they reached the Ross Sea, so a skeleton camp staff and Twin Otter crew would need to remain after 18 January to make sure they were safe. As the longest crossing of Antarctica ever attempted without dogs, snowcraft or air support, their immense journey of 3499 km was shrouded in uncertainty.

ANI staff keep the base open as long into autumn as necessary to make sure all clients safely leave Antarctica, but when winter grips the continent and planes cease operation anyone still in the interior risks remaining there until the next spring; even the US South Pole base is isolated during the months of darkness. Prudently the ANI camp is prepared for such an unlikely event, with stocks of food and fuel stored in tunnels excavated under the ice. These catacombs also hold all the tentage and other equipment between seasons.

When the meeting broke up, the staff scattered over the camp on various frigid chores. Four or five, their faces iced and steaming, extended the dining tent by adding another section and moving the kitchen back.

The Patriot Hills base runs on Chile time, a delightful pun! At 11 a.m. Steve King, the Twin Otter pilot assigned to take us the 750 km to Berkner Island, followed a blast of cold air into the cook tent to report on our prospects, emerging gradually from thick mitts and coat, icy goggles and head coverings. We gathered round expectantly.

"The satellite images show a belt of high cloud stretching over the Antarctic Peninsula and up past Patriot Hills," he said. "It may clear in the next 24 hours and we could go tonight."

So, with no prospect of an early departure, we could relax a little. Steve is a swarthy, drawling Canadian whose easy-going but professional approach to flying is highlighted by a mischievous small-boy look in his eyes. He is one of a four-man team contracted by ANI from Kenn Borek Air in Calgary, Canada, to supply the two orange and white Twin Otters, each with its own pilot and engineer. The Twin Otter is a powerful and versatile plane specially developed for the demanding conditions of the Arctic – and therefore also perfect for Antarctica.

Even a short stroll to the outside toilet required full protection for hands, face and head. Steve had explained earlier that all waste, including human waste, was returned to Punta from Patriot Hills on the Hercules. For men, the "wet" toilet was an undistinguished empty 200-litre fuel drum standing on the snow with a tin funnel. Women were given wide-mouthed plastic bottles that could be emptied into the funnel.

At various times we all walked up to visit meteorologist Anthony Machado in the frigid, unheated radio tent. Hired by ANI through the Uruguayan military (with an agreement that Uruguayan Antarctic Division could use the information collected), Anthony was huddled in full polar clothing, minus goggles, over a computer warmed by hot water bottles. In the rosy glow coming through the red tent walls, awkwardly punching the keyboard with mittened hands, he showed me the cloud images he had recently downloaded from a weather satellite. In tones of grey I could make out Berkner Island and the Antarctic Peninsula. Another punch of the keys brought up a world map showing satellite orbits. Because satellites mainly service populated areas, there were many hours between passes over our area of interest. It would be a while before we'd get the all-clear for our flight.

There was some benefit in our forced wait in that we were acclimatising, but Peter was itching to get going. "I just wish we could get the flight over with and get on with it," he said.

We fiddled with our gear a little more between luxurious interludes in the dining tent. Peter went for long walks around camp, even when the wind was howling.

Outside the radio tent, Doug gave us the HF radio we would carry and instructed us on using it. "We have four frequencies programmed in, channels 1 to 4 on this switch here," he said. "You'll find that, as you get further away, we'll need to move up the channels to get best reception."

We agreed to schedule calls every second night to advise our position, progress and condition. The wire dipole aerial would need to be strung out at camp, and we knew this would be an inconvenience on the ice. Some parties just take either a radio or an Argos beacon, but we decided to take both for safety. The radio would enable us to communicate with *The Australian* journalists who planned to contact Doug by satellite phone for regular reports of our progress. The Argos is a one-way system only, transmitting position data and a limited range of agreed messages via satellite to ground stations. Doug and Steve Pinfield maintained we should treat the Argos as our main means of communication and the radio as a backup only.

We certainly did not want any glitches in communication. It is a standard ANI requirement that if there's no contact with expeditioners for 50 hours, or if the Argos reports no shift in position for the same period, the company sends a plane to the last indicated position. This was even written into our contract. It is an essential condition for ANI, whose continued operation depends on permissions from the Antarctic Treaty nations. A life-threatening delay in the rescue of a party in difficulties would seriously damage ANI's reputation and jeopardise the tenuous existence of private adventure on the continent. Such an agreement also eliminates the responsibility of deciding whether to send help or not. An unnecessary rescue was the last outcome we wanted. Even if we turned the plane away without any passengers, the flight would be charged against our rescue insurance. Once our insurance was used up, we might have no choice but to get on the plane in perfect health!

The radio was bigger than we expected, and we were alarmed when Doug showed us that it took 11 D-cell batteries, with 11 spares. The batteries were heavy alkaline units. This was a minor tragedy because, had we known this, we could have brought lighter lithium batteries from Eveready, who had helped us with batteries for our GPS receivers and compact cameras. Still, at this stage we had no choice. Keith, who was to carry the damned thing, was especially distraught and trotted off to the kitchen to weigh it.

"Seven and a half kilos!!" he reported in disgust.

Keith continued shaking his head and muttering inconsolably throughout the afternoon. This was four kilos more than we had allowed. I went through another round of calculating our sled weights.

Helen Thayer had been packing up for the short flight to Hercules Inlet, her starting point for the Pole. Some 20 km from the Patriot Hills camp, this is the closest spot on the geological "coast" of Antarctica, where the permanent Ronne Ice Shelf, floating on the sea, meets the solid continent. It is the third most popular place for modern ski expeditions to begin a traverse to the Pole, after Berkner Island and Patriot Hills. These are the accessible locations because they are serviced by ANI, and the choice of various expeditions between the three jump-off points comes down to three fundamental factors in polar adventure: cost, practicality and the "rules of the game".

Cost is the most straightforward factor, with Patriot Hills being the cheapest. The extra flight to Hercules Inlet adds cost and very little distance to the trek, but there's a strenuous and hazardous climb through a steep crevasse zone to regain the altitude of Patriot Hills. Berkner Island adds greatly to the cost as well as 300 km to the trek. The quaint ethics of polar adventure ordain that starting on the real edge of the continent, where the permanent ice meets the open sea in high summer, is pure and superior, because this is the closest the explorers of the heroic age could get without aircraft. Thus Berkner Island is favoured by those who wish their traverse to the Pole to remain untainted and can afford it.

I consider these ethical considerations quaint for several reasons. Firstly, nearly all traverses from Berkner Island have actually started slightly inland from the coast of the Weddell Sea, on the pretext of being latitudinally level with where the seaward margin of the permanent Filchner Ice Shelf meets the southernmost limit of the Weddell Sea (on the eastern margin of the island). Apart from reducing the distance to the Pole slightly, this has another sly practical benefit: it avoids a little of the climb over the island from sea level.

A second reason the "rules" are slightly awry is that the poor souls of the heroic era never gained a foothold on the continent in the southern part of the Weddell Sea anyway, though they tried. There are two points around the margin of the continent where the sea penetrates furthest south, in the Ross

Sea and the Weddell Sea. Both points are on 78°S and therefore the same direct distance from the Pole, about 1330 km. Scott's and Amundsen's teams successfully reached the Pole from the Ross Sea, but the only attempt in those days from the Weddell Sea, Shackleton's, failed.

Thirdly, the harsh purist rules of engagement for modern polar journeys were born of competitive attempts to make the first "unsupported" journey to the North Pole. When competition is involved, along with nationalism, sponsors, the media and intense public interest, the importance of fine distinctions can easily become exaggerated. The concept of "unsupported" has generated controversy in both the Arctic and the Antarctic. It is worth noting that all "unsupported" traverses to either Pole routinely use aircraft for the return. They also have aerial rescue backup, which the explorers of yesteryear never had. The psychological benefit of this is enormous. If the accepted "support" of extraction by air from the Pole is removed, there has really only ever been one completely pure journey to the South Pole – Børge Ousland's 1996–97 Antarctic crossing.

The debate becomes even more complicated and farcical if the use of wind power and technological aids is thrown in. The Footsteps of Scott expedition, which walked from the Ross Sea to the South Pole in 1985-86 without radio communications, rescue backup, GPS or sails, almost gets through this sieve. However, the team flew back from the Pole – and they accepted a couple of free meals from a US geological party they stumbled across!

Having said all that, and acknowledging that an unpowered journey to the Poles, or over any other significant distance, is a great human achievement, it is important to understand that the rules give some comparative measure of quality, for both participants and observers. In this sense, a journey without depots to the South Pole from Berkner Island is superior to one from Hercules Inlet, which is clearly but marginally superior to one from Patriot Hills. A full crossing (such as Børge's) or a return journey (not yet accomplished) would be superior to all. It might also be argued that a totally muscle-powered journey is a greater achievement than the same journey accomplished with the help of the wind via sails of some kind. But what if the sail journey is completed in half the time and without radio communication or satellite services? Finer points like these are best left to the pundits to debate. It remains important that those engaged in these types of games are totally frank about the parameters of their own journeys and that they avoid criticising others.

The 1997-98 season illustrated the distinctions beautifully. Helen was going from Hercules Inlet because she regarded this as more worthy than a Patriot Hills start and did not think Berkner Island provided sufficient distinction for the extra cost and effort involved. The Icelanders were starting from Patriot Hills because Berkner Island was too expensive and the difference between Patriot Hills and Hercules Inlet immaterial. We were going from Berkner Island because we wanted to be beyond criticism as the first Australians to reach the South Pole on foot and without support.

Late in the afternoon we stood beside our tent and watched Steve King taxi the ski-equipped Twin Otter across the snow with Helen aboard. The plane lifted off so suddenly it hardly seemed to be moving. The Twin Otter can take off in about 100 m and land in about 200 m, which means it can go almost anywhere. When Steve returned, he reported a blisteringly cold wind at Helen's drop-off point. "She's a tough lady," he said, shaking his head.

The high cloud cleared to leave the camp basking in sunny calm. Steve checked the weather with Anthony and came back with bad news. "An ice fog is forming over Berkner Island and there'll be no flight tonight." He explained that one thing that puts the wind up him is the possibility of flying into cloud with the sun so low at "night". This sounded good to me; I like a pilot with strong survival instincts. To emphasise the point Steve told about flying to the far side of Filchner Ice Shelf a few seasons earlier. He was nearly at the destination, an abandoned base on the Luitpold Coast where ANI has a fuel depot.

"When I get that far out, I don't have enough fuel left to get back, so I have to land and refuel. Suddenly I ran into low cloud, I couldn't see a thing. I knew where I was, I knew the terrain and I knew I could land down there at the base, so I just lowered the plane as slowly as I could until I felt the skids touch the ground. I didn't like that one little bit."

Our last chore for the day before tucking into another great dinner was to video a promotion for the scouts' Trekathon, which John wanted to take back to show on television. As we tried to relax in the dining tent after our sumptuous meal, pilot Steve came over to make an offer.

"You know one thing we can try if you're keen to get there is hopping to Berkner Island. We set off even though the weather is not great and get as far as we can. Then we set down and wait for the weather to improve. One problem is I don't get to see the satellite images that way."

This seemed to me like a dubious proposition, but it is apparently routine. Peter wanted to keep the options open.

"Lets see what happens tomorrow," he said.

Peter's diary:
We are getting no closer to the Pole by sitting here. Despite my trepidation, I'm keen to start.

2 NOVEMBER

My diary:

So, we may go today to Berkner. I have not quite fathomed my emotions on this point, but I am certainly not one with this journey yet. There is no doubt that I will go through with it, but I am disappointed that other feelings seem to be drowning any chance at excitement. Fear is there certainly, more now of the cold and unpleasantness than of the hauling and pain. But there is also a detachment, an unreality, like this is all a dream and I will wake up soon back home in bed with my wife, warm and secure. I cannot really tell whether I prefer to fly to Berkner or not to fly. As Peter said yesterday, at least when we are on our way we can suffer with a purpose, because we will be walking towards the Pole, at last. The conditions here are pretty unpleasant. Peter is finding the cold very hard to deal with and is obviously worried about it. This is his first time in such severe cold. If action is an antidote to anxiety for most people, then in Peter this must be writ very large. He hates waiting and wants to be on his way.

Keith is fine, in his element working on the best options for his gear and probably coping the best of all of us – a survivor. I think John is becoming bored and will take the next plane out if he can, due in a few days – as long as we have left by then.

The early-morning satellite photo did not show enough of Berkner Island to be useful, so we waited for the next passage of the satellite at 2.30 p.m.

Peter was sleeping cold. He said to John on our first morning at Patriot Hills: "Jeez, if this cold keeps up I'll never make it." Keith suggested he might be warmer in our small tent rather than the roomy one with John, but he was inconsolable. After breakfast, I overheard him talking to Steve Pinfield.

"How do you keep your feet warm at night in these temperatures?" Peter asked.

Shrinking under the table, I thought to myself, "Oh my God, how embarrassing! The man has no shame!" But Peter has a philosophy of learning as much as he can no matter how silly he risks looking. As I crept away to protect my own sensitivities, I heard Steve offering suggestions. I suspected that Peter's difficulty with the cold was more than just inexperience. People like Peter who have immense physical ability may also have slow metabolisms, and perhaps their bodies have difficulty keeping warm when at a low ebb. Maybe there is some truth in his adage about keeping warm through movement.

We were sitting in the dining tent at about 3 p.m., waiting expectantly for news from the satellite, when Anthony bustled in. Before he could pull off his headgear, he blurted out: "The weather is perfect!"

There was much to be done in a hurry to prepare for the flight: filling vacuum flasks with hot water, pulling the tent down and packing the sleds. I was holding the bag as Keith stuffed our tent into it when Steve Pinfield came crunching across the snow from the dining tent.

"We've got a problem," he announced, looking serious.

He suggested we meet in the dining tent to talk it over. We dropped what we were doing and filed in, wondering what it could be. Doug was there and they explained they had just heard from Punta that the Argos positions had not come through from Australia. We'd been activating the device daily at Patriot Hills to test the system. Our helpers in Sydney were to receive our coordinates each day and then report them to ANI in Punta.

"Punta had to go to the Argos ground station in Toulouse, France to get the data," Steve said.

"We have two contacts in Sydney who should be managing the process," John said.

"It's the weekend there and neither are answering," Steve replied.

I'd feared this might happen – that some fine organisational detail would be overlooked in the hurly-burly of the previous weeks. It seemed our helpers in Sydney did not clearly understand that the contact system had to be functioning before we set off. It was just a small but serious and embarrassing breakdown in communication. Failure can be built on such mistakes.

Steve was worried. "Twenty-four-hour contact with Australia is essential, so that if you activate the emergency button we can respond as quickly as possible," he said. "We have a plane here to send at any time, but it cannot leave instantly and will take some time to get to you, especially if the weather is bad. Any additional delay in getting the message to us is very serious. Unacceptable."

He seemed ready to cancel our flight. He was absolutely right, of course. It was his job to ensure unnecessary risks were eliminated. It was also right that his risk management was based on the assumption that something would go wrong, but I suspected again that ANI really believed we were heading for certain trouble. After all, the contract with ANI specified only that we had to maintain contact by either radio or Argos.

The communications glitch certainly did nothing to impress ANI staff. They probably doubted our ability to even use the radio! In spite of some undefined fears of my own, Steve's concern contrasted with my thinking on safety, and I'm sure with Keith's and Peter's view. We were more confident and better prepared than outward appearances might suggest, and I could not visualise anything seriously life-threatening happening, especially early on in uncrevassed country. With the radio as backup, it did not worry me that it might take a couple of days to get the Argos contact system functioning efficiently. We had all been in far more serious situations, in remote wilderness, with no contact, and rescue many days away, and we were used to relying on ourselves. Nevertheless, the incident was embarrassing, because it showed that indeed we were less prepared than we would have liked.

After some tense discussion, it was agreed that we would radio Doug every night until the problem was sorted out. Steve was still unhappy, but we left him and went off to complete our packing while John explained how he would resolve the contact system when he returned from Berkner Island. We were on our way – slightly chastened.

We stacked the sleds in the front of the plane behind the cockpit and wedged three 200-litre drums of fuel among the four passenger seats left for us. With a nominal payload of 900 kg, there was not much freeboard on the cramped flight. With Steve up front was engineer Lionel Rossi. The fourth passenger was John, who had long intended to fly with us to Berkner Island to watch the troublesome expedition child take its first shaky steps.

Without delay the Twin Otter wobbled across the wind-packed snow and lifted into the wind, turning away from the looming Patriot Hills and any further organisational problems into smooth Antarctic skies.

Dwarfed by the imposing backdrop of Patriot Hills (top) one of the Twin Otters from the base takes off from the bare-ice runway. We were flown to our starting point on Berkner Island in one of these sturdy aircraft. Canadian skier, climber and communications technician Doug Woods (above) looked after ANI's radios and satellite telephone at Patriot Hills, and would keep in touch with us during the polar journey. Later a 150 km/h blizzard demolished the tent and scattered Doug's equipment across the ice.

This DC-6 aircraft (left), abandoned near Patriot Hills (but not by ANI), is a reminder that Antarctica rarely forgives mistakes. Failing to find the blue-ice runway in a white-out, the pilot was forced to land the wheeled plane on the snow, knowing he could not take off again. Determined to avoid our own mistakes, Keith (top) adjusts his sled-hauling system at our base camp below Patriot Hills on a magnificent −28°C day. The expedition's fund-raiser, manager and mentor John Leece (above) is ecstatic as he steps onto Antarctic snow − his dream and ours at last turning into reality. John was caught in a blizzard at Patriot Hills before returning to Australia to close more deals.

JOHN LEECE

At meal time an international camaraderie fills the insulated and heated dining
tent (top) at the busy Patriot Hills base. Tourists, expeditioners, researchers and
staff satisfy cold-weather appetites on piles of home-cooked food. Wind-blasted
snow and ice glistens under a low sun on the Marble Hills (above), seen from
the Patriot Hills camp at 80°S. Beyond this rampart lies the vast wasteland
of the Polar Plateau.

When a southerly blizzard blasts down onto the camp (top) from the high plateau, it becomes an exercise in survival just to move around outside. The blue and white mess tent can be seen on the left. After inspecting the ski-equipped Twin Otter aircraft (above) that would fly our 900 kg payload 750 km from Patriot Hills to Berkner Island for the start of the trek, we try to present a confident air.

61

CHAPTER 3

BEASTS *of* BURDEN

In the tracks of Sisyphus, we haul our ambitions
in our sleds. We are vulnerable, determined
and insignificant to everything except each other.

LINCOLN HALL, THE LONELIEST MOUNTAIN (1989)

1 NOVEMBER

We left the mainland quickly and flew north-east over the Ronne Ice Shelf, which is as big as the state of Victoria. Through the frost-rimmed windows we could see a vast expanse of snow, fading unbroken to the horizon, wind-patterned into intricate interlocking textures. I noted that we would be able to read the prevailing wind direction from the patterns when we crossed them on the ground. Occasionally crevasse fields appeared where some rock or other hidden obstruction disturbed the shelf's smooth northward drift, much as a submerged reef creates a bombora. The worst crevasses were huge and frightening, treacherously hidden by windblown snow. From above, it was easy to pick a route through them; down among them it would be impossible. Peter muttered what we were all thinking: "I hope we don't have to cross anything like that."

Antarctica is perhaps safer than some other places – there are only a few ways to die. Crevasses are one of them. We'd come prepared for such obstacles but hoped we wouldn't need to call on our rope and climbing equipment. The thought of being dragged backwards into a blue-black abyss by a plunging 170 kg sled was most unwelcome.

The extent of the nothingness was overwhelming. I tried to visualise three person-sized dots crawling over the surface down there like fleas on a sand

---

Wearing ice-climbing crampons on an uphill slope of very cold, "sandy" snow, Keith struggles to drag his 170 kg sled just 7.3 km on our first day.

dune. Space alone can't harm you, but it loomed before me as an inescapable expression of the continent's grand indifference.

I passed a pencilled note forward, confirming to Steve where we wanted to get off the bus: "On 78° line (or slightly north, not south), between 45° and 46° west. Pick a nice spot!" We had earlier agreed to a drop-off close to Børge Ousland's starting point the previous year, and Steve passed my note back with "78.23°S, 45.48°W" written on the back. He turned and yelled from the cockpit, though I could only read his lips in the noise, that it was where Børge got out.

I had the maps on my lap and tried to spot when we crossed the "coast" between the ice shelf and Berkner Island. I couldn't; the incline was just too subtle. Soon I noticed the texture of the snow below growing more distinct. We were losing height. Nearly four hours after leaving Patriot, the plane's shadow rose to meet us. We hit, the plane bucked and shuddered over the humps and stopped in a matter of seconds. Steve looked back, grinning, and said: "Within a kilometre of Børge's landing – how's that?"

We tumbled out of the relative warmth into the glacial cold. My first act was to empty my bladder and stain the perfect whiteness. The sun, low in the sky, cast a golden light over the unbroken snowfields. Although it was around 10 p.m. local time, two hours ahead of Patriot Hills, we would continue to operate on Chile time for convenience.

We struggled to unload the heavy sleds without bending them dangerously. Although they were made of very strong kevlar, we were wary of causing hair-line fractures that might develop into breaks later. We laid our skis out, not sure in which direction to point them. Keith turned on the GPS so that it could zero in on some satellites and figure out where we were – a process known as initialisation. John was filming, I was taking photographs and Peter was ready to go. Steve called out that it was –30°C. In spite of the penetrating cold, conditions were ideal, with full sun and complete calm. We were blessed to have such gentle weather to ease us into life in the Antarctic wilderness.

Looking around, I felt disoriented. There was not a landmark in sight, and although I knew the sun must be a little west of south, and the wobbly tracks of the plane pointed back south-west towards Patriot Hills, none of this made much sense. Keith got an answer from the GPS and shut it down to conserve batteries. "A hundred and eighty-two degrees to the Pole," he yelled at me as I reached for the compass and strapped it on my chest.

"Come on, let's go," Peter said. "I'm freezing!"

I took the compass off again to get into my hauling harness. I wasn't sure whether to put my skis on before or after the harness. I also wanted to sling the camera around my neck at this historic juncture, and strap the camera pouch on somewhere. Sledging was going to be a confusing business! I had trouble cleaning the snow off my boots and wedging the square toe into the tight-fitting ski binding, which I hoped would loosen up with use. I clamped the arm of the binding down, realising I was fumbling, and one of my stocks fell over. I could hardly bend down to pick it up because my torso was swaddled in paraphernalia. Lionel and Steve were watching us, inscrutable in their masks and goggles.

Keith led off and I followed to keep him on the bearing. We waved our stocks to the aircrew. "See you at the South Pole in a couple of months," I yelled. John came over and shook our hands and slapped Peter on the back. "Good luck guys, I know you'll make it!" he said.

I looked at a horizon as empty as the sea and my stomach tightened with fear. I gave a tentative tug. My sled shifted slightly. "At least they move!" I cried out. I sighted the compass on Keith's back. He had gone 10 m towards the Pole already. "A bit to the right," I said. "That's it!"

A scream over our heads and the plane was gone, leaving us utterly alone with the silence.

Steve told me later what he'd thought after he'd left us:

I've dropped off a lot of expeditioners, and when you see someone like Børge head off, you think immediately, yeah, he'll get there. When I watched you guys putting on your skis and heading off from Berkner, well, I looked at Lionel and he looked at me. He shrugged, and I thought, These guys may not make it. But John said to us, "Those guys will do it. It will take them a few days to work things out, then they'll be right. They'll get there." I guess John was right.

Despite the lateness, we agreed to travel for an hour, just to make a start. The sleds dragged appallingly over a gravelly surface that created high friction. It was like pulling a cast-iron bathtub along a beach. We quickly discovered that, rather than using our leg muscles to move the sleds forward, it was better to stand on the spot, skis together, and bend the torso forward. This would move the sleds just 15 or 20 cm. Then we'd step forward without pulling the sleds and repeat the process. This way we obtained maximum traction, our skis being in full contact with the snow. They were fitted with climbing skins, not the traditional sealskin strips of former days but a synthetic substitute, with backward-pointing nylon fur.

Any attempt to pull the sleds through this "sand" by walking normally would risk a backward slip and often an undignified face plant. Keith, very aptly, called our new technique "winching". It was about as slow as a mechanical winch too, but effective. We were forced to resort to winching over small humps every few metres. To add to our difficulties, all our skins came unstuck from the skis. They were too new and stretched under the strain.

Trying to keep Keith on the right bearing by yelling to him as we grunted and sweated was futile. When we took a breather I handed him the compass.

Somewhat chastened at the end of the hour, having covered a miserable 1.1 km, we stopped and pitched the tent ... or tried to. The shock cord linking the tent pole segments had lost its stretch in the cold, making it difficult to keep the poles together. So much for "low-temperature" components. It was stunningly cold: Keith's small thermometer bottomed out at −35°C with a speed that suggested it would have continued falling if it had been able to. It was nearly the middle of the night, and the sun hovered just 10° above the horizon due south of us.

The first few camps on any trip are usually a little disorganised until a routine develops, and this one was even more so. After we were safely ensconced in the tent, Keith martyred himself by cooking dinner in the vestibule. Cursing but dogged, he suffered two frostnipped fingers for his trouble. It was so cold that the fuel would not vaporise in the stove, making it impossible to light. Peter warmed the stove in his sleeping bag (initiating an evening ritual followed thereafter). Once it was alight and roaring, with a billy of snow aboard, a horrible smell filled the tent, followed by smoke. Something was burning! The heat had blasted through the plywood sheet we'd brought as a stove-base and begun to melt Peter's foam mattress!

"Thanks Peter," I said. "Your mattress saved the tent floor."

Peter surveyed the damage stoically. It was a seemingly minor mistake, but one that really put us on guard. Any mistakes were to be rigorously avoided in such an unforgiving environment. We agreed in future to put the baseboard directly on the snow through a special zip-out section of the waterproof tent floor that we had arranged for just this purpose.

I got into my sleeping bag with my fleece clothing on but woke up later sweating. The bag was just wonderful!

3 NOVEMBER

On the morning of the first full day of our journey, it took us four hours to get organised. We would have to speed up our routine. We melted about 10 litres of water from snow and heated it for our breakfast muesli and chocolate drinks as well for two flasks each of hot soup (fortified with olive oil) for daytime drinks. Keith did all the cooking with just one stove. We had a second stove as backup, as well as spare parts, and decided in future to use both stoves for breakfast.

Ready to go at last, I leant forward at 45° against the weight of the sled, bent my torso down even further and moved the load just a nudge. We were wearing crampons to improve traction after the heartbreaking toil of the previous evening. I kept winching until the sled cleared the patch of sticky snow, then I moved on in regular but short, staccato steps. I felt like a heavy truck grinding uphill in bottom gear.

Keith was in the lead. I followed his tracks as he veered slightly to one side of our bearing and then to the other to avoid gently sloping wind ridges that might just as well have been Olympic hurdles. With the sled about 2 m behind me on the hauling ropes, I could not predict when it would bog down and need another winch, but I noticed that I could read Keith's footprints: when the going was hard they were very close together or fumbling. In places his sled had ploughed 10 cm into soft drifts. We had to climb gradually from near sea level to the 974 m crest of Berkner Island, and although the slight incline was undetectable to the eye, it was glaringly obvious to the body.

The coarse snow crystals sparkled in the hard sunlight. It was calm again but crackingly cold. Sledging was proving surprisingly noisy: the stock-points squeaked in the snow and the sled creaked and groaned; the blood thumped in my ears and my breathing was heavy, interrupted by occasional grunts of effort. Without these sounds of our snail-like passage across the landscape, I'm sure I could have heard a snowflake fall and settle upon the jewelled surface. Occasionally, when the sled came off a hump, it surged forward for a metre or so like an eager husky puppy. What blessed relief!

After an hour and half we had our first break. We'd agreed that Keith would lead for two of the day's four 90-minute "shifts", after which I'd lead for the other two. At the end of each shift we would take a short break to munch on biscuits and chocolate and slurp our soup.

I brought my skis together and stopped, throwing my shoulders back to shake out the stiffness, stabbed the stocks into the snow and wriggled my gloved hands out of the straps. I shuffled my skis backwards to the side of the sled, careful not to tread on the still-attached ropes. Then I whipped open the zip of my sled cover and extracted my down jacket, pulling it on over the harness to conserve warmth. I sat down gratefully, my back to the slight breeze, on the soft part of the sled where my sleeping bag and insulation mat were packed and took out a vacuum flask, a packet of biscuits and a small plastic bag of chocolate. Our specially designed biscuits contained wholemeal flour, egg, macadamia nuts and dried fruit, as well as olive oil to boost the energy content. What they did not contain was water, because Keith knew we would not appreciate hauling excess fluid or eating frozen biscuits. As a result, they went down slowly. The frozen chocolate was also a challenge, as was the first slug of soup with all the oil floating on top.

I had eaten only two biscuits when it was time to go again. I forwent cleaning my sunglasses, but quickly smeared on some lip cream and put the food away, removed the jacket and stuffed it into the sled, zipped it up and shuffled forward again, reversing all procedures.

It was always a relief to pause, but our bodies cooled down quickly even though we kept the breaks short. Moving off after each one, I could feel the heat draining from my hands into the stock handles. As I worked my arms, blood pumping down from my body, the chill bottomed out and began the slow climb back to warmth. It was half an hour before they were comfortable again. My body continued to feel slightly chilled. As for the soup, even in the stainless steel vacuum flasks it was cool by the third and last stop of the day.

I was wearing fleece pants without overpants, and a fleece jacket under my parka. Keith and Peter just had thermal tops under their parkas and reckoned they were quite warm, yet I was cold. I realised condensation must have been forming ice inside my parka. Although our parkas were of breathable material, a big difference between inside and outside temperatures is needed to drive the moisture through, and too much insulation inhibits this process. During the last shift I stopped and tried to struggle out of my parka. I got into a terrible tangle, with my head still stuck inside, and could not figure out what was wrong. Keith came over and helped me out. The parka had frozen to the fleece jacket. When I'd taken the jacket off I found I was much warmer without it. Ranulph Fiennes, the British polar expeditioner, maintains that it is important to be "bearably cold" when sled-hauling. This keeps sweating to a minimum but it also leaves one vulnerable immediately one stops hauling.

Towards the end of the last shift, I made an extra effort to get ahead of the others. At 5 p.m. I left my sled and skis and, dizzy from the strain, trudged back to photograph the long shadows of the other two on the snow. I asked how they were going.

"I'm rooted!" Peter replied.

"Bloody hard work, eh?" Keith said.

Once we had our down jackets on, it was really quite pleasant in the calm. We strung up the radio aerial from skis jammed into the snow and established a good connection with Doug at Patriot Hills. John came on and Peter told him: "I can't remember a harder day ever!"

Surely this can't be true, I thought to myself, but it did mean he was finding the going tough. Peter and I had developed rub spots on our heels, despite the soft comfort of our boots. We would have to manage our feet carefully to avoid being crippled.

In our six hours of toil we had made just over 7 km. We intended slowly to increase our hours and distance each day as we established a routine and became accustomed to both the climate and the effort. Our second dinner went well under Keith's direction and we were all in good spirits despite the hard day. We figured it could only get better. I felt sure we would get there. Peter was finding it tough but confided this only to his diary:

> I can't remember a harder day and very disappointing in relation to distance. We walked 1.5 hours then rested. The rests only take a few minutes as we get too cold. I feel worn out and fatigued. Guess it's getting used to it or it may have something to do with the diarrhoea I've had over the last couple of days. I've got no energy and my feet hurt terribly. I wondered during the day how I would face 70 days of it. The reality is that hopefully this is the worst type of snow we'll get and our sleds are at their heaviest.

Cloud advanced until the sky was overcast. Soon there was a white-out. By bedtime it was snowing gently, the flakes pattering softly on the tent.

4 NOVEMBER

A magical day. Five centimetres of fresh powder had fallen overnight. The cloud was low; we could see for several hundred metres to where the ground merged with the sky. There was no horizon and the snow was an unfathomable blank. Keith led all day over fairly good surfaces, an improvement over yesterday. The fresh snow must have buried the sandy stuff. I felt we were covering more ground. As the light wind fell away, the scene became serene and beautiful, caressed by clouds of gossamer. I almost forgot the drudgery for a while – a luxury of following – and ambled happily along. Perhaps, I thought, I was finally arriving in Antarctica.

Peter, too, was happy to give Keith his head. Still nursing a sore leg, strained running up a sandhill in Australia, he wrote in his diary:

> Keith is skiing very well and does most of the trail breaking. I'm concerned about my calf and feet in general. I'll take it easy during the next couple of days.

The cloud cleared to reveal the most wonderful snow surfaces, wind-packed and crystalline. It was pleasantly warm, −20°C, and I lashed some clothes on my sled to dry. A sled can be quite convenient as a wardrobe, clothes line and seat. I also found it comforting to have everything we needed for many weeks in one secure package.

Later some thin cloud moved in and a few fine snowflakes drifted down, glimmering in the sun. On the back of my glove I noticed each was a tiny but perfectly formed hexagonal crystal. This was the most delicate of snowfalls in a world of shifting ephemera. I thought of Antarctica as a land of vapours, a fluid country made only of air and water. Snow falls from the faintest wisp of cloud, the sky reaching down to become part of the land. At the end of the day I cruised into camp behind the others. An ice fog moved at ground level around the campsite and the sun swept low, setting the fog aglow. The sense of space and purity was overwhelming: our camp was the only feature in a vast circle of whiteness.

Keith drew from the GPS a disappointing tally of 11 km for the day. Peter squatted by the radio, waiting for the call from Patriot Hills. On cue, Doug's voice crackled out: "Aussies, Patriot Hills. Good evening. How are you guys? Over."

"Good, Doug. We went really well today," Peter replied. "We walked for 8 hours, and whilst we're pretty tired, we're not as wrecked as we were yester-day. What we plan to do from here on is walk for about 8 hours a day for the rest of this week and gradually increase that daily average to about 10 or 11 hours a day."

I wondered if the radio was rivalling the video as a confidant, because the three of us had not discussed the strategy in exactly those terms. Ten hours was okay by me, but 11 sounded a bit much.

We all sat outside while Keith cooked dinner, creating a cloud of steam in the still air, and I didn't want to go to bed.

5 NOVEMBER

We got away in three hours on this our third morning with the help of two cooks and two stoves. We could improve on this because we had taken a while to re-glue the skins onto Peter's and my skis. They had given us a hard time yesterday, flapping loosely and causing plenty of slips.

I led for the whole day in variable light and weather. At first it was overcast and I had difficulty maintaining a compass bearing with nothing to aim for, particularly when my rhythm was broken by lumps and bumps concealed by the universal greyness. When the light was strong, I'd stop to let the wobbling compass needle stabilise in its spherical housing. Swinging my torso, I'd look up in the direction of the bearing and fix on a shadow better defined than the rest or a spot of sunlit brightness. Then I'd trudge towards that beacon, each slide of a ski taking me 40 cm or so closer. After a few minutes and several re-alignments, I'd reach the feature, often finding it to be a tiny ridge of sastrugi smaller than a cat. Occasionally I would sight on a cloud feature, as long as it was a slow-moving one.

Later the cloud lifted and, with the more distant view, I could see we were on a gradual slope leading down into the head of a broad valley that opened to the east. Keith and Peter were sick of second-guessing the subtle deceptions of the landscape and thought it was merely a trick of the light, something already very familiar to us, but I was convinced by the languid cloud-shadows moving across the opposite slope and the eagerness of my sled to follow me. It was encouraging to have something more than an ever-receding horizon in front of us.

The sun and breeze came and went all afternoon, and it was a battle to keep clothing properly balanced to stay warm but not too sweaty. The leg and underarm zips that provided ventilation in our windproof shell clothing were a real boon.

I pushed ahead as hard as I could when I led off for the last shift. The travelling was good (surely we were going downhill!) and a slight following wind was strengthening. The light steadily dimmed and soon thickening snow began to blow against my back. I looked behind to make sure the others were not out of sight in the gloom. After eight hours we had travelled 15 km. This was our best distance yet, but it confirmed a downhill run. More proof came from our watch-altimeters, which showed we had dropped 200 m during the day. I wondered what had become of the climb to the crest of the island.

Peter's diary:
I found the day long and tiring, but was pleased with the distance covered. Ian led during the day, he did a great job.

Keith and I had a hand-freezing time acting as human supports for the radio aerial in driving snow as Peter made the radio sched with Patriot Hills. Doug said our positions from the Argos, which we had been activating at every camp, were now coming through from Sydney. We agreed we would radio only every second night from then on.

The tent was a haven from the storm that strengthened through the night.

6 NOVEMBER

No progress at all today. Strong wind and a continuous stream of snow buffeted the tent. Unfortunately the wind shifted in the night and began rocking the tent quarter-on, causing the poles to buckle ominously inward. Fresh snow piled up around us. Keith and I dressed and ventured outside to see what we could do to make our situation more secure. We were greeted by thick snow streaming sideways from the NNE, enmeshed in a stinging head-high ground blizzard. Visibility was down to a few metres and I could only bear to point my goggled face downwind. Some 30 cm of fresh snow blanketed the ground and our sleds were nearly buried.

Keith bravely filmed the rocking tent. Using stocks and skis, we pegged out more guys to improve its stability, then dug out the vestibules and built a snow wall around the windward side, quarrying snowblocks with a small saw and a snow-shovel fitted to an ice-axe. While we worked outside, Peter tried the zip-out tent floor as a toilet. "Difficult but achievable" was his verdict. However, we would continue to conduct our morning evacuations outside. When we were satisfied that our camp would not now get blown away, Keith and I crawled back inside.

We went on short rations and ate some biscuits left over from previous days (none of us was consuming our full daily ration). Later the wind eased until the tent was merely vibrating, but snow continued to fall, gradually filling the gap between the snow-wall and the tent, climbing half-way up it and threatening to push it in. Keith went out again to dig away several cubic metres of accumulation.

To fill in time in the tent we filmed some video interviews. I recorded an intro for Peter, who was buried in his sleeping bag. Tortoise-like, he slowly shoved his head from the bag, sunburnt and stubbled, to make his statement:

At the moment it's still total white-out outside, but the barometer is rising and we're hopeful the weather is going to clear up because we need to get some miles under our belt. The further away from the coast we get, the better the weather will get, we hope, and the further we get into November, towards December, the better the weather should get — more consistent. Although with all the snow that's fallen ... it's probably going to be really hard to pull the sleds tomorrow. So that's something I can look forward to. In the tent it's reasonably comfortable because of the good bags, but if you can imagine, it's really cold. On the inside walls of the tent we get this rime, like snow on the inside ... outside is covered in snow, and inside the rime sinks down and gets all over our sleeping bags and clothes and things.

The rime developed unpleasantly in cloudy weather and was impossible to remove, so it travelled from camp to camp with us until the sun shone. When warmth sublimated the frost it passed straight out through the breathable tent fabric. It persisted on the dark side of the tent until the sun came around.

I welcomed the day of rest after the grunt of our first few days. Physically I was faring pretty well, better than I had expected. Previously I had suffered in the early part of a strenuous journey until my body got used to it. The fact that I'd trained more than ever in my life must have paid off. My legs were weary at the end of each day, but no muscle aches or stiffness had developed. My heels were tenderly hovering below blister level and hopefully toughening up. They are the hardest to prepare adequately for this kind of exertion as there is no substitute for sliding up and down in boots all day.

7 November

Light winds and snow during the night sealed our fate for the day: hauling sleds across the blankness again. We feared the soft new snow would make our task tougher than ever.

We crawled from our cocoon into gently falling snow and a slight breeze from the east. It was a complete white-out, an underworld where sky and ground merged. In such conditions there is so little to fix the eye on that it is easy to lose one's balance and fall over while standing still. It's been compared to being inside a ping-pong ball.

It took some time to dig out our sleds. I had to shape a ramp in front of mine so that I could haul it up to the surface of the snow plain, now raised 30 cm by the fresh snowfall. To our delight the sleds sat cleanly on the new surface, which had been packed firm by the wind. We set about extricating the tent, taking care to find all the pegs and other assorted anchors. At times like this it can be very easy to lose things in the snow.

At one point during the day, Keith, who was leading, stopped to gaze around, arms outstretched to the tops of his stocks, his back arched. As I caught up, he turned and said: "Just admiring the view."

With Peter behind me, Keith and his sled were the only things in sight. "Yeah, it's great isn't it?" I retorted. "Lots of variety; one minute it's snowing and the next it's not snowing so much."

The travelling was not too bad. The temperature was about −12°C, with either calm air or a light breeze. The surface was solid, wind-packed snow with patches of velvety powder. We had decided it was too demanding for one person to lead for the whole day, so we adopted a system of shared leads over four shifts. Every third day one of us would lead two shifts. It was Peter's lucky day.

On his first shift, Peter stopped to regain his breath and turned around to us in exasperation. "Are you guys finding this tough, or is it just me?" he asked.

"No, it's hard all right, and probably a bit worse in front" I replied.

Keith consulted his watch-altimeter (like me, he had it hooked onto the sled with a karabiner rather than on his wrist, where it tangled with clothing). "And it's uphill," he said. "We've climbed 20 m."

When you're pulling 155 kg, any incline is debilitating. Peter brought some perspective to our task. "You know," he said, "you've got to hand it to those early explorers, knowing that every step they took towards the Pole was one more they would have to repeat on the way back."

For us, the idea of returning was unthinkable.

We pulled all day through a void of greyness. Ahead, nothing. Behind, the landscape was defined only by our weaving tracks for 20 or 30 m, then nothing. It was easy to believe that nothing existed except for our halting and quixotic caravan of warmth. Peter staggered off, eyes glued to the bubble on his chest, groping in the gloom to find the lumps and bumps he could not see. Crystal-ball gazing, Keith called it.

Peter's diary:

Pulling was very difficult in complete white out all day ... I found the going very slow and frustrating. We were generally moving uphill which didn't help. Distance was again disappointing as a result ... Ian and Keith are very courageous and pull determinedly.

We toiled uphill for six of our eight hours of hauling. In the tent in the evening, Keith put a pile of snow on the stove to melt and then warmed the GPS batteries in his sleeping bag before installing them and switching on. The reading from the oracle at our sixth camp was 78.784°S, 46.340°W.

"Eleven kilometres for the day and 45 km total," Keith announced.

The GPS also computed our bearing from our last camp. Amazingly for a day of weaving through the gloom, we had tracked exactly on our intended direction of 181° magnetic. The last chore we asked of this impressive piece of technology was to advise our bearing for the next day. The LCD display, sluggish in the cold, suggested the same, 181°, which sounded fair enough. Keith shut the machine down after just a few minutes. It was capable of much more than this, but we wanted to save the batteries. If the GPS were to fail, navigation would become very difficult, if not impossible. That was why we carried a spare device and four sets of batteries.

For the first time I plotted our position on the best map we'd been able to get of Berkner Island and the surrounding ice shelves. It was a 1:2,000,000 glaciological chart published in Germany and produced from satellite images. I marked a spot for each of our camps, discovering to my dismay that our starting point was further from the northern coast of Berkner Island than I'd thought, and even some 16 km south of Børge's starting point on 78.23°S. It looked to me as if we'd jumped the start a little, and I said so. I felt responsible because I had overlooked this discrepancy in the hurly-burly of starting out. There had apparently been some disparity between our GPS and the Twin Otter's. Keith was a little disappointed, too, but philosophical. Peter didn't think it mattered.

"They said they put us down where Børge started," Peter said. "If it was good enough for him, then it's good enough for me! You wouldn't really want to be dragging even further through this sand, would you?"

He had a point, and there was certainly no going back to salvage purity now. Børge's starting point appeared to have been very precisely aligned with the current edge of the Filchner Ice Shelf, which has retreated south in the past 10 years as chunks have broken off and sailed away across the Weddell Sea.

More positively, my red dots and the line joining them showed us making a beeline for our intended departure point from the southern end of Berkner Island. The GPS had this destination programmed into it so that it could give us the bearing to follow each day. It also became clear that we were crossing the valley behind McCarthy Inlet, a deep bay in the east coast of the island, which explained our ups and downs and also perhaps the snowy weather.

We'd had the choice of starting on Berkner Island's eastern or western sides, or anywhere in between. All were ethically acceptable, based on the precedents set by previous expeditions, provided the latitude was close to the 78th parallel. Because he intended to parasail, Børge started near the eastern side, which his research indicated received more wind from the north-east. The western side offers a slightly shorter route. Two previous Norwegian expeditions had chosen this side: Sjur Mørdre, the pioneer of the Berkner route to the Pole, started with his team there in 1991–92 at around 78.25°S, and Erling Kagge, who made the first solo journey to the Pole, set off from there in 1992–93. This route has the added advantage of avoiding the worst of the climb over the island's 974 m high southern summit, not to mention the climb up the lower northern dome. Nearly all this height is lost in the descent to McCarthy Inlet. Choosing to follow Børge's route was one of our first major mistakes, the penance for which was the grinding ascents. Børge's own planning was impeccable. He picked up good winds and parasailed rapidly up most of the ascents.

Late in our hauling day we had noticed a strange band of light to the east.

Because it was the only variation in a world of grey, we watched it closely as it slowly approached us. While we were struggling up the last slope to our campsite, the band turned into blue sky, sandwiched between the flat horizon and the trailing edge of the infernal cloud under which we had suffered for two days. At the same time the temperature plummeted.

Later, as we sat comfortably relaxed in the tent, the sun finally came out from behind the cloud, bathing our hovel in the blissful warmth of a calm, clear evening. The dark green tent acted like a greenhouse, absorbing the solar radiation and trapping the warmth inside, to our great pleasure.

Before snuggling in to sleep, I switched on the Argos beacon and placed it in the vestibule. Here it would spend the night sending a signal up to a passing satellite that would compute our location and download it to the ground station at Australia's Casey Station, on the far side of the Antarctic continent. I switched it to zero, the routine "all OK" code, again.

Harnessed with sled and compass I prepare to leave camp on Berkner Island for another exhausting day, my face fully protected from the cold and sun. Strapping the compass to his chest allowed the leader to maintain direction, in the absence of landmarks, without using his hands.

Late evening shadows reach across the eternal snows of Berkner Island (left) as we take the first of three million footsteps to the South Pole, abandoning any thoughts of retreat along with our last tangible link with the rest of the world – the plane. It took 1–2 hours every morning to prepare breakfast (top) of muesli with warm milk and olive oil, melted from a frozen block, and vacuum flasks of soup for the day. To ensure an early start, Peter took over this task. Keith (above) prepared the evening meals, which we finished with a welcome warm drink.

JOHN LEECE

Our 5 November camp (right) is blessed with a golden ice fog, as Keith tends pasta boiling on the stove. Finding a campsite on Berkner Island was never an issue, we just stopped at the allotted time and pitched the tent. From the comfort of his sleeping bag, Peter (top) reports our progress to Patriot Hills on the 7.5 kg two-way radio that was our main communications link – a ritual repeated every second evening. Navigation over the featureless snowfields depended upon our battery-powered Global Positioning System (GPS) receiver (above), which computed our position at each campsite, the kilometres travelled and the bearing to be followed.

*In a stinging 60 km/h blizzard, Keith (top) shovels away heavy snowfall
that kept us stormbound on 6 November and threatened to collapse the tent.
On a calmer day but bundled in a down jacket against the −25°C chill
(right), he melts a huge pot of snow, and his frozen balaclava, over our
critically important small petrol stove. The Argos unit (above) was activated
at every campsite to transmit our position, the temperature and a message
code, selected by a switch and listed on the unit, via orbiting satellites to
our supporters in Sydney, and then to ANI.*

Chapter 4

A VIEW *at* LAST

Such a journey takes you prisoner.
Every fibre, every thought, trapped in the ice.

REINHOLD MESSNER, ANTARCTICA: BOTH HEAVEN AND HELL (1991)

8 NOVEMBER

My diary:
I don't know which is worse: to have no visibility and therefore no concept at all of progress, or to have a wide horizon to prove that any apparent progress is totally inconsequential.

I was sitting up, crosswise in the tent, with my delicious sleeping bag up to my waist and my down jacket warming my top half, writing in my diary after a day of calm, big-sky sunshine. I was finding it hard to keep my hands warm, so I wore thin polyester inner gloves.

Peter had been very efficient at organising breakfast and getting us out of the tent this morning. He was keen to get away earlier than we had been. "The quicker we get started, the earlier we can stop and camp and get into the tent," he insisted. Since clock time was totally arbitrary in our situation, his logic bemused Keith and me, and we told him so. But he remained adamant, and I decided it must be psychologically important to him. I certainly agreed with him that we needed to reduce the time between waking and moving off.

We'd had a punishing day climbing out of the McCarthy Inlet basin. The numerous bumps made it tougher, as did patches of soft snow that gripped the

"I feel like I'm on the Burma Railway," Peter said, plodding along the tracks to the Pole. It was easy to plot a straight course when the sun shone because distant features were clearly visible.

sled hulls. The storm two days ago had created drifts behind every little hump. On the steepest our ski skins lost traction and we slipped backwards. This was disheartening and gave our overworked leg muscles extra grief. We contemplated swapping to wider skins for the next day. We were all very tired at the end of eight hours. Peter's and my heels had rubbed badly. This was worrying, though mine didn't seem to have blistered yet. Peter didn't say much about this at the time.

Peter's diary:
I had trouble again with my [shift] leads due to the extreme pressure on my bumps. Felt very tired today as all of us did. Can only hope that conditions improve off BI [Berkner Island]. Hope the weather remains good to us… Ian and Keith are performing better than me. My heels are letting me down. I want to do well for Beth, Marnie and Kimberley and Australia. This gives me strength.

At least we'd had some scenery to appreciate. There was a huge view back to where the inlet's northern shore ran down to the ice shelf, a vast and gently sloping landscape. I felt gratified to have my map interpretation of the lie of the land confirmed. The air was very calm for most of the day, but when a light wind did pick up we all had trouble getting our hands warm. According to our instruments, we gained some 220 m in height, which was at least gratifying. I hoped we would maintain the height gained until we dropped off the far end of the island.

When we spoke with Doug and John on the radio, they told us that while we had been languishing in our pathetic blizzard two days ago, they'd suffered 150 km/h winds that flattened much of the Patriot Hills camp. We could only be grateful that we copped nothing like that.

9 NOVEMBER

After a week of pulling, we were gradually settling into a routine. As on previous mornings, Peter woke first to start the stoves for breakfast. He roused me by dumping a food bag at his feet, near my head, and in my bleariness I struggled with knots in plastic bags while still lying down, passing him the required items. I could hear a wind vibrating the tent and there was little inspiration to forsake my sleeping bag too soon. Keith started stirring and groaning, his face half covered by an airline sleeping mask. He and I slept along the walls of the tent, heads towards the rear vestibule. Peter slept in the middle, with his head at the main entrance. The large vestibule was a good space for preparing breakfast, leaving the rest of the tent free for our morning preparations. Peter usually dislikes cooking, but after instruction from Keith, he quickly learnt to light the stoves reliably and figured out a good sequence of juggling the billies, bowls and vacuum flasks for the morning cook-up.

I retrieved my gloves and inner boots from the net hanging from the roof of the tent (where they dried out overnight) and stuffed them into my sleeping bag, replacing the thin thermal socks and liner gloves that I had dried out in there as I slept. Slowly I came out of my shell like a reluctant cicada, making sure every bit was clothed as soon as it was exposed. Heat was not to be squandered, and body parts kept warm all night in the bag needed to have that warmth protected. Heading off into the white horizon with feet already cold, for instance, would be asking for trouble. I pulled my feet out one at a time for their morning prep. An experienced outdoorsman and chiropody lecturer, Alan Donnelly, had advised us in Sydney on foot care. Peter arranged this, knowing that other ski expeditions had suffered from major foot problems.

Removing my dry night socks, I swabbed each foot with alcohol and rubbed anti-perspirant powder over it before fortifying my heels against blisters. I rubbed a few quick-drying layers of friar's balsam on and added a layer of plastic artificial skin before slipping on thin thermal socks. Over them I pulled a plastic bag, salvaged from our daily rations, to act as a waterproof vapour barrier. Then came the thick, greasy-wool felt inner boot, which had already moulded perfectly to the shape of my foot. The insulation provided by these was phenomenal and they resisted moisture absorption very well. Unfortunately they also moulted alarmingly when new and for the past week we had been picking wool fibres from our mouths after every meal and drink!

I shoved the completed feet back into the sleeping bag so they would be toasty warm when I finally put on my outer boots to go outside. The outer boots of light nylon canvas absorbed little moisture and had a low thermal mass, so the warmth of my felt inners was not immediately sucked out as it would have been by heavier cold boots. I had built up the inner soles of the main boots with several layers of closed-cell foam, both to insulate and to fill up the space and thus reduce the up-and-down movement of my heels.

The vapour-barrier principle is widely used in very cold climates to prevent moisture from sweating feet reaching the main layers of insulation, there to accumulate, freeze and reduce the insulating ability. Keeping the felt inner boots as dry as possible was critical for warm feet. However, having your warm, sweaty feet in plastic bags all day has other complications, starting with "prune feet" and progressing to trench foot. The alcohol and anti-perspirant controlled this problem. In fact, the liner socks whose job was to absorb the moisture of the foot were damp but never wringing wet when we took our steaming feet out of our boots every evening, and they dried quite quickly in our sleeping bags. Obviously the thin socks would eventually deteriorate from this treatment, and we could not waste fuel washing them, so we were carrying 10 pairs each.

Our faces needed care, too, and as I was working on my feet Keith was putting on sun cream and lip salve. He was having no problems with his feet, using manufactured vapour-barrier socks instead of the plastic bags, and some perfect outer nylon bags made by Leanne. After a week, his inner boots looked pristine, perfectly protected between two layers of nylon. The tip of my nose and lips were quite sore, but I didn't know if this was from sunburn or a touch of frostnip. I put some tape on my nose to protect it from both extremes.

It was my turn to lead two shifts, the first and last. I started off feeling weary already, a bad sign. It was hard work again, but this was more bearable than the cold wind. I was glad to reach the end of the first shift and pull out the 'huddle tent' to shelter us during the break. This dome-shaped plastic bag, found by Keith in a Sydney hardware store, began life as a patio-furniture cover. In the lee of my sled, the three of us sat close together on the bottom edge of the bag and pulled the rest of it over our heads. It shut out the wind perfectly and we could enjoy our soup and biscuits and discuss progress. Peter referred to it as the "cone of silence", from the old *Get Smart* television comedy. Although we only stopped for 10 minutes and kept our big gloves on as much as possible while eating, it took half an hour of hauling to warm my hands up again after the stop.

My diary:
This is an extremely uncomfortable business. I plod along, with a number of little requirements demanding attention – a boot needs adjusting, my goggles are iced up and need scraping, I need to urinate and replace the cream on my lips. But I know I can only stop for long enough to attend to one of these chores or my hands will cool down too much. If we find −14 [°C] with a 20 kph wind only just bearable, how will we cope with worse?

My heels were a bother. The plastic vapour-barrier bags kept slipping down into my boots as I walked. The wrinkled plastic rubbed my heel as it passed over it. Without the plastic to separate the two, the liner sock would stick to the inner boot and rub at the skin, and sweat would dampen the crucial insulation of my inner boots. I had to figure out a better system.

A black cloud began to move in from the north-east during the afternoon, a sheet of steel sliding overhead like part of a cosmic machine. It obliterated the sun and then, with glacial slowness, continued to close down the remaining blue sky, squeezing it onto the horizon with the weight of a planet. We skied towards the narrowing band of blue with a sense of impending doom, hoping to escape underneath.

When the blue sky disappeared, so did the ground definition. The cloud was featureless and grey, absorbing all detail from the snow, but it lent the wind strength. The last shift became a slog. The only thing to focus on was the diminishing band of light. One lens of my glasses was frosted up. I was tired and there were many low icy ridges to winch over. I was not enjoying myself. I longed for much better sledging conditions: hard snow, sunny and windless weather, a downhill slope!

It had been mostly uphill again all day, with 140 m of altitude gained. At last, towards the end, we seemed to reach a less steep part of the island's ice dome. I began the day weary and finished despondent. I could only hope to feel better on the morrow.

10 NOVEMBER

The evening was superb. We sat on our sleds eating another enjoyable and well-earned dinner, this time rice curry. The air was cold but still, and there was warmth in the hard sunlight. In the vast circle of white under the arching blue, there was just us, our tent, sleds and motley gear strewn about. It was flat in all directions, the snow stretching away, textured and glimmering. A three-quarter moon hung 30° above the horizon to the north-east, and the sun hovered just half as high in the south-west. Antarctica seemed benign, almost friendly. I felt privileged to be there. When we raised Doug on the radio, he had journalist Jennifer Foreshew from *The Australian* on the line and relayed her questions.

"Can you describe your surroundings?" she asked.

Words were inadequate. Attempting to convey a sense of the place through such convoluted communication was hopeless.

Doug told us the second Hercules had finally arrived at Patriot Hills that day and John was on his way back to South America and further complex negotiations with our partners. He had his own burden to haul. I gave Doug a message to send to my son, Cale, on his 12th birthday.

It had been a far more comfortable day than the previous one. We'd had perfect cold weather, with cloudless skies and no wind. The skiing was better, too – still mostly uphill but with fewer soft "sandy" patches and some flat going towards the end. For some periods, dragging was almost enjoyable. I'd been advised that the slopes on Berkner Island were not noticeable. Well, what the eye couldn't see the body certainly could. Slopes of just one in 100 or less made the sleds significantly harder to move. Compared with the flat, where there was a little bounce from the haul ropes with each step, the slightest slope turned the sled into a slug.

Whenever a small hump or ridge momentarily increased the slope even more, the only way to clear it was to jerk with the hips and winch. Slowly the sled inched up the incline to the crest, groaning and crunching, the nose climbing into the air. When the centre of gravity reached the crest, the sled seesawed and the front crashed down. On the flat this moment of release was pure delight, for the sled slid down just a little under its own weight. But not on a climb; there, even the downward side of a hump had to be negotiated with muscle power.

The pleasant conditions prompted a rush of filming. At the end of one shift, as Peter and I munched on biscuits, I aimed the video camera back along our tracks at Keith in the distance and joked to the microphone: "Keith's lagging behind because he's a slack-arse. No, actually he was called to nature. He's done his damnedest to try and catch up, but we, of course, have run on ahead because we didn't want him to catch us, we wanted to get this shot."

After he jerked his sled over a bump, I saw Keith stop and stand in his characteristic pose, hands on stocks planted wide.

"He's having a blow now, probably cursing and swearing at us, the poor bastard. He'll accept it's for the good of the cause when he gets here," I said.

When he did reach us, a huge Fu Manchu icicle was hanging off the chin of his balaclava. He had the video camera strapped to the sled so he could film himself hauling towards us. Alone with the camera, he had voiced his feelings: "Fourteen hundred km. I don't know whether we're going to make it or not, to be honest with you. At this stage it's just damned hard work."

He was more positive in his diary that night: "Great day. −20C all day, but sunny, glorious ... Peter's feet are sore, left heel. Ian and myself are travelling OK. A bit tired but in good spirits. 84 km travelled 1215 to go!!!" (Keith was making his calculations according to the readings of the GPS, which measured a straight line to the Pole. We expected our course over the ground to be longer.)

I turned to shoot Peter giving a rundown of our progress.

We're averaging at the moment about 11 km a day [Peter said]. Yesterday was all uphill, today it's been a bit flatter and we're hoping to do about 15 km. We need to get that average up to about 20 or 25 km a day to get this trip done, because we've got a helluva long way to go. But we figure the snow conditions here are perhaps a little bit softer than they'll be up on the plateau and our sleds are definitely heavier, so we figure we'll be able to move across it more quickly. At least we hope so, because this is a real effort to get up each morning and trudge for 8 hours …

We actually carried on for eight and a half hours, the longest yet, but it was a strain for all of us, relieved by the delightful evening. Peter was really suffering with his heels, something he had feared from the start. He said to the video: "I never wear boots, because I have these bumps on my heels that always rub … they're really giving me hell. They make it really hard because when you're pulling the sled, all the weight's against your heels … But anyway, we'll get there."

Peter was twice forced to halt to adjust his socks and dressings. He hated stopping and showed intense frustration, but he seemed to cope with the pain well. He also had a nasty frostbitten patch on his left cheek, about the size of a 50c piece. It was scabbed and cracking and must have been very sore, but he didn't talk about it. We were all keeping our worst fears to ourselves. In his diary Peter wrote: "My heels, especially my left one, hurt like hell … The last two and half hours were a real struggle. I'm worried about this because it could cause me to slow up. I can only battle on."

By the time we had finished our hot chocolate and fruit biscuit dessert, the temperature had fallen to −24°C and we retreated to the tent.

11 NOVEMBER

Peter's 40th birthday. As a special present he got to trudge for another eight hours across Antarctica. At least this might have protected him from the feeling of going downhill with age!

I started off feeling physically better today. It was sunny and there was a slight breeze from the north-east. My latest ailment was a bruised rib cage, perhaps caused by the sled harness being too tight when we had been struggling over the humps a day or two earlier.

On his shift Peter showed a tendency to 'go for it', heading off quickly and hardly stopping to look back. I struggled to keep up, and this aggravated my blisters. I wondered how Peter's feet were doing. He was showing his remarkable ability to ignore afflictions and push through difficulties. Keith continued to plod steadily, without rushing. "It was the same in the Simpson," Keith said of Peter's approach. "You just have to ignore it, otherwise you'll go mad."

Peter's style concerned me, because mine was more like Keith's, measured and cautious. I was confident I could get to the Pole on the food we had brought and barring major problems, but at my pace, not rushing, whether it took 60, 70, 75 or even 80 days. I reasoned that northern Berkner Island had delivered difficult travel and that we would certainly get faster. Peter wanted to go fast to have as much time as possible up our sleeve as a safety margin, and he was beginning to worry about a perceived lack of commitment in us.

Later the breeze turned north-west, bringing a low fog up from the Ronne Ice Shelf. Silence engulfed us and we spent an ethereal afternoon under a hazy sun in a golden mist. By then I was really tired and I found the last hour tough. I was having hot and cold flushes and feeling vaguely ill. My sled felt 100 kg heavier. As well, my heels had blistered and, by trying to reduce the lift of my heels, I put more strain on my legs. I only just made it to camp and felt like crawling straight into bed and going to sleep.

As we relaxed in the tent, thoughts inevitably turned to the day's effort and what it meant for our chances of reaching the Pole. I felt pretty depressed about blisters and my performance. The plastic bags were bugging me. I had been taping them around my ankles and instep. This helped but did not entirely solve the problems.

Peter's diary reflected his mixed feelings: "My feet were a little better today, but still very sore, particularly the heels ... Other than that I feel OK. We all agree that it was a hard day ... Great distance – our best yet."

Indeed, 17 km was a good result and it was gratifying to put our first 100 km behind us. Peter entered the day's data in his notebook, carefully calculating the amount of food left and the distance remaining against our rate of travel. He had drawn up a detailed table to monitor these vital statistics.

"This is terrible," he exclaimed. "We have to average 20 km a day if we're going to make it to the Pole, and after eight days we've only made 101 km."

I tried to be positive: "We always knew the first week and Berkner Island would be tough, and the distances are increasing. I reckon we'll start making good progress soon."

Later, as we ate dinner, Peter reflected on the strangeness of our existence. "When I'm plugging along behind with my goggles on and watching my skis in the tracks, I feel like there's a wall down either side of me and I'm travelling down a corridor," he said. "I feel like I'm on the Burma Railway."

12 NOVEMBER

We emerged from the tent this morning to find our sleds and other gear decorated with crystals of rime, a legacy of the fog. The snow surface glittered with diamonds, too, but the beauty concealed a dark side. Leading the first shift, I turned to Keith. "Very high friction today," I said.

"Yeah, it's like someone's thrown sand over the snow."

His description was perfect. But he didn't seem too affected by the "slowsand", as we called it, punning on quicksand. When he took the lead, he romped away so that Peter and I struggled to keep up. Peter found his shift tough and even stopped for breathers.

Keith and I accepted that Peter's greater strength would mean we two would eventually have a tougher time, even though for the moment Peter seemed to be suffering with us and Keith was pulling strongly. Peter, too, recognised Keith's performance, while being overly critical of his own.

Starting at 8.18 [Peter wrote in his diary] we pulled until 6 o'clock with 2 hour 20 min shifts each making 8 hours 40 mins in total. Keith pulled one, Ian two and me one segment. My segment was hopeless as I did not perform very well. No energy and heels hurting atrociously ... Keith performing the best out of us as far as skiing is concerned.

As I was leading, I heard a sudden loud "Whump!", and the snow under my skis gave way. My visceral reaction was that we'd hit a crevasse, and I instantly went into a half crouch, tense and ready, adrenaline pumping. But nothing happened. A dull roar rolled away from us, like the sound of a passing jet. The surface appeared unchanged but for some small cracks around my skis. There was no crevasse.

I had read about snowquakes and realised we had just experienced one. New layers of snow may have air gaps between or inside them, especially if the wind is strong. These airy layers are unstable and can settle if extra weight is placed on them. In this case, our bodies and sleds had caused the collapse. On the flat slopes of Berkner Island, it was not possible to tell how far the snow surface had collapsed, but it felt like about 10 cm. To judge from the noise, the area of subsidence must have been the size of several football fields. It was a most unnerving experience but one we would eventually get used to.

We gained no altitude in the day, which we counted as a blessing, as the hauling would clearly have been horrendous if uphill. But I felt all the hard yakka had been for little result. I found this lack of reward most disturbing. We plugged away all day with no scenery to indicate progress, and we arrived at a spot to camp that to all appearances was identical to where we began nine or 10 hours earlier, as if nothing had happened in between.

Apart from the textures of the snow and the sky, there was nothing to look at. It was easy to imagine we were part of some cruel cosmic joke, marching on a planetary treadmill that just kept turning over the same terrain. The circling, never-setting sun added to the sense of disorientation.

We wondered when we might see something for our troubles, and we looked forward to the view across the flat ice shelf to the mountains beyond, as prisoners might await their release. If we kept walking on the treadmill, the mountains would be delivered; that was the promise that drove us.

Only the abstract GPS figures gave an indication of progress. Nightly we consulted the oracle. The numbers, originating from a realm beyond our understanding, began to assume a mystical power. The oracle revealed that, in spite of the hard travelling, we had done 17 km again. We had no option but to believe it, and were well pleased.

I was missing Marianne and our children painfully, especially when slogging away with little else to think about. I wondered what they were doing, and I contemplated all the things I'd like to be doing with them. I looked forward joyfully to the time after my return. I'd still be on leave and the kids would still be on holiday. Maybe we should go to the beach for a week. The beach!

It was Cale's birthday that night. At 7 p.m. on our watches – 9 a.m. at home – I sent a special birthday thought.

13 NOVEMBER

Setting out this morning, we were confronted by a cold wind, heavy overcast and falling snow. Nevertheless, the horizon was partly revealed, and even that amount of visibility was a boon to travelling. As we walked south, the wind quartered into our faces from the left. With such a wind it was very difficult to arrange my clothing so that I was warm but not sweating too much. With my parka and overpants on and all zips open, my arms and shoulders were hot, but the wind chilled my chest as it whistled through my front zip and out of my right armpit vent. My nipples felt as if they were being chewed off by an ice maiden. The contrast in temperature between different parts of the body was almost physically painful.

The hauling was quite good, a light cover of silky smooth snow lying on the infernal dry crystals of sand. A thin ribbon of blue hovered on the horizon. During the next few hours it gradually grew, spreading over us until the sun emerged to spectacularly highlight the hissing, living flow of spindrift over the ground. The wind picked up and soon all the fresh snow had moved on, leaving our old enemy, the firm, sandy surface.

It was still cold and windy when we stopped to pitch the tent.

"Where should we camp tonight, guys?" Peter asked.

"Let's keep going to the next nice spot," Keith replied sardonically.

"Yeah, a shady tree and a little creek would be good," Peter said.

"With soft banks of sun-warmed snowgrass to lie on!" I added.

The place we chose looked like all the others, and we wasted no time diving into the tent. We had by then developed a standard way of arranging ourselves during cooking. Peter sat with his back to the side of the tent, legs across the main entrance. There, on a good day, he could try to dry his boots and gloves in the sunshine (which came in through the doorway at this time of day because the other end of the tent always faced north-east, the direction of the prevailing wind). I sat similarly, but facing the other way in the middle of the tent. Keith was backed into the far corner of the tent with his legs diagonally towards me, leaving the triangle of the other corner, where the floor unzipped, free for kitchen duties. This arrangement gave us all enough room and enabled us to sit quite comfortably in our sleeping bags while Keith tended the stove.

We all felt we had covered a good distance during the day and expectantly awaited the oracle's verdict. Looking like a wizard behind the steam of our cooking dinner, Keith peered at the GPS. Then he broke into a huge grin and punched the air. "Hey, 21 kay," he yelled.

We all whooped and cheered as if we'd won the lottery. For the first time we had broken the critical 20 km barrier. It was an enormous psychological boost.

Through the elation, I surveyed the damage. My thighs had been chafing slightly. My heels seemed stable, but by the end of the day my feet had begun to ache with the strain and pounding. The tip of my nose was really burnt and sore, but my lips were fine because I'd kept my balaclava pulled up over my mouth. The nose was a difficult one: it was so hard to protect and still breathe freely. My general physical condition was more pleasing: although tired at the end of the day, I had developed no soreness in my critical leg muscles, the engines that had to drive me to the Pole. It was the accessories that were suffering! Peter's feet were still deteriorating and Keith had two black toes - from pressure, thankfully, not frostbite.

14 NOVEMBER

Ah, the tedium. Hard days were becoming a habit. We trudged all day without scenery to look at, having little time to even appreciate the snow textures, which often changed by the hour. Sometimes as I plugged along the railway tracks, my gaze was drawn to the horizon, where I expected, for some reason, to see something. The edge of our world became particularly sharp and well-defined in the afternoon when some stratus cloud moved in. I was singing the

Railroad Work Song, which had become my sledging anthem. It's a rhythmic song that captures both the drudgery and the almost mystical beauty of physical labour.

As we settled into the tent, I set up the video camera in the annexe to film us all for the first time, clamping it to an ice-axe that I rammed into the hard snow. Peter began by reporting on the day: "We've just settled down at the end of day 13, after another good day's travel."

Keith interjected, laughing: "Speak for yourself, my feet are bloody sore!"

Peter continued:

The day started off reasonably warm in terms of temperature but there was a pretty stiff wind blowing that made it pretty cold to travel this morning. The wind died down and in fact it got pretty hot at −15 [°C] for us to walk ... We've done a second day of 21 km, which is great, because to do this thing in the 69 food days that we've got, we've got to average 20 km a day. The only down side of all that is that our feet are pretty sore. Our feet have got blisters and black toenails and all that sort of stuff, which we've got to come to grips with as we go further on, because we don't want any of that to cripple us.

This is the best part of the day, getting into the tent and relaxing and writing up diaries and having soups and having tea and a chat. Because you can't really have a chat during the day when we're walking because its all too noisy ... and we're too puffed out anyway to talk. So we trudge along with our own thoughts ... "

During Peter's commentary I had been plotting our course on the map. "We're well past our halfway point on Berkner Island," I announced. Then I turned to the camera and said: "We keep looking towards the horizon hoping we'll see something one day. In a couple of days, hopefully, when we come over the top of the island, we will get a view, maybe, down the other side and towards the mountains on the far side."

Peter went on: "Our day starts at 5.30 when the alarm goes off and everyone springs out of bed." He laughed and I was moved to explain: "Peter's being sarcastic. Peter springs out of bed and does a sterling effort of getting breakfast together from his bedside. Keith and I wallow and moan and groan and eventually emerge from the pits in time for breakfast."

Keith and I are not strong morning people. However, as a result of Peter's fortitude, we have cut our pre-start routine down to three hours, at least two of which are taken up with melting snow.

We discussed other aspects of our walk. Peter asked me how many days I thought it would take us to clear Berkner Island on current progress. I said six. The talk then switched to our health.

I had felt from the start that the greatest threat to our success lay in our own bodies rather than the external environment, as harsh as it was. The records of other expeditions made it clear that progressive physical breakdown resulting from the sustained strain of manhauling was the insidious enemy. As we extended our hauling hours and the distance travelled, we drew closer to that indefinable line that marked our physical limit and which was probably different for each of us. The danger was that the line may not be detectable until it was crossed.

The afternoon had been beautifully calm and warm, with the sun shining weakly through the stratus. The temperature climbed to a balmy −11°C, and it was so quiet you could almost hear it rising. This was delightful after several days of wind, and we didn't have to rush around on arriving at camp trying to get warm and do a dozen other things all at once.

15 NOVEMBER

My diary:
It is late in the afternoon, and I really have the shits. It is the last lead of the day, my second, and I'm finding the going really hard. My goggles are iced up, a new wear spot in my crutch is smarting and my trudge-worn heels have deteriorated markedly. Every few steps the sled drags terribly and I have to strain to keep it moving, the reluctant slug! Is it just me? Gasping, I look back in search of some absolution or excuse. Keith seems to be cruising and behind him I can't tell how Peter is faring. I can see my tracks cutting through frequent soft patches, gouging up to 10 centimetres deep. Either side of the sharp grooves cut by the high spec polyethylene runners, just one centimetre thick, the fibreglass hull of the sled has rubbed a wide rounded channel. It is the large surface area of the sled hull that seems to be dragging like a block of concrete against the cold snow.

When I stopped at the end of my allotted two hours and 10 minutes of sweltering in the lead, I checked the altimeter for a redeeming surprise. Thank heavens, it really was hard work! We had gained 80 m of altitude during the shift, making a total of 130 m for the day.

It was perhaps the balmiest day we had experienced. Although the mercury did not rise above −15°C, it had been mostly calm and the sun was growing noticeably warmer as high summer approached. Our normal hauling garb now consisted of one layer of thermals on the lower body and two layers on the upper, all under full windproofs. When we overheated we would open all the zips for ventilation. Today we sometimes overheated even without parkas. We certainly could not complain about the weather so far.

The pleasant conditions at camp that evening found Keith mucking about outside. A very industrious fellow, he constructed a mini incinerator from our first empty fuel drum and set to burning some rubbish. He seemed to be up to something else more secretive but I could not see what it was. Peter was in the tent, attending to all the little clothing chores required at the end of each day, when Keith called out: "Hey Peter, come outside, it's beautiful!"

Keith's encouragement failed to make an impact. Then I saw what he had been up to. Giving up on getting Mohammed to the mountain, Keith put four cigarette lighters on the cake he had constructed from sawn layers of ice, and carried it in to Peter, singing "Happy birthday". The singing was of Keith's usual standard but the cake was superb. Peter was delighted, even if it was a couple of days late.

"Make a wish," Keith said.

"I'll make it out loud," Peter said. "I wish for pain-free feet for the rest of the trip."

We put the cake in the pot for dinner.

Peter's diary:
My feet as usual were the main complaint with many more blisters resulting. This makes walking very uncomfortable. In the first two hours I had to adjust my boots five times to try and alleviate a couple of new pressures on my right foot. This I was partially successful at, but still the pain continued. My feet are a continuing irritation. Otherwise, I feel OK, plenty of energy, etc ...

Despite his foot problems, Peter always seemed cheerful in the tent at the end of the day. Leaning back on his clothes bag, he sighed: "Ahhh. This is always the best part of the day!"

16 NOVEMBER

My diary:
There has been lots of soft shit to drag through today, mostly this afternoon in the sessions led by Peter and me. By the end of the day I am in

total struggle mode, bone-weary and blistered. My heels are giving me hell, especially on the harder going, and I seem to be getting more and more tired each day. This is a worry. I think I need a rest.

Peter noticed it too. He wrote: "Ian found the trudging difficult today after lagging way behind. He's having trouble with his feet as well."

At the end of the last shift, Peter wanted to go on but Keith was against this. Unable to keep up, I had fallen behind and did not hear the conversation. Even on my leads I seemed to be holding the others up, since they kept close behind me. When I had earlier asked them about this, they said it did not bother them if I was a bit slower. I wondered what they would say if I asked for a rest day. I knew Peter was dead against the idea. Not that he said so; he just remained silent when Keith mentioned it. I hoped my condition would begin to stabilise quickly and then improve.

It became almost hot at times. In the afternoon we all stripped down to single thermals for the first time. It was only at these sweaty times that we noticed the stink of our bodies. I was moved to have a quick "snowbath" as soon as we reached the campsite and before I cooled down. Whipping off my shirt, I quickly rubbed snow over my torso and just as quickly got dressed again. It was a token but refreshing effort.

We had really hoped to see something today because we expected to come over the top of Berkner Island. But though the ground rose and fell somewhat, there was little overall change in altitude and we saw no sign of the alleged summit. We ticked off our second 100 km and crossed the 80th parallel. These milestones were becoming important as measures of something achieved beyond the mere GPS numbers. As we set up camp that evening I noticed a strange double horizon to the south and south-west. Could this be the first sign of the mainland, or was it just another illusion, a trick of Antarctic light? I wondered. Perhaps we'd find out tomorrow. I was dreading the grind and pain of another day.

17 NOVEMBER

My diary:
It is becoming more and more difficult to emerge from the pit each morning. Today will probably be really hard, after yesterday's experience. I glue some thicker pads to my heels, and call a short halt during the first session to adjust them. At the first break I try loosening the bootlaces around my ankles. This seems to ease the pressure and the pain.

Patches of soft snow continued to plague us early on, but as I led off for the second session, conditions eased and we entered a realm of magnificent swirling patterns in the snow, dusted with a coarse, crystalline layer of sparkling powder. This provided a sleek skiing surface that allowed reasonable progress into the afternoon even over the soft patches. We had definitely broken the back of Berkner Island and were on the downhill run.

Peter led the third shift, taking no prisoners. He wrote: "I was very pleased with my pull as I walked the whole 2.10 without stopping … I think this will add significantly to the distance we covered today."

Keith and I dawdled a little at the start, photographing each other on the superb crystal snow, and briefly discussed Peter's style.

"You can't flog it out for 60 days without a break," I said. "I don't think Peter realises that."

Keith said it had been the same on their Simpson trip. "He just doesn't stop, no rest days. The way I deal with it is to take it easy some days. That way you have a rest while moving and Peter stays happy."

Peter became a tiny dot in the distance. As we headed off in pursuit, I pondered our discussion. In spite of what I'd said, I suspected Peter probably was capable of going hard for 60 days straight. I didn't know whether the same could be said of Keith, who can be inscrutable at times. I doubted that he would ever ask openly for a rest day, because he deferred to Peter as leader and perhaps did not like to see himself as less capable than Peter. I had no shame on this point but enough pride to put off requesting a rest day for as long as I possibly could.

When we reached Peter, waiting at the next rest stop, he was not happy. We had come in 25 minutes behind. Keith then led the final shift, taking it steady. It was a pleasant relief to plod along his track, Peter at my heels. I sensed shadow-boxing between Peter and Keith, an unspoken theatre played out in their actions. I felt this left me awkwardly on the perimeter to survive as best I could. The pounding, bruised feeling in my heels intensified occasionally, forcing me to stop briefly and shake the pressure away. The pain reminded me of a similar sensation I'd had when walking long distances on hard roads with a heavy pack, and I suspected it was caused by the pressure of the hard ski against the foot.

I was keeping an official log as well as my personal diary. When I finished the official entry for today, Keith added on the bottom: "Ian is learning how to handle Pete's obsession with time/speed/kms."

We made 23 km – a record.

18 NOVEMBER

A doggerel haiku for Berkner Island (from my diary):

> *Berkner, buggerer*
> *breaks my back*
> *bend to crack*
> *Berkner: buggered now.*

Berkner must be the most featureless island on earth. Half the size of Tasmania, it has not a single rock or crack to break the unrelenting monotony of its surface. We longed for a view of the mainland, or even the island's end. I dreamt that a crevasse field would be a relief, a source of interest and something to engage the intellect beyond putting one foot in front of the other.

At the start of Peter's shift he was impatient for Keith and me to rise from our feeding. "Come on! Chop, chop! Kilometres rule our lives," he said.

My inquiry as to the reason for the panic was met with silence at first. Then Peter said he did not want to start until we were ready, "… to avoid yesterday's debacle."

We had another heatwave in the morning, with no wind and the temperature well up into single figures. We sweltered in single thermals. A wave of cloud rolled in from the north-east and stayed for the afternoon. Ground definition was lost but there were some beautiful features of light and shade on the horizon; there seemed to be some topography out there. The ground was very humpy and, with no contrast to help us, we were swerving all over the place. My sled was resisting like a kid being dragged from a lolly shop. All afternoon we rocked and rolled, our legs struggling on without information from the eyes. At the end of the day we walked around camp on wobbly legs like sailors coming ashore.

At one stage Peter trained his video camera on my diminishing form as I led into the greyness. He spoke quietly and confidentially into the microphone, as if afraid of disturbing the peace:

> *Today it's the warmest it's been, about −5 [°C]. There's no wind and it's silent, absolutely silent, except for the noise of our sleds. We only talk at all in our own thoughts … daydreaming, thinking about home. When you stop, when we all stop, its absolutely silent …*

It was a better day for me. My feet were not too sore and I was able to keep going at a steady pace. It was intriguing that as soon as one affliction diminished, another took its place. My glasses were the latest irritation. I was sick of seeing only 30 per cent of Antarctica. Eyewear poses enough of a problem for anyone in such cold: goggles fog and freeze up with the most subtle changes of wind and temperature. For Peter and me, these difficulties were magnified by the need to wear prescription glasses inside our goggles, offering the ice gods twice as many surfaces to play with. For this reason I wore my prescription sunglasses as much as possible instead of my goggles. But when the frigid wind blew, only goggles could protect the eyes from the cold.

Peter's frustration with our performance was starting to show in his diary:

Berkner Island just goes on and on and I think that it is killing us. Keith and Ian seem lethargic and despite good conditions and relatively light sleds, just plod away. We should be moving to take advantage of the good conditions, not let them slip away. I'll hold my tongue for the time being. Ian in particular is slow to start from each rest and generally lethargic during the day.

19 NOVEMBER

My 43rd birthday. I felt more like 63.

As a special gift, all my petty physical ailments improved and I was less weary. Peter even agreed. "Ian seems to have cheered up and his legs were well done," he wrote.

I found that my thin silk balaclava, which I had brought for keeping my greasy hair off the sleeping bag, effectively protected my face from the sun. The overcast conditions continued through the night to the middle of the day. I found them very pleasant, with more interesting white-line horizons and an intimate, enclosed feeling rather than a sensation of limitlessness. Peter, on the other hand, found them very uncomfortable.

Berkner is not giving up its prey easily [he wrote]. I led two stages today, the first I was pleased with, completing the 2.10 min non stop. Going was fast and downhill. It was difficult, however, in that the light conditions were very poor, making the snow relief very difficult. The second stage was just hard work. Flat with lots of soft snow and bumpy. I did another 15 min to make up for the slow progress.

We supposedly passed quite close to a bay in Berkner's east coast, as we approached the southern end of the island, but we could discern no sign of it. We lost more height and ended up not far above sea level.

20 NOVEMBER

A landmark day on which we expected to cross Berkner Island's south coast onto the Ronne Ice Shelf. And good riddance to the tedious place! We were not sure what to expect as we came off the island, but we knew that in such regions the ice is often disturbed and we needed to beware of crevasses. There the Ronne Ice Shelf, a massive extension of the mainland Antarctic glaciers floating northwards over the hidden sea, runs into the island and diverges to either side. Our crossing point was close to where the flow divides, which we hoped would minimise the disturbance. Even so, our glaciological map showed crumpled pressure ridges on a vast scale formed by this collision.

I estimated we would reach the coast around midday. As we packed up, we made sure our climbing gear was handy in case we struck crevasses.

While we were pulling gently downhill during the second session, I thought I could see a very slight break in the slope running parallel to our course on the left. Fortunately it was sunny, with a few clouds, and their shadows lent some shape to the land. Peter and Keith were so used to the illusions generated by that subtle world of light that they thought I was imagining it. When we stopped for our break I sensed we were on the brink. If so, the junction was incredibly subtle and did not seem to offer any hazards. Peter led off down a slight slope. Squinting ahead at the flat horizon, I made out some dark smudges.

"Hey, there are some little black bumps on the horizon!" I yelled.

Keith stopped to peer. "Looks like land, guys," he said.

The sight was just as I thought the headlands of the Pensacola Mountains escarpment might look, and it was on the right bearing. These mountains are part of the Transantarctic Mountains, the vast range that spans the frozen continent.

After a few minutes we moved off the slope out onto flat ground. That was it. We were skiing over a dark and secret sea. On either side I detected a few long seams in the surface, straight lines running from our course for hundreds of metres. We had seen nothing like them on Berkner Island and I decided they were old fractures that had closed up under pressure. The going was noticeably harder, much to Peter's disgust.

The dark smudges had vanished over the horizon when we'd reached the ice shelf, but we made the planned change to our bearing from 178° magnetic to 168°. Our next objective was Wujek Ridge, our pass through the Dufek Massif into the Pensacola Mountains 180 km away. It had taken us 16.5 days of hauling to traverse Berkner Island (not counting the day in the tent). We'd covered 282 "killer-metres" at an average of 17 km a day.

Our hopes for firmer skiing on the ice shelf went unrewarded. The snow was soft and slow, and slight undulations on a vast wavelength added to the toil as we crossed the gentle pressure ridges shown on the map. Peter found his shift a real slog, but Keith still seemed to be cruising. He took over and shot off on the last session after downing some chocolate.

"Chocolate always affects him like that," Peter explained.

It had been warm all day at the low altitude, and although I had been travelling pretty well, in the last hour I hit the wall. For the first time I was forced to stop between scheduled breaks. I downed some chocolate and soup and whinged into Peter's video camera. We had agreed the night before to extend our daily schedule to nine hours – four shifts of two and a quarter hours each. Including rests, we would be on the road for 10 hours. Disappointingly, we covered only 22 km despite the extended time. This I attributed to the ups and downs and slow snow.

I filmed Peter pulling into camp. He seemed to lack his usual strength, his arms and legs working wearily. He stopped and lifted his goggles.

"Today's been really uncomfortable, through some pretty soft snow on the ice shelf," he said. "And it was bloody hard going. My feet are sore, my legs are sore, my bum's sore – with a rash that threatens to consume all my vital organs. I'm glad we're in camp."

The radio call was clear and chatty. Doug relayed a wonderful message for me from home, received the night before: "Happy 43rd, good travelling and lots of love from Marianne, Cale, Holly and Ruby the Dog."

I was thrilled and touched. I had been thinking earlier that I had nearly forgotten about our first and new dog. I wondered if she would not know who I was when I returned – and hoped she would be the only one! Keith made me a birthday ice-cake, with "43" carved in it.

Keith (top) doles out soup water as the main course cooks. On windless evenings we dined outside to enjoy the overwhelming space and clarity. On our tenth day we move through a glowing ice fog (above), in a circle of light that seems to travel with us. The monotony of 380 km long Berkner Island, where not a single rock breaks the snows, was relieved by the changing atmospheric displays.

Peter suffered severe blisters, caused by natural bumps on his heels and the strain of hauling. He bore the pain stoically but was frustrated by having to stop from time to time for repairs.

Our "huddle tent" began life as an outdoor furniture cover but gave vital shelter during hurried stops in the wind. Peter called it the "cone of silence", a reference to an old television series.

Photography was challenging when we were lashed to a heavy sled. Keith leans into position (right) with one of our two compact cameras. At the end of a day's hauling we enjoy the comfort of our small tent and thick sleeping bags (above), a secure haven from the harsh Antarctic environment. The warmth of sunny evenings was trapped inside the wind-sealed tent and lifted the temperature above freezing. "This is always the best part of the day," Peter said.

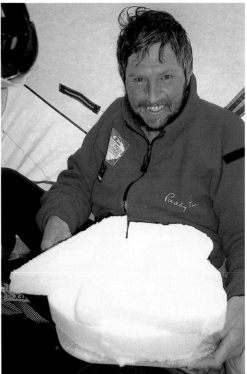

KEITH WILLIAMS

On 18 November we pass through a magical zone
of coarse ice crystals bejewelling the snow (left). We'd
broken the back of Berkner Island's rise, and the
calm air combined with a slick surface made travelling
pleasant. It was so warm we even dispensed with
our windproofs. "Happy Birthday to you!" On
19 November Keith's singing heralds my birthday.
His present to me (above) of a beautifully constructed
ice cake, was similar to the one he had given Peter
on his 40th birthday eight days earlier. We put the
cake in the pot to melt into water for dinner.

CHAPTER 5

ACROSS *a* SECRET SEA

The daily routine enabled us to draw a veil over the infinite scale of the landscape and our pathetic insignificance ...

ROGER MEAR, IN THE FOOTSTEPS OF SCOTT (1987)

21 NOVEMBER

I never thought it would be possible to feel so hot in Antarctica. I stumbled along in single thermals, without overboots but with liner gloves and a silk balaclava to protect me from sunburn, sweating like a pig in a sauna, goggles fogged. The fog condensed and trickled down before my eyes like rain on a window. Sweat dripped off the end of my nose and for once did not freeze into a chin-icicle. But the temperature was still −10°C, and I cooled down after only a few minutes of rest. The low altitudes are the tropics of Antarctica.

It was strange to see objects 170 km away. Lumps of the Pensacola Mountains hovered on the horizon, disappearing and reappearing like islands seen over an ocean swell as we negotiated the gentle rises and falls of the ice shelf. They seemed no closer at the end of the day but at least Berkner Island had shrunk to a shimmer on the horizon behind us.

Keith found the sight of the mountains inspiring. They should have inspired me, too, but my mind was dulled by the heavy hauling. Keith confided that he also felt tired during the last hour or so of each day. He didn't show it but I wanted to believe him for my own sake. As a reward for our 22 km effort we passed both the 81st parallel and the 300 km mark. Though reasonably satisfied with our recent progress, we wished it might be a little easier to achieve. The next day we expected to clock up a quarter of the total distance (329 km).

As we approach the Transantarctic Mountains, a glassy surface of rock-hard ice mirrors Keith's stride. He is in crampons for the second time.

Tonight, as Peter was working on his diary, Keith and I spoke of our dreams for a rest day in the mountains.

"I'm writing down how you're always bullshitting about rest days," Peter said. "I couldn't believe it, even before the trip started, you guys were on about rest days! I'd like a rest day too, but you just can't afford it on a trip like this; you've got to keep the average kilometres up."

"Hang on," I countered. "Rest days don't affect our food days or your calculations, because we use the spare food." We had all accumulated a number of packets of uneaten biscuits. But Peter had stopped listening.

We had been hauling hard for 17 consecutive days since the storm – longer than I had ever gone on a wilderness journey without a rest. I found Peter's approach irrational and annoying, but I also knew he was accustomed to daily averages of 130 km on his endurance speed trips, day after many a day. I was sure he was finding our rate of progress snail-like, and no doubt any rest he regarded as inessential would be very frustrating for him. He wrote in his diary that he was feeling stronger each day.

It seemed to me that Peter liked to execute some journeys in a particular style: you start, you finish, and you spend as little time as possible in between. For me, the journey itself is as much a part of the goal as the finishing of it, and I have always enjoyed just being in the wilds. Rest and appreciation of the environment make a happy combination that moulds my style. However, because I seemed to be surviving our restless existence, and in view of the conflict that would certainly result, I decided not to insist on a day off at that time. A rest day was precious currency I wished to hoard until absolutely necessary.

22 NOVEMBER

Peter's diary:
Started walking at 7.10 am with complete cloud cover which made snow definition extremely poor. I led the first 2 ¼ hours and found the snow good for sled travel, but I could not see where I was putting my feet. Keith led the next session and had to sit down several [times] because he was dizzy and was seeing things … We felt about 8 snowquakes today, some of which were very surprising.

I led two sections today and felt very strong on each. The second session was difficult in that it was as if the snow had frozen with waves and troughs everywhere. Very rough going. Could not see the mountains today as the clouds moved that way. Ian and Keith also led good sections and despite the difficulties, I'm hopeful of a reasonable kilometrage.

As we sat on our sleds during a rest break, Peter said to me: "That last kilometre to the South Pole is going to be great! I'm not going to pull the sled another inch and then I'll retire from skis."

It is a sad sort of trip where everyone is thinking of the finish. Generally in the wilderness I don't want the trip to end; this time there was dread that it wouldn't. But in spite of the drudgery, there was no thought of backing off; we were all determined to finish what we had set out to do.

Although the terrain had been monotonous on a grand scale, there was remarkable variety in the detail. The snow textures and patterns were constantly changing in subtle ways and were often supremely beautiful. This was a redeeming feature for me, even if many of the textures resisted the passage of a loaded sled. Occasional snowfalls delivered fresh particles that airbrushed away old patterns and created new ones. In stronger winds, the spindrift powder became a cutting agent that sandblasted grooves and sculpted the snow between them into knife-edge crests, polishing to a marble-like translucency any parts hard enough to rise above the surface. These features are called sastrugi, a Russian word. As the sun swung around the sky, the light varied constantly, throwing shadows and highlights in a million shifting tones of white and grey, blue and silver. What was opaque in dull light became luminous, then invisible, then sparkling as a wind-clipped sea on a bright summer day.

I was reminded of a choppy sea when the humps and ridges of wind-carved snow dipped and rolled before us. But the whitecaps and waves were snap-frozen in time. Wave after breaking wave on a half-metre swell made for heavy hauling.

Earlier in the day it was overcast and oppressively warm. It was just below 0°C and we pined for cooler weather, which followed in the afternoon. We must have been acclimatised by now, for any temperature warmer than −15°C seemed too hot for hauling unless accompanied by a cooling breeze.

Camping was luxurious in these conditions, with no frost inside the tent. The only difficulty was that the steam from the stove condensed on the aluminium tent poles and froze later in the night, locking the poles together.

In the evening I broached a subject that had been bothering me for the past week. My consumption of biscuits had fallen well short of the allotted ration of two packets (400 g) a day. Not only was I not hungry enough, but there was also not enough time for eating during the breaks. About 25 spare packets, or 5 kg, had gathered in the back of my sled. Peter and Keith had until recently also been failing to fulfil their eating duties. We had spare soup too, since Peter preferred just hot water during the day. But my biscuit hoard was becoming ridiculous and growing day by day. I asked Peter what he thought I should do with it, and he suggested throwing it away. I found this surprising and unacceptable. My hoarding instincts were offended.

"That's ridiculous, to chuck out good food that we have carried so far, when food is the limiting factor controlling our chance of success," I said.

I saw the spare food as useful insurance against hold-ups. Keith agreed we should hang on to it. Peter then concurred up to a point, and I moved onto the next issue. "Okay," I said. "If we agree to keep them for the common good, it seems fair that the burden of carrying them should be shared."

At this point Keith and Peter focused on practical matters to do with dinner and I got no response. So I continued to drag the biscuits. I did not mention my hoard of chocolate, which I intended to consume myself.

On the radio sched we were pleased to hear about our fellow expeditioners in several parts of the continent but shocked to hear from Doug that Helen had been evacuated with a slight head injury. Apparently her sled had knocked her unconscious after coming off a bump. Though we said nothing, we were all prompted to ponder our vulnerability in a land of immense indifference.

The three Icelanders were going strongly from Patriot Hills towards the Pole and were near our latitude about 500 km to the west. It must be a busman's holiday for them, I thought. Not so for the Belgians, who were struggling painfully slowly up into the mountains of Queen Maud Land and had asked for two new sleds to be flown in. The going must have been tough, and we wondered how they would make their immense 3500 km crossing to the Ross Sea. They had hardly begun, and balmy midsummer was nearly upon us.

On warm nights on the sunny side of the tent I sweltered in my sleeping bag and had to unzip it. It was one of those nights, and as I nodded into blissful sleep I contemplated the vagaries of human physiology, wondering why I was condemned to wake up at least once in the night, sometimes two or three times, to use the pee bottle. It was a very unpleasant duty, emerging into the cold, half asleep, finding the bottle, taking extreme care not to spill it or miss, then unzipping the annexe and tipping it into the corner – carefully avoiding the boots and the Argos. At the other extreme lay Keith's bladder, which could hold over a litre. I did not believe him when he first confided this to me, but later I'd witnessed him filling our one-litre bottle, emptying it and adding more. I was holed up in Antarctica with two physical freaks!

23 November

The day was punctuated by many snowquakes, some rattlingly big. The localised ones that began from our track were not too disturbing and were often foreshadowed by small tremors. The ones that attacked from some distance away, although also set off by us, really gave us the willies. No matter how familiar they became, they caused an instinctive reaction in us, as when a falling rock whizzes by your head.

The heatwave seemed to have passed, and we were back to −18°C, with a biting wind. On his lead Peter had started off before Keith and I had finished our break, and he just kept going. As we packed up to follow, Keith told me that he was going to take it easy because the ankle ligament he had sprained a few months ago was sore. I would hate to see Keith going flat out, because I still couldn't quite keep up with him. At the end of the shift, Keith was 15 minutes behind Peter and I was another five minutes slower. By the time we finished our feed, poor Peter was freezing. He constantly suffered from cold hands after our breaks, not only because he seemed to become chilled much more quickly than Keith or me, but also because he often had to wait longer.

The final lead was Keith's, and he did take it steady, as he said in his diary: "Sore ankle ligaments in both ankles. Took it easy today – more consistent but slow!! and still made 24 km!!!"

24 November

Peter's diary:
By any standards today was a horrible day. We woke to −20[°C] and a 20 kph wind. Breaking camp was difficult, but achieved by 7.30.

My glasses constantly fogged and I couldn't see where I was going. The conditions were cold, stops in particular were cold. My hands after each break were difficult to warm up. The main problem was the composition of the snow, it was sticky, like glue, and it was difficult to move the sleds and the skis. Also, the terrain was like a frozen ocean, up and down. The travelling was extremely difficult, a real grunt. It was simply a relief to get the tent up and to move in. The time in the tent, particularly the evening meal is the best time of the day...

Morning by contrast I find frustrating. I get up early, 5.15 am and start the breakfast so that we can reduce the preparation time and get going early. The guys, however, never cooperate and sleep in for more than reasonable. My objective is to maximise the efficiency of breakfast. I had a go at them today and generally let my displeasure be known.

As we stopped to camp at 6.15 p.m., I too cursed a day of hard-fought progress. "Well, that was a real hoot, wasn't it? About as much fun as extracting your own appendix!" I said.

A 20 km/h wind had been blowing from the west all day, bringing a ground blizzard and spindrift and forcing us to use the "cone of silence" during stops. We were wearing single thermals on the bottom, double thermal tops and windproofs. In fact, while we were moving, conditions were surprisingly bearable. Except, that is, for the ice that formed on the face and goggles. Life in Antarctica would be so much easier if you didn't have to breathe. No goggle-fogging, no masks of ice, no frost in the tent; you could just cover your face for the whole day and forget about it.

The slugs were extremely reluctant today. It was like being back on Berkner Island and struggling uphill again; it felt as if there was someone sitting on my sled who applied the handbrake every few metres.

It wasn't all hard. Around us a grey fog of ice crystals flew in the wind but we moved in a shaft of sunlight that streamed down from above like a searchlight. This was no illusion; the windblown snow hugged the ground, so there was less of it overhead than to the side. A wide halo encircled the sun, caused by refraction from the airborne ice, and bright spectral sundogs (parhelions, or mock suns) appeared on opposite sides of the halo.

In spite of the display of meteorological beauty, we wasted no time in crawling into the tent after 10 hours out in the killing wind.

Doug was taking a day off from radio duty at Patriot Hills and Lisa took our call. She said that at Patriot Hills they had us "up on the board to get to the Pole first".

25 NOVEMBER

You can freeze and burn on the same day in Antarctica.

The wind abated during the night but returned in the morning, along with low cloud and a half-strength sun. We disliked waking to the sound of the wind buffeting the tent and spindrift spitting against the fabric. It was so much harder to get up and force ourselves outside. When I awoke, my right hand was numb, swollen and stiff. Both hands had been deteriorating for a while – from the strain of pushing on the wrist-loops of the stocks, I supposed.

In the middle of the day the cloud moved aside and the mountains stood clear again after hiding for nearly two days. They were much closer, and we thought we could discern our pass, Wujek Ridge, among the rock buttresses and icefalls that made most of the escarpment unassailable with sleds. With the mountains looming and faster snow conditions, I was feeling strong again. The last shift was over flat snow with a texture like plastic, hard and slippery. I began to think we could make the distance. What appeared to be the sudden gradient of the mainland coast from the ice shelf looked very close, and the rise of the mountains beyond was more dramatic than I ever expected.

On the delightful last shift I stopped to video Peter and Keith skiing ahead of me towards the mountains less than 60 km away. Looking through the viewfinder at their small black shapes before the mountainous mass allowed a certain detachment:

> *Here are our brave adventurers, heading in a beeline towards Wujek Ridge, desperate to come to grips with the mountains as some way of measuring their puny progress against the vastness of the landscape ... against what's been going on previously – just a desolation of ice. We now have some scenery to measure ourselves against. It does make our ambitions look pretty puny and pathetic.*

26 NOVEMBER

> *My diary:*
> It's great to have the mountains – something else to occupy us other than the insides of our own minds, with their petty animal concerns like heat and cold, aches, pains and tiredness ... and the constant thinking about other places to be: the organism's way of telling us we are not doing right ... frigging around in an environment hostile to human health ...

On the ice shelf we had been crossing the grain of the wind-carved surface, and often the grain had been strong and thick. On our last day on the shelf we "struck paydirt" (as Keith put it) – beautiful hard, icy snow, mostly flat, on which the sleds became happy, willing partners, almost wanting to move.

After only a couple of hours, we crossed another indistinct shoreline and set foot on mainland Antarctica, 413 km from our starting point. As on the edge of the ice shelf off Berkner Island, I spied a couple of hairline cracks running straight across our path into the distance. These "strand cracks" are formed by the tidal movement of the ice shelf against the land's edge. We began climbing immediately and moved into a zone of supernatural calm and silence, where the ground was strewn with chunky crystals of ice. I felt a sense of unreality and wouldn't have been surprised to see weird beings, carried on giant insect steeds, approaching us over the next rise.

The Ford Ice Piedmont rises 600 m in a series of benches from the edge of the Ronne Ice Shelf to the foot of the great escarpment of the Dufek Massif. The going was excellent on a hard translucent surface on which the sleds barely left a mark. The mountains rose and fell behind the slope in front of us, disappearing as we climbed, reappearing as the slope eased. The hide-and-seek was exciting, as on each reappearance the crags grew. The travelling, even though quite steeply uphill, was noticeably easier than on the flat but lumpy, sandy surface of the ice shelf. They were the best ground conditions we'd had on the entire journey, and we ate them up. We climbed 350 m in the day, over half the height to the base of the pass, and yet we still managed to cover 26 km horizontally. Our best distance and our greatest ascent.

In all pleasure there must be a little pain, and mine came in the last shift when the ground grew slightly lumpy. My hammered heels rapidly deteriorated when required to give the extra lift for the climbing and began to hurt badly. Peter and Keith continued strongly, but I slowed down to reduce the pain and the damage. They set up the tent on a crystal field before the mountains and I photographed the camp against the backdrop of the escarpment. A beautiful evening settled around us, auguring well for the next day.

I apologised for dragging the chain. The others did not seem to mind, and Peter said graciously: "I think we'll all be in that situation at some stage."

Nevertheless, I wondered if they had other ideas, if they ever thought they might be better off without me. Although I had contributed a great deal to the expedition's planning, I was not putting as much into the chores of the journey as I would normally expect of myself.

Peter's diary:

Ian continues to be a major problem, always being slow. He's last out [of] bed, last to start, disorganised and always slow on the move. We had to wait on each stretch up to 20 min for him. He can't seem to lift his speed to suit the better snow conditions. We are going to have to do this if we are to complete the trip. He's got too much junk in his sled which he refuses to get rid of. For example upwards of 30 packets of biscuits that he has not eaten. I told him to get rid of them but he refuses.

Keith produced another excellent meal, of dried vegetables and chunks of salami (soy grits for him) in a cement of dried potato, which we consumed voraciously. Of our three main meals, this was becoming my favourite.

27 NOVEMBER

For the first time on the whole journey my sled felt light. We revelled in a glorious day of hard and fast surfaces, zooming towards the mountains that dominated the horizon. For once the compass was almost unnecessary as we homed in on Wujek Ridge, the easternmost bastion of the long escarpment. Above the sloping piedmont, the crags rose 1200 m. Summits of broad ice plateaus were festooned with wild rock spires, with icefalls plunging through the lower bluffs. I pulled out the binoculars at our rests and marvelled.

The day gradually became overcast, the stratus cloud creating spectacular effects over the mountains. As it slid down the slopes, it thickened into a purple gloom. At the same time we found ourselves on a surface that looked as if it had been gouged by a giant claw. The claw was the wind. It had blasted and eroded the hard snow into intricate sastrugi. This was not the mild sastrugi – or rather the remnants of it – of Berkner Island, which had been mere bumps 20–30 cm high; here were ridges that rose a metre above the grooves.

The snow remained hard and continued to provide good sledging. In places the knife-edged ridges were close enough together to allow the skis and sleds to bridge them. Elsewhere the grooves became deep swales and climbing out was laborious. In the gloom it was difficult to spot the higher bumps ahead, and sometimes the skis would dive unexpectedly into a wide dip. Maintaining balance in such conditions was difficult, and we stumbled frequently.

Sometimes, when rushing off a slope, the sled would ride over the backs of my skis and ram my legs. Naturally we tried to keep the sleds running freely over the beautiful surface by skiing ahead of the slides. This style of travel was invigorating and fast and an enjoyable contrast to all that had gone before, but it was also exhausting in the long run.

On the third shift I set up the video on the ice-axe to film all three of us sledging towards the cloud-shadowed mountains. After that Peter took off like a scalded cat, with Keith in hot pursuit. I had no chance of keeping up but went as hard as I could between taking telephoto shots of the two black dots against the purple-clouded mountain wall. They were the most spectacular images of the journey so far. Careering over the sharp ridges, racing ahead of the advancing sled, I covered ground faster than ever before and soon realised I was gaining on the other two. I pulled into the rest spot just 10 minutes behind them, which translated into a little more than 500 m. They said they had put the brakes on a bit when they realised the potential for injury in the reckless pace. None of us wanted to wind up like Helen Thayer, hit by her own sled, and it had become obvious how this could happen.

Peter's diary:
Keith put a good effort in and covered many kilometres. I started well but was slowed by poor light and snow contrast as it clouded over. I was also concerned about Ian who had dropped many kilometres back and was only a speck on the horizon. If it had whited out we would have lost him, so it was decided to slow the pace and allow him to catch up.

Racing over the icy snow, I had been carefully watching the rate at which the rock outcrops of Wujek Ridge were growing. I had also noted the parallax shift as ridges protruding from the escarpment moved relative to the background. I predicted that we would almost certainly reach the bottom of the pass that night. Since the GPS had given the distance to the pass as 32 km last night, the others considered my prophecy unrealistic.

During the last shift we began to descend to a wide basin at the foot of the mountain wall. The sastrugi gave out and the sleds moved smoothly on the slight downhill slope of hard snow. Soon the snow became threadbare and patches of blue ice began to show through it. We realised that, as at Patriot Hills, this was caused by winds funnelling around the base of the mountains and carrying away everything but the ice, leaving it looking like polished marble. We were on the rim of a vast windscoop.

Outcrops of rock drew alongside on our left like dark wooden ships. They were the outlying nunataks (from an Inuit word meaning an isolated rocky peak surrounded by ice) of the Boyd Escarpment, an ice slope that extends northwards from the main escarpment. It was exciting to see rocks so close, and we laughed and yelled as we slid down the gentle incline with little effort. It was a wild ride, and so delightfully easy. Hairline cracks appeared, and others even a few centimetres wide – our first tiny crevasses. After this we looked carefully on either side as we proceeded. The ice was extremely old, evidenced by its deep transparency and the lack of crystalline structures. Faint cracks wriggled through it like quartz veins in metamorphic rock.

Soon the snow became patchy and gave way to pure blue ice. The sleds skittered like cakes of soap on glass, and we had to take care they didn't run us down. We indulged in an orgy of photography, such was our joy at this change to our surroundings after nearly four weeks of whiteness.

The slope gradually levelled out, after which we started very gently to climb the far side of the windscoop into the mountains. I was now more certain than ever that we'd reach the base of the pass as predicted. Our skin-equipped skis skidded about uselessly on the icy rise, so we donned crampons. Walking on the rock-hard surface felt strange and awkward after the weeks of moving our legs in a sliding action. The sharp spikes of the crampons bit less than a centimetre into the ancient ice, and we teetered along as if on stilts.

Keith and I worked on video shots. Peter waited impatiently for a while before going ahead. He quickly changed back to skis when he found himself among snow patches again, and he weaved around to link them. After we'd taken our photographs, Keith and I took a straight line across both ice and thin snow to catch up.

My diary:

These days while sledging, I seem to spend more time fretting about being the slowest and trying to fathom Peter's approach. He seems to treat everything as an obstacle to be overcome as quickly as possible. He hates stopping. I love stopping! I live to stop, I rejoice in it, I walk only to justify stopping in a different place! I love to understand the landscape, to observe and to learn. Peter said the other night that he always knew this would be a terrible grunt of an unenjoyable trip, just because that's the sort of trip it is. I knew too that it would be like that at least in part, and at other times it would be glorious. While disappointed that Peter's prediction has proved to be more accurate than mine, I also resent the fact that it could be otherwise. I know even as I think these thoughts that they are unworthy, that I cannot blame Peter for anything more than perhaps imperfect communication. I knew enough about his preferred style before I came, and I know how much of a burden he carries in his absolute commitment to succeed on this journey. You make your choices and you have to try and live with them.

So I cursed and stewed as I strode along, but my resentment usually evaporated when we stopped and the other guys wouldn't seem so bad any more for moving on when I was taking photos or for zipping off as soon as I arrived at a comfort stop. If I'd been in their boots I would probably have done the same.

At 6 p.m. we reached a flat patch of snow on the ice and decided to camp. We were well positioned at the foot of the pass, a wide glacial slope leading between the crags of Wujek Ridge on the right and the smaller rocks of Bennett Spur on the left. But we were very exposed. Worried about the strength of the wind that might whip down from the heights, Keith wanted to go on to the foot of the first outcrop.

I argued that we had no way of judging how far away the outcrop was, that it might take us another hour to reach it and that we should not finish too late before a big day on the pass. I also reckoned that the winds that gouged out such basins blew mostly in winter and that the outcrop would not necessarily provide better shelter.

Keith's disquiet was reinforced when he uncovered a small crevasse a few centimetres wide while digging out the entrance pit to the tent. "Look, it goes right under the tent on my side!" he said. There was laughter in his voice, but though not seriously worried by the crevasse, he was obviously nervous about the location. I wondered if I should have deferred to his intuition.

As well as clocking up a remarkable tally of 31 km for the day, we had climbed nearly 300 m before losing some height in the windscoop. A third of the distance to the Pole now lay behind us.

As I stood outside the tent taking in the magnificence, clouds and light moved slowly through the mountains. I was entranced. Nearby to the east a huge cliff of dark brown columns loomed out of the bedrock promontory of Bennett Spur, which itself broke through the ice-slope of the Boyd Escarpment. With nothing to provide scale or distance, I found it impossible to judge the height of the crags. The protruding bones of the earth confirmed that this nebulous icescape did in fact rest on a solid foundation, that it was rooted on our planet.

To the south a string of other bluffs formed the Wujek Ridge complex. Between the two lay our path, a wide valley of glacial ice creeping down from the Sallee Snowfield on the plateau above, mostly covered by a layer of snow. We would follow a slope of continuous snow on the far right of the valley, hard by the brooding cliffs of Wujek Ridge, to avoid the open crevasses and steep rises of bare ice that we had seen shining further out on the slope.

From Wujek Ridge round to the west the massive rock escarpment led into the basin of Davis Valley. Our map showed the whole valley as exposed rock, with a few eternally frozen lakes. Ice-free areas are rare in Antarctica and of great scientific interest. I longed to explore this remarkable country, where probably only a few geologists have ever trodden. Beyond Davis Valley the long, exposed arm of Forlidas Ridge reached out, the lower slopes patterned like honeycomb. This polygonal ground is also a scarce phenomenon.

My diary:
Over the whole scene, an ethereal light drifts and changes through clouds that in places are solidly dark and sombre, in others bright and sunlit. We have had some light snow showers during the afternoon, and now a few more flakes are drifting down, squeezed from the swollen purple bellies of the clouds. It is calm and peaceful beyond description.

Peter called out from the tent: "What are you doing out there, Ian?"
"Just looking and taking photos," I replied.
He probably regarded me as a strange fish.
Concerned that our route up the pass might disappear in the lowering clouds, I took a compass bearing for the next day and then retired to the tent.
By the time we lay down to sleep, a heavy snow shower was falling. We all pondered what the next day would bring. The pass was the keystone of our route to the Pole and had only been ascended once before.

As we crossed the Ronne Ice Shelf, the distant Dufek Massif of the Transantarctic Mountains began to take shape and lure us onwards. I point out to Peter (top) our intended route through the mountains. Our excitement grew as we reached the mainland and ascended the Ford Ice Piedmont, spying the icefalls, crags and peaks of the range, before camping in this idyllic setting (above), 300 m above the "coast" of Antarctica.

*27 November was our most exhilarating day. Having climbed the final 200 m
rise of the piedmont, we head across superbly fast snow towards the 1200 m
escarpment of the Dufek Massif, just as cloud descends on the mountains.*

Keith (left) prepares to poke one of the specially made Arnott's biscuit through his frosted beard. We consumed biscuits, chocolate and soup at our three scheduled breaks between four shifts of hauling every day. Fast travel (top) allows us to cover 31 km across the last of the wind-scoured, blue ice piedmont and reach the foot of the Dufek Massif, where a freeze–thaw pattern of cracks on the barren Forlidas Ridge (above) was dusted by light snow.

CHAPTER 6

TOIL *and* TROUBLE

Strength, perseverance and patience.
Time passed, one day I'd get there …

BØRGE OUSLAND, ALONE ACROSS ANTARCTICA (1997)

28 NOVEMBER

Keith's diary: "UP UP UP all day. Up Wujek Ridge. 1200m. *Very* hard haul up the pass. One slip and you would have been part of the scenery in no time. Scenery fantastic. The Pensacola escarpment is really GRAND."

Snow continued to fall through the night and we were greeted in the morning by a day of heavy cloud. Fresh, light snow softened the ground, and the crags of Wujek Ridge were shrouded in fog, their shapes ghostly and without detail. This was not an inspiring day on which to face the most strenuous and scenic part of our route. For months we had feared the physical challenge of this climb – 500 m up into the heart of the mountains and the edge of the Polar Plateau. Our sleds were losing, on average, 1.3 kg every day as we consumed our food but they still weighed at least 130 kg. The worst of the climb had looked fearsomely steep the day before. Now we couldn't even see it.

Keith donned his climbing harness in readiness for crevasses, but Peter and I decided to leave ours handy in the sleds. We believed the fresh snow would allow our skis to grip what had been bare ice the day before but, as we pulled away from camp, we quickly discovered our mistake: the thin cover just slipped away under the skis to expose bare ice. So we switched back to crampons until the ice disappeared under the snow, at which point we resorted to skis again.

Skirting a huge, corniced windscoop, Peter throws himself into the desperate 500 m climb of Wujek Ridge. The climb tested our strength to the limit.

We climbed gradually at first through snow showers towards the first rock outcrop, which we needed to keep on our right. Keith was leading and kept heading towards the rock, but Peter and I turned leftward and headed more directly towards the looming cliff. This was the main landmark of the route.

During his 1996-97 crossing, Børge Ousland became the first person to use Wujek Ridge, or rather the slope beside it, as an access point to the Polar Plateau. In his previous attempt he had used Frost Spur, 19 km along the escarpment to the south-west. When he'd recommended the Wujek Ridge route to us, he had written: "Go straight for the white wall, and then close to the mountain, follow the face of the mountain up to the top. You will see where to go, it's a nice walk on the top itself, after the climb." I had been looking forward to the nice walk ever since. The precise identity of the "white wall" was open to some interpretation, but it was obvious that we should make for the big cliff and then keep the rocks close to our right to avoid crevasses.

Keith turned left below the first isolated rock outcrop, which was at least 100 m high and about 2 km from our camp, and we took parallel courses towards the main cliff, he a little higher up the slope. He soon pulled away, so it seemed he had made the better choice. As we climbed, the snow became deeper. More had fallen on the higher parts, and it was still coming down.

We passed beneath more dark masses of rock. They squatted like office blocks. Peter continued to follow me as we entered lumpy terrain. In the poor light it was difficult to find our way through the chaos, which seemed to be a field of sastrugi obscured by the fresh snow. The wind must really whistle down that pass at times. Stumbling and feeling our way, we weaved through the maze of obstacles. As Keith approached the main cliff, I could see it was at least 300 m high and almost vertical. In another world it might be a fine rock-climbing crag. I kept expecting him to stop and wait so we could agree on a line of attack for the steepest part of the pass, which reared up at the end of the cliff. But he was a man with a mission, a mountaineer used to the absorbing challenge of route-finding through steep terrain, and he was keen to check it out up close. Too far away to be heard in the snowstorm, I waved my stocks to indicate we wanted him to stop, but he didn't notice. Peter told me not to worry. "Let him go, he'll find the best way," he said.

As Keith approached the steeper incline, he turned away from the cliff and moved across the slope towards its centre. This looked like a bad idea to me as I thought he would certainly find more fractured ice out there. Then he turned again and dragged his sled back towards the cliff. This was perplexing, to say the least. Why was he zigzagging? Was he not sure where to go, or was he was trying to avoid a crevasse?

Meanwhile the snow was getting thicker, both in the air and on the ground, where it was causing significant drag, although we had now escaped the worst of the lumpiness. The work was already hard – and this was the easy bit! Despite the snowfall, I was sweating freely in the relatively high temperatures.

We had passed the last island of rock, and the main cliff was rearing up ahead. As we came close, a giant chasm between the cliff and the slope we were climbing came into view. It was a windscoop many times larger than any I had seen before. It had to be at least 100 m deep and a couple of hundred wide, extending the full length of the cliff, or about half a kilometre. The chasm could swallow a small village and several office blocks in one gulp and come back for more.

There was no way of approaching the base of the cliff, which lay deep in the pit. The edge of the scoop was abrupt and vertical. In one way this was good news. The formation of such scoops involves two mechanisms: concentrated high wind sweeps around an obstruction and scours away snow near it; at the same time, the wind deposits snow on the scoop's outer edge, where it is moving more slowly, and creates a ridge. Heavy deposition on the slope we were on meant any crevasses would be well buried.

We kept far enough away from the edge of the scoop to avoid any risk of it collapsing under us. The cliff reared overhead, split by vertical cracks and seamed horizontally with pale veins.

Keith eventually stopped and sat down on his sled. Good, I thought. Our first food break was overdue and I really needed to replenish my energy. As we approached him, the reason for his bizarre course became clear: the slope had become too steep to tackle head-on, even though the gradient remained well below 10°. We were forced to start zigzagging too. The deepening snow amplified the difficulty; so did the slight underlying lumpiness, which periodically increased the angle over which the sleds had to climb, obstructing the front of the sleds as effectively as a brick wall. These "stoppers" were hidden in the snow and often we couldn't detect them until we felt the sleds jam against them.

Wobbling and straining, zigging and zagging, we took at least 10 minutes to cover the last 100 m to Keith. He was near the base of the even steeper main slope. Compared with the incline on which we were already suffering, this looked impossible. Years of mountaineering had taught me that snow slopes always look steep when viewed from the front. However, this knowledge made little impact on my horror.

"Bloody hell, this is horrendous!" I exclaimed to Keith as I threw off my harness, unclipped my skis and dived into my sled for some food and drink.

It had been very thirsty work. "I couldn't figure out from back there why you were wandering around, but now I know."

Keith had finished his morning tea and, as he packed up, he explained his plan. "I wanted to make sure this was the best way," he said. "I'm going up to check it out, so wait here till I see if it's possible."

Wearing neither skis nor crampons, he took the ice-axe-cum-shovel and waddled up the slope, in his element and absorbed in finding the best route. Quite quickly he reached the top of the steepest section, perhaps 100 m away, beyond which the slope dipped out of sight. With Keith's deep track now defining the slope for our eyes, the real angle was more apparent and it looked as if we might just do it. Planting the shovel, he wallowed back through knee-deep snow. The snow was falling heavily by this time, and we were cooling off.

"It'll go, but only just," Keith said. "If we go up towards the shovel that's the steepest bit over."

As Peter and I packed our food away, Keith put his crampons on and began dragging his sled up the rise, first this way and then that. I clipped on my crampons, strapped the skis to my sled, gritted my teeth and followed.

At first I stuck to the trench Keith had gouged. Crampons ensured secure

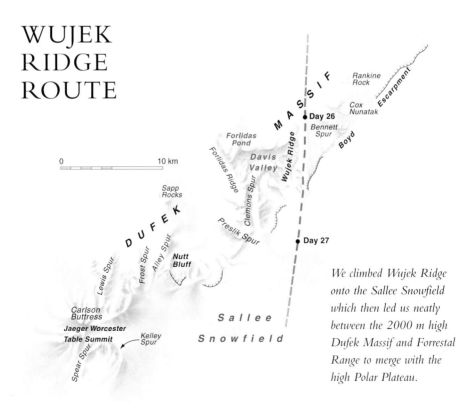

WUJEK RIDGE ROUTE

We climbed Wujek Ridge onto the Sallee Snowfield which then led us neatly between the 2000 m high Dufek Massif and Forrestal Range to merge with the high Polar Plateau.

footing, but there was still the unbearable resistance of the sled. We continued to use our stocks for balance and extra power. Without skis, our feet sank into the snow up to the ankles. Splay-footed and bowing low to overcome the sled's resistance, I lurched slowly upwards.

I realised that to get good photos of the struggle I would need to be to one side looking back at the others. With my camera around my neck, I extended one of my leftward traverses. Cutting my own track seemed easier than following Keith's because I did not sink so deeply. Beneath the soft new snow, now 15 cm deep, the base snow was coarse and unconsolidated. My boots sank instantly through the top layer. The next level offered more resistance but usually not enough; it often crumbled only after I had transferred my full weight onto it. If my next step didn't sink as far, I had to make a strenuous high lift. Usually, however, the forward foot did sink. It was exhausting.

The sled bulldozed through the soft snow. I could take only a dozen or so steps at a time without stopping to relieve my muscles and recover my breath. At one stop I snapped a few shots of Peter against the backdrop of the wall. Even when stopped, it was essential to keep tension on the harness lines to prevent the sled from sliding down the slope. By leaning forwards to balance the sled's weight against my own, I was able to free both hands and work the camera. I couldn't move to a better position or even twist from the direction I was facing; I just had to make do with the fleeting opportunities presented.

We could gauge the height gained in our awful labour by sighting across to the cliff. We were gaining; we would get there.

The turns were the worst. They had to be sharp and quick to minimise the time the sled spent facing directly up the slope. That was the point of maximum danger, where muscles could lose the battle against gravity and the sled might start to toboggan down the hill, with unthinkable consequences. A judicious mix of upward and sideways movement was the best way to make the turns. Although this cut the time spent in the danger zone, it demanded a gut-busting effort because it entailed dragging the sled broadside through soft snow.

Progress was painful and slow. My feet ached from the enormous pressure, and the strain on my legs was so intense that I feared I might snap a tendon. There was no avoiding the climb, so I tried to work my limbs steadily, minimising sudden exertion. Although the temperature had fallen and a stiff breeze was whisking across the slope, my face was streaming and the sweat dripped from the end of my nose. I hated the sled, even though it was my lifeblood.

When I saw that we were leaving the cliff behind and the good photo opportunities had passed, I rejoined Keith's trench. The snow seemed to be getting softer and deeper as we climbed and it was difficult to find any firm footing. I was floundering, hanging heavily on my stocks as I lifted my feet.

Suddenly one foot gave way and I fell sideways onto the side of the trench, panting and cursing simultaneously. As I struggled to recover, I saw that I'd stepped into a crevasse less than 30 cm wide and that my right leg was jammed between its icy walls. Sardonically, I noted that the leg made a perfect anchor and the sled could not drag me down. I relaxed for a moment and leant my bottom against the snow, quite comfortable.

But I had to get moving again. Planting my stocks on either side of me and pushing on my left foot, I wriggled my right leg free of the crevasse.

Keith and Peter had stopped to rest above the steepest part of the slope. Keith pulled away just before I arrived but Peter was still fiddling with his clothes. He had been filming me struggling up towards him. For a moment the clouds blew apart to reveal the lower crags of Wujek Ridge and the ice valley below. It was the finest view of the journey.

We were almost level with the top of the main cliff now. Although the slope eased above us, its summit was at least 100 m higher. Peter trudged off while I restored my energy with biscuits and soup. When I followed, he was a zig and a zag ahead of me. I had not yet seen Keith stop for a rest, but Peter did so regularly. It was some consolation to see he was finding the going hard too.

Although the gradient had eased, the sled's resistance seemed the same, and exhaustion began to slow me down. I was sure I would make it, but I had to stop for more rests, hanging gasping in my stocks like a flogged prisoner while the others pulled away and vanished over the top. Fortunately it was fairly calm, the sun was shining and the velvety new snow was magnificent.

The crest turned out to be ever so subtle. Peter and Keith were sitting on their sleds as they slowly hove into view. At last the snow flattened out. Peter filmed me hauling towards him. "Grunt-cam" we called it. I was stuffed, and must have looked it. I glanced up at the camera and said: "I've carried some big packs up big hills in my time, but that's the hardest thing I've ever done."

As I pulled my sled up level with theirs at last and collapsed on it, Keith made a welcome announcement. "We've been talking about it and we're going to have an early mark tonight," he said. "We'll just ski for another hour and then camp."

This was good news for me and, I suspected, for Keith too, since he had led all the way up the pass. It had been a supreme effort and he had done it in fine style. I assumed Peter's silence confirmed his agreement with the idea. It was 2 p.m. It had taken us nearly seven hours to complete the 500 m climb. We had reached an altitude of over 1100 m and were delighted to have overcome such difficult conditions to get there. We wanted to name the pass after our greatest and most committed supporter, John Leece. Of course it would be presumptuous to do that without Børge's approval, so for the time being we would just refer to it as "John Leece Pass" among ourselves. We thought of John overcoming his own "grunt" back in Australia.

After a good rest, I led off onto the plateau of the Sallee Snowfield, which rose very gently for some distance. The new snow was 12 cm deep here and as light as gossamer. Our skis slid underneath it, only the tips breaking the surface. Although it was beautiful, we were disappointed that the hoped-for firmer snow and easier travel on the plateau were not to be.

We now headed for an ice scarp several days away across the snowfield. I was in the lead and found the pulling hard. Before an hour was up I was tiring fast and felt I was going too slowly. It was typical of such terrain that the rise constantly gave the impression that it was about to relent but never did. We agreed to go on a little longer, until 4.30, to see if we could breast the rise. It was becoming apparent that Peter was not keen on an early stop. Perhaps he was frustrated with the slowness of the day's travel and the inevitably few kilometres it would add to our total. I suggested to Peter that he take over if he wanted to go a little faster. He did and I pulled in behind him, finding the going much easier. Keith ambled along at the rear for a well-deserved rest.

Shortly before 5 p.m. Peter suggested we go on till 5.30. I was annoyed and said so. My view all along had been that if we could achieve the pass in one day we would be doing well, and any distance beyond it would be a bonus. The climb had taken a lot out of me, and the idea of an early stop had become attractive. Keith remained silent and seemed, to my surprise, to be unconcerned with this change of plan. (Much later Keith told me he was exhausted and that the change had really irritated him.)

Peter turned to me. "I don't mind. I'll stop if you want me to," he said.

I became exasperated at what I perceived to be a lack of forthrightness. "That just isn't true, Peter. Why can't you be more honest?" I paused, my frustration vented, and added more evenly: "OK, keep going to 5.30, then."

Without further comment, Peter moved off and we continued slowly up the slope. Slight bumps began to develop and we were all having trouble pulling over them. Suddenly, at 5.15, Peter stopped, planted his stocks and started taking his harness off. "You're right, we've done enough today," he said.

I took this as a welcome sign of compromise but then noted that we had, in the end, walked for our allotted nine hours.

The sun came out and the evening was calm and warm. Peter moved efficiently into the tent while Keith and I were still mucking about outside in the pleasant conditions. Peter and Keith had been consuming their entire daily biscuit ration for a while now. Over the past few nights, as a kilojoule bonus, they had also begun reducing my surplus pile. I had increased my consumption to a whole packet during the day and a few extra biscuits at night. Peter asked if they could help me out by eating some more of my hoard this evening.

I said: "No worries, as long as you guys realise this is not sustainable. Consuming my cache means we're eating beyond our means at the moment. Then you'll get hungry, Peter."

Peter had become the hungriest of us all. Keith was in the middle, satisfied with the standard ration. He offered a loaded observation: "Then we'll have to do less miles."

I expanded on the gentle jibe. "You don't think a small thing like being hungry will slow him down, do you?"

Peter joined in from the tent: "That's right. I'm totally focused on one thing."

"One thing? What's that?" Keith asked, knowing the answer.

"The Pole," replied Peter.

"There must be more to the trip than just getting to the Pole," Keith said. "You can fly there much easier. What about enjoying the scenery?"

"Oh, I do as we pass through it, but it's really just an obstacle."

Peter must have been disappointed that Keith and I did not seem sufficiently committed to the primary goal. After the episode at the top of the pass, I began to wonder if Peter was too committed and not taking into account the very real risk of physical breakdown. I supposed it was to be expected in such circumstances that each member of the party might try to compensate for the perceived shortcomings of the others by asserting more strongly his own attitude, even if indirectly.

Having started out this morning a little weary after the previous long day, I was pleased not to feel completely worn out at the end of the day. I was certainly very tired and would wait with interest to see how I felt in the morning. I wrote in my diary: "My feet feel like they've been gone over with a sledgehammer. We were like Hannibal crossing the Alps – except that we had to drag our elephants!"

Peter's diary:
Kilometres will not be impressive today, about 11 km, we estimate. If this is the case it will be an excellent result given that we have climbed the pass, the worst climb of the trip, in one go, 600 m. We still need to rise, but this, hopefully, will be distributed over the remaining 800 km, not in 11 km like today.

The snow came down again. We felt a sense of loss at having our hopes of firm conditions so decisively destroyed.

29 NOVEMBER

Keith declared this would be one of his "rest days". He would "work to rule" and take things easy as an antidote to Peter's drive.

The light snowfall that had persisted through the night tailed off to a few dustings during the day. The surface improved as we travelled, the new snow thinning out and becoming firmer. A slight breeze brought perfect hauling conditions – clear goggles and no sweating. Clouds came and went in all shapes and sizes, hiding and then revealing the mountains.

We passed the tiny outcrop of Petite Rocks well off to our right, with the 2030 m high dome of Worcester Summit rising behind, some 20 km distant. This high point of the Dufek Massif rises 800 m above the flat Sallee Snowfield in a complex of ridges and icefalls, with a satellite rock spire off the northern end, before plunging 1400 m down the other side towards the coast. It was hard to keep our eyes off the shadow and light show on the mountain, and Keith and I took many photos.

The tops of the Dufek Massif ran away to the south-west in an almost straight line. On the sunlit horizon south of it, but well to the right of our course, sailed an armada of coal-black nunataks, each perfect in its triangular symmetry. Ahead, to our left, we glimpsed the approaching Forrestal Range, forming the eastern limit of the Sallee Snowfield.

The nomenclature and structure of these mountains is confusing. A number of distinct ranges, including the Dufek Massif, the Forrestal Range and some others separated by icefields, are grouped as the Pensacola Mountains. These in turn form part of the Transantarctic Mountains, a sinuous 3500 km range that divides the continent, extending from the western side of the Ross Sea to the eastern side of the Weddell Sea. It is one of Earth's great cordilleras. For half the length of the range, in the region of the Ross Sea and Ross Ice Shelf, the mountains rise proudly from sea level to over 4000 m, but for most of the remaining half the peaks are swamped by the ice fields of the interior, occasionally pushing their tops out of the whiteness.

The beauty of our route lay in the ease with which it breached the Transantarctic Mountains and neatly sidestepped large glaciers, with their complexities and crevasse zones. Its efficiency was proved by five Norwegian explorers who crossed Antarctica in 1990-91. Dubbed Shackleton's Dream and led by Sjur Mørdre, the expedition travelled from Berkner Island to the Pole with dog sleds. From there three members skied on without dogs to the Ross

Sea via the Axel Heiberg Glacier to make the fourth crossing of the continent. After our expedition Sjur wrote to me explaining how he had discovered the route. After studying the maps for a long time, he concluded that the valley between Dufek Massif and the eastern mountains would provide perfect access to the Polar Plateau, though he chose Frost Spur to reach it. Only when skiing towards Frost Spur did he spot what he called "nice slopes" to the east, near Wujek Ridge. Børge Ousland later found a good route there from maps and aerial photos, which he used on his second, successful, expedition to the Pole.

Tonight's camp had an inspiring setting. Beyond the tent's front door the peaks of the Dufek Massif ranged across the horizon. From the rear entrance we could see the icecaps of the more distant but more extensive Forrestal Range. It was a great place to be.

Peter's diary:
We had a good start with me starting breakfast at 5.15 and we were away by 7 am.

I'm becoming increasingly annoyed with Keith and Ian's lethargic attitude to our main goal – The Pole. All day they dragged the chain and on both of my leads were several kilometres behind me at the end of the sessions. In the last session I lost sight of them totally and as there was mist moving in I decided to wait. It took them 35 min to catch up (disgusting). They've generally been going slow and taking photos of one lump of rock. I will [call] this the 500 photo rock.

It was good that I led 2 sessions today as it meant that I could push the pace and cover the distance. They had to walk longer to complete the stages and we achieved the distance required.

The weather was cloudy and overcast all day, very threatening as far as storms are concerned.

This is our 28th day and by my rough reckoning if we maintain 25 km roughly each day to the pole, we will do it in the remaining 32 days, resulting in a 60 day or better total for the trip. 60 days is the time we planned to complete the trip. If only I can keep the others going!

I'm focused on the Pole. Focused and efficient. Whilst the mountains are nice to look at, as far as I'm concerned they're just something to be overcome in order to achieve the main goal. The quicker I see the backside of them the better, because this means I'm closer to the Pole.

I hope the weather remains cloudy. Perhaps this will distract the others from the constant photos. All they talk about is rest days and taking it easy. All I think about is kilometres and efficiency.

GPS reading for today shows 28 km travelled. My pushing my sections paid off.

That evening Peter discussed the photography with me: "Obviously in the mountains is where you'll be getting the best photos. Perhaps it would be better, when you want to take a lot of photos, that I do your leads for you, so you can hang back and get your pictures. Then you can take over some of my leads later. That way you'll be satisfied, and so will my focus on kilometres."

I replied: "Well, I wasn't aware that my taking of photographs has impacted on my leads significantly or very often, except maybe on the ice when we were approaching Wujek Ridge, but that was exceptional. And I want to make kilometres too, you know."

But it sounded like a reasonable suggestion, so I told him I'd think about it.

Photography for me is more than a routine function. It gives me great aesthetic pleasure and satisfaction and is thus an important contributor to my sense of wellbeing. To be honest, I also welcomed it as respite from the monotony of hauling.

I was conscious of the importance of good photographs as a means of fulfilling our responsibilities to sponsors and providing a comprehensive record of our journey. Taking pictures was one of my assigned functions on the expedition and I felt a strong responsibility to do my best. But this was proving extremely difficult. If I was lucky I had just a few minutes free during the day for photography. Often I gave up valuable eating and resting time for it. My difficulties were not alleviated by my frequent separation from the others during our travel and their unwillingness to cooperate with positions or waiting. It was obvious that Peter found photography stops irritating.

One aspect of Peter's suggestion that did not appeal was piling up a shift-lead debt that I would have to repay. Not being good at thinking quickly on my feet, I decided to assess the situation over the next few days.

30 November

The nights were a blissful respite from the rigours of our days. The fears for the morrow could be pushed aside by dreamless oblivion. Last night the peace was shattered by my bladder, which roused me three times to service the piss bottle. As well, my right hand kept me awake for an hour as alternating waves of dull pain and numbness coursed from wrist to fingertips. My hand was stiff and useless for more than an hour after I woke this morning. I tried wrapping the stock-strap around my wrist in different ways and doing less pushing with both hands when hauling.

My diary:

It is a bloody slog of a day, with shitty slow snow of breaking crust and high friction sand. We climb 240 metres, most of it on my two shifts of leading, plus ups and downs. My feet hurt quite badly again after a good day yesterday – who would think that the same pains could persist for four weeks!

Peter's diary:

Snow conditions were not perfect, in that they were slow and a terrible strain. Deep snow with a crust that we and the sleds kept breaking through making it a very strenuous day. The others don't think that we have done very well, but I estimate that we travelled at least 25 km. We need to make 25 km now to maintain our average. If we can do that in these conditions we have a good chance of making it for the rest of the expedition ... We have left 500 Photo Rock behind and are camped below the Pensacola Mountains ... There have been many hundreds of snowquakes over the last couple of days. One huge one that we could hear moving across the valley for several minutes.

We actually covered 26 km, but even Keith admitted it was tough, delivering his verdict to the video camera after leading his shift:

Every step was an effort. In fact every step reminded me of going up Wujek Ridge the other day, and we're going along supposedly on the flat. It was just damned hard work. I'm glad it's time for a soup and biscuit break. Yeah, it was one of the hardest sessions of the trip so far.

But light moments and beauty again compensated for the pain and drudgery. It was a great delight to be able to observe our progress among the mountains. An hour before camping, we crossed the 83rd parallel. The previous day we had completed the 500th kilometre. At the end of the day we had under 800 km to go, or so the GPS reckoned, and were two-fifths of the way to the Pole. As the journey progressed, our joy and satisfaction in these measures of progress grew. Just about every second day we found a milestone to celebrate. In another two days we hoped to reach the next: three-sevenths of the journey. We were creeping up on half way. Half way would give rise to much rejoicing.

It was −10°C but in the calm, sun-drenched air I was sweating freely as I plodded along in the rear wearing only light thermals. We were approaching both the summer solstice and the Pole and, as a result, the sun was describing a circle around us at a constant height above the horizon. Our shadows swung around us through the day, pointing west in the morning and east in the evening. My moustache had iced up and clouds of breath coated my beard in frost. In an exotic contrast, the stink of sweat filled my nostrils and condensation trickled down my goggle lenses. I knew that if the slightest breeze sprang up, the moisture would freeze instantly.

Noise surrounded me: the chunk-screech of the stock-tips driving into the snow, the rhythmic slide and shush of my skis. Behind me, the sled bumped and ground and groaned over and through the snow. Every now and then a snowquake whoomped across the plain. Snowquakes were so frequent they had become routine, and we hardly took fright any more, except with the big ones. Hauling was tough; the harness tugged and jerked on my hips and shoulders with every step.

Peter and Keith were about 10 minutes ahead, chugging along like machines. When I had stopped earlier to adjust my clothing to cool down, Keith overtook me, muttering as he went: "I'd better keep going because if I stop I may not be able to get up again." He was looking tired, his usual fire burning only dimly. I speculated that climbing the pass had affected him.

Peter was trying to put as many kilometres behind him as possible in the shift of two hours and 20 minutes. The previous day I had even seen him change gloves without breaking stride. I knew that again I would pull into the rest stop 10 or 15 minutes behind. Although my slowness was marginal, I surmised it had to be as infuriating for Peter as much as it was a relief for Keith.

I was thinking how good it was going to feel to reach the Pole and dreaming about being home again when my reverie was rudely interrupted by a series of low ridges that demanded a concentrated effort. I found the best technique was to use momentum, skiing faster and pulling harder as the sled approached the rise. Then, when the momentum was spent, I would lean forwards just at the right moment and heave the sled the last bit over the top.

Various parts of my body were trying to tell me things. There were twinges in my legs, which had suffered on the climb up the pass. My feet ached from the constant pounding. My right hand seemed to have sustained some sort of nerve damage and I tried to avoid straining it. Occasionally I had pins and needles in my fingers but the sensation quickly passed. Listening to my body was vital if I was to survive the punishing pace as well as the harsh environment.

I stopped to wipe the moisture from my goggles and ease the ache in my feet. The surroundings were stunning. We were just drawing level with the bluffs and shimmering blue and white ice tables of the Forrestal Range.

In places the ice reflected the sun with a mirror-like gleam. Behind us, the Dufek Massif was fading to a silhouette. The mountains rose abruptly on either side of the flat snowfield, which was punctured by scattered nunataks in other directions. After weeks of visual deprivation on Berkner Island and the ice shelf the mountains were an aesthetic lifebuoy. I swung my skis around, flicked the haul-ropes out of the way, pulled the camera from the sled and captured, for one last time, the wonderful symmetry of the Dufek Massif.

My diary:
As I hold my breath and the camera shutter clunks, I am suddenly aware of the intense silence. Without my busy sounds, there is nothing. The mountains shimmer, the snow stretches away like a sequined sheet of silk, the sky is an aquamarine. What an absolutely pristine and pure, yet lifeless and inhuman place. How can humanity possibly threaten this? I wonder if we should even be here, leaving our trail of buried turds across the unsullied ice.

The lads were getting away. I grabbed my stocks, shouldered the harness and moved on, carrying the scene and my thoughts with me to ease the burden.

Though I am deeply moved by the heart-rending and impeccable beauty [I wrote], it does not invoke in me an urge to protect. In other lands I have been so moved – in Tasmania, and Cape York Peninsula, where the biological riches seemed so fragile, the perfection so imminently threatened. Here, in the interior of Antarctica, the only ecology is the inert ecology of air, ice, space and rock. Børge met an adventurous snow-petrel as he approached the mountains, but we have seen nothing: not an insect, not even a lichen exists here. This immaculate land seems at the same time incorruptible. It is taking care of itself perfectly well, thank you very much. Inland Antarctica exists in a wondrous state of grace that lies beyond human concerns, aloof and unyielding...Thoughts turn to the condition of the rest of the world, that once was all as sublime and undefiled as Antarctica. It is a colossal tragedy that only here can such sublimity be revisited. What have we done ... What have we done?

A long radio sched this evening covered much ground. Peter told Doug we'd had a hard time in "fairly atrocious conditions" making the 26 km. Doug seemed genuinely impressed by our progress. He reported that the Australian media were watching us closely. "You've got a great response back home, a lot of people following you," he said. "The Trekathon, which I think was the other day, that was doing very well. A lot of people involved in that…"

Peter turned from the mike to Keith and me. "That's great, isn't it? I hope they make a lot of money. It'll make this big grunt worthwhile."

Finally Doug relayed some questions to Peter from Jennifer, who was on the satellite phone, for a report in *The Australian*. Peter said: "Morale is high, we're enjoying the expedition but it's a lot of hard work… At the moment we're surrounded by these fantastic mountains, and that's been a real inspiration to the three of us. Once we leave these mountains we get back into much more plain conditions with no scenery."

1 December

The first day of summer, but I expected no swallows. The morning began in sunshine but steadily became heavily overcast. The mountains remained discernible, at least in outline, but the ground was invisible except where our skis defined it. Our route lay between the mountains, so there was none to sight off, and we all struggled in the lead. Even following was difficult, as the tracks ahead could be seen only for a metre or two. As Peter put it in his diary:

> Each person leading each shift had a great deal of difficulty navigating, but particularly telling what one's skis were doing. You couldn't tell what the ground was doing and as a consequence where the skis should be. Very demanding physically.

Our 1:250,000 scale map showed a rise in the ice field, marked as a "steep slope", lying across our path just a few kilometres from our camp. After some hours we had seen nothing and wondered if we could have missed the scarp in the dreary light. We had climbed to nearly 1400 m, but gently.

Typically Peter tried to go as fast as possible during his lead, and consequently staggered and veered around in the gloom, groping over the uneven terrain like a blind man with two flailing sticks. At one point he turned and apologised for going so slowly and holding us up. Keith and I accepted his apology with grace before resuming the hard work needed to keep up with him. I managed to stay with him by stopping only when he did.

When Peter's time was up, Keith said: "That was a very relaxing shift. Thanks, Pete. Also quite entertaining."

Later, passing too close to Creaney Nunatak, an outlying knoll of the Forrestal Range, we blundered into a steep incline. It was obvious from the accumulation of snow hereabouts that the prevailing wind came from the north-east. Mountains on our right showed us windward faces of bare rock, but nunataks on our left extended long spurs of snow that had built up in their lee. It was such a spur that we had crossed near Creaney Nunatak.

We camped shortly afterwards. Despite our unsteady course, and at least partly owing to Peter's efforts, we had covered another 26 km.

I raised Peter's suggestion about my photography. I had been giving it some thought and avoiding interrupting my leads with photo stops. It had become obvious that Peter's strategy would not work. I would end up even further behind, have shorter rest stops and still not get close-up shots of the others sledging. I didn't think the back of the line was the best place for the expedition photographer. Peter's solution satisfied his priorities but not mine. I told him it was not a good idea. He just said: "Oh, okay." Perhaps he was happy because there had been no recent problems and we would soon leave the distraction of the mountains anyway.

Tomorrow, according to Børge's notes and the map, we had to climb two more jump-ups in the snowfield. They lay between crevasse zones and navigation would be critical, so we hoped for better conditions. We pinned our hopes on an ever-so-slowly widening band of blue over the northern horizon, where the cloud originated. From the tent door, we could see the distant Dufeks shining on the edge of the sunlit land. To our surprise, the tops around Davis Valley and Wujek Ridge were also still visible, though now 80 km away.

Peter had become obsessed with reaching the Pole in 60 days. Keith and I had tacitly concurred, or at least we had not vetoed the idea, since it seemed achievable at our current speed. Keith would ultimately defer to Peter as leader, but I was more pig-headed and expected more consultation and consensus. Peter had seemed more relaxed today, even accepting some lingering at our breaks. As long as we were clicking along at 25 km or more a day, he seemed satisfied. This rate would put us at the Pole on 31 December. It was now day 30, so by that schedule our traverse was half over.

My hand kept me awake again. It was beginning to seriously concern me.

2 December

The sky was clear, as we'd hoped, but a nasty southerly was blowing straight in our faces. One of the ice scarps was clearly visible, running straight across our path. There were broken ice cliffs on the left of it, against the Forrestal Range; on the right were smaller disturbed areas, where the ice flowed over buried rocks. There was open terrain between, consistent with Børge's notes. In front of the scarp I could see a small outcrop of dark rock that just broke the surface like a wave-washed reef. It would be exciting to explore but I thought our route lay too far to the side. We took a bearing between the broken areas and agreed to change direction at the first rise, just 3.5 km from camp. This would put us on a more directly southward course towards our exit from the mountains. The previous night we had entered these locations as waypoints into the GPS. Again we kept our climbing gear handy, ready to rope up if necessary.

With Peter in the lead, we marched on 177° magnetic (197° true) to the first rise. We didn't know it, but we were heading into a serious incident that would bring to the boil all the tensions that had been simmering between us.

The climb seemed to take longer than we expected. A hundred metres below the crest I heard a yell and looked up to see Keith, out of his harness, skiing quickly back and waving his stock. I could not make out his words but looked over to where he was pointing. I now saw that the rock outcrop was only 20 m away. I quickly unharnessed myself, snatched my camera and raced across just as Peter disappeared over the rise.

It was the first real land we had touched since starting out. We were as thrilled as two kids at Christmas. The few dozen square metres of geology barely rose above the surface of the ice but they displayed an impressive variety of red and brown sandstones and quartzites. We ran all over the outcrop, picking up chunks and yelling about what we'd discovered. I was absorbed by the richness of the textures and colours after the endless monotony of snow. I spied a rounded chunk with black flecks and for a moment thought I had found lichen, but then recognised a metallic mineral. A search revealed not a trace of lichen anywhere; the stone was as clean and unweathered as if freshly shattered for our pleasure. I had promised Cale I would take back a piece of Antarctica for him, so I carefully selected a few choice fragments and pocketed them for both of us. Precious treasures.

Reluctantly we returned to our sleds. We were surprised not to find Peter waiting beyond the top of the rise. We spotted him in a slight basin below the next ice scarp, a kilometre or two ahead. We now realised we were on a bench that separated the two rises. This had been invisible from our campsite because the deceptive light had merged the two jump-ups.

Simultaneously, both Keith and I saw that the best route lay to the left of Peter's path. A subtle valley led to the top between steeper slopes, one of which Peter faced. Not only did the valley offer much the easiest way up, but Keith and I also agreed it would be the safest. Glaciers are always more crevassed on convex slopes, where the ice is being stretched. The valley was concave, and the ice was certainly being compressed there and unlikely to be cracked.

At that point we also realised we had passed the waypoint at which we intended to change our bearing more to the south (and directly towards the valley). We shifted direction by about 10° to the left and made for the valley, hoping Peter would see where we were heading and join us.

A short time later we saw him traversing to the left across the foot of the slope towards our line of travel, so we continued on our way. Then he turned back and began climbing the scarp. He was zigzagging. It looked very steep, and as we watched through zoom video and binoculars, he stopped to change into crampons. He laboriously zigzagged towards the top, stopping every few metres to rest. I could see by his movements that the ascent was as difficult as at "John Leece Pass", though only about 100 m high. Peter's way led to the highest part of the scarp; ours would take us to the lowest. He would be on top before we could even reach the bottom, so we saw little point in following him up a poor route.

Keith and I continued towards the valley, watching Peter until we could see he was safely up. I reckoned that when we got to the top we would be 500 m to his left. Our ascent was strenuous but straighforward: we walked directly up it without zigzagging. At the crest we expected at any moment to see Peter, who was probably waiting for us to appear. I knew he would be furious and that our separation was potentially serious, but Keith seemed less concerned.

"We should cut across and link up with him," I suggested.

"No, that will mean going off our line and more distance," Keith replied. "Let's stick to the correct route. He'll be right; he'll see us soon and come across."

I said: "We should get back together as quickly as possible. He won't have a clue what we're doing."

Just then Peter came into sight, almost directly to our right, sitting on his sled. While waiting, he gave us both barrels, straight into the video camera:

Right now I'm about as annoyed as I've been with the attitude during this trip. We've had to negotiate a pretty major crevasse field, the first major crevasse field, today. I would have expected the other two to support me through that. What happens? Just before the crevasse field they go wandering off into a pile of rocks, and I had to find my own way through the crevasse field, which is damned dangerous. And when I turn back they're picking a different way through the crevasse field, so heaven knows where they are at the moment. All I've done is I've come to the top of the rise and I'm sitting here waiting for them to pop out somewhere. It's bloody dangerous, and they should be supporting the leader through this, not wandering off playing pansies in the bloody rocks. Meanwhile I sit here and freeze my butt off.

With the physical obstacles behind us, Keith and I stopped to consult the GPS and get a bearing to our next waypoint. Peter did not stir, so we moved off on the new bearing, still slightly uphill, using the spare, hand-held compass. At least we were all in sight of one another now, and our reunion was only a matter of time and who would give in first.

We waved our stocks to encourage Peter to join us, but for a while he didn't move. Keith agreed to a compromise and we adjusted our course so that it was slightly to the right of the new bearing. Peter began to haul almost parallel to our course, perhaps still following the original bearing. We were ahead of him, and eventually I persuaded Keith to stop when the slope flattened out and some nunataks appeared ahead, confirming our bearing was sound. It was 11 a.m. and way past time for our first food break. I was starving.

Peter changed course and came across. He was absolutely livid. Stopping 10 m away, he threw his stocks down and launched into an angry tirade.

"I waited half an hour while you guys were collecting frigging rocks for your garden! And then you went off on the wrong direction," he exploded. "Can someone tell me what is going on? ... The leader sets the pace; it's up to the others to keep up ... What if I'd fallen in a crevasse without you guys to back me up? ... The worst example of incompetence I've ever seen!"

Keith and I weathered the storm without saying much, except to point out that we took an obviously better route. Keith protested that Peter's view of leadership was wrong. I decided it would be injudicious to say that if he had been seriously worried about crevasses he should have waited. Peter was not in a receptive frame of mind. Keith kept eating, unperturbed. I remembered that Peter had told me he and Keith had an understanding about their differences. I decided it would be best to let them deal with this conflict in their own way.

Peter was entitled to be browned off on several counts. He was quite certain he was on the right route, and in the circumstances it was unwise for us to have separated. But Peter was mistaken about the waypoint position, and I would not apologise for stopping at the rocks. In my experience, fault can usually be found on both sides when these things happen. There was obviously some misunderstanding over the route and pig-headedness on the part of all of us in persisting with what we wanted to do. The fact that trouble emerged in a key section of the route, one that involved some potential risk, was unfortunate, but with hindsight I can't help feeling it was inevitable.

The incident brought to the fore all the tensions that had existed between us from the start as a result of differences in approach and priorities. We had never discussed or dealt with them adequately and this event showed me that, left unresolved, they could become dangerous.

Peter signalled that he would sustain his anger: "You guys can do all the navigation from now on."

In silence we packed up and I led off. Keith followed closely but Peter hung back, keeping his distance. He remained silent and aloof for the rest of the day. Although I regarded our actions as justified, I felt a twinge of guilt at allowing the situation to develop. I had an urge to come clean and turned to Keith. "We need to discuss this," I said.

"Yeah, we'll have to talk about it."

The freezing wind had abated and the day became magnificent – one of our finest – as we hauled parallel to the Forrestal Range, passing close to the steep bluff of Mt Stephens (2066 m), the region's highest point, and a series of nunatak outliers. Haskill Nunatak was a particularly striking trapezoid only three kilometres off our track. It rose about 200 m above the snow plain in sweeping slopes of ice-cream flecked with chocolate rock. I would have killed for the chance to dance along that voluptuous summit ridge, sledless and free.

The snow was quite good for hauling. Aside from the emotional tension, the travelling was immensely enjoyable. Our bearing would take us close to the last nunataks of the range. Yonder lay the great white void of the Polar Plateau, which we must soon confront. We would leave the mountains with great sadness; they had been magical and kind, almost friendly.

As Haskill Nunatak fell behind, we encountered a series of ups and downs across our path. They were associated with windblown ridges in the lee of a series of smaller nunataks close by. We climbed several, descending through sticky sand, dragging hard even downhill. Away to the right, fine black peaks of the Neptune Range marched across the horizon like a column of nuns.

The last ascent of the day brought us to the top of the ridge that ran from Ray Nunatak. We camped below the sublimely curled summit cornice that looked like a breaking wave of foam. Ice is a remarkable and plastic substance, able to mutate into infinite forms, many of exquisite beauty. Just beyond, standing before the void, swelled the equally gorgeous Beiszer Nunatak, last bastion of the range. It was good to camp close to these hills, to share some time with them before leaving them in our quest to be somewhere else.

Peter became talkative, and the atmosphere in the tent was relaxed, as usual. I was waiting for Keith or Peter to raise the incident on the ice scarp, but it was not discussed. Peter put his case to his diary. After writing down much of what he'd said to us and to the video camera, he concluded: "All in all we wasted a lot of time ... We should have done a lot more than 24 km."

That night I fingered my stones with furtive pleasure. There would be nothing but ice from here.

On our radio sched two days earlier I'd asked for ANI's resident doctor to be available for a remote consultation next time around. When we answered the call from Doug this evening, Dr Kate Brown came to the microphone at Patriot Hills and said how good it was to hear another Australian accent. We thought so too. Kate was from Western Australia.

I described the symptoms I was experiencing in my hand. After asking some specific questions, she said: "It sounds like carpal tunnel syndrome, nerve damage with inflamed tendons." She reassured me that continuing to use my hand would not cause long-term damage. "It should heal up completely with treatment." She endorsed my tactic of reducing strain on the wrist and prescribed a 1–2 week course of anti-inflammatories (which we carried in our medical kit) as well as a supportive bandage during the day.

After I'd finished talking to Kate I felt a great weight had been lifted from my shoulders. Worries about long-term damage can be morale-sapping. I went to sleep more relaxed than I had for weeks.

3 DECEMBER

An absolute stunner of a day. I hauled myself out of the tent early to take some photographs I had been after from the start. This was the first time we had camped on anything but flat ground. I skied, sledless and free, a short way up the slope to look back at our tent, puny-looking in the vastness of its surroundings. My legs felt wearier than they had on any other day of the expedition. It seemed strange how my body reacted in a way apparently unconnected with my perception of how difficult each day was. Yesterday had felt good, except for the continuing foot pains. Perhaps 32 days of grunt, 27 of them without a break, were taking their toll. But it is amazing how legs will keep on walking if you insist, even when they know better.

Our departure from the mountains was memorable. The sun was at just the right angle to highlight the glittering snow running up to the aesthetically curved slopes of the two nunataks and their deep blue cornice shadows. The visual feast mitigated the initial hard grind across the undulating ridges that spoked out from the peaks.

Keith's diary: "Great day weatherwise ... but SOFT SNOW made sledging very hard. Left mountains and headed into the white void."

Peter's diary: "Sledging into nothing is extremely difficult after having mountains to look at for the past couple of weeks. We need to get used to this again. Nothing more was said after the problems of yesterday. The guys seem more focused today."

We passed east of a low, crevasse-riven hillock of broken ice. Further to the west, nunataks of several colours stabbed the horizon, one a perfect red-brown pyramid with a black cap. As we sat on the sleds at our first break, looking ahead to the blankness of the plateau, I waved towards the southern horizon. "It's amazing to think that the next thing we'll see in that direction will be a bloody American aerial – and not for another 700 km!" I said.

Our high hopes for better snow on the windswept plateau were dashed yet again. As the mountains fell behind, the snow became increasingly soft and slow. At worst the bindings of our skis became submerged and the bellies of the sleds dragged mercilessly, like fat elephant seals. Undulating ground added to our woes; it was a blow to have to drag hard to force the sleds downhill.

We were all disheartened by the grind and the disappointment. Keith was subdued and did not say much. He seemed to be finding it tough. Perhaps, like me, he felt the loss of the mountains. I was surprised to see Peter, during his lead, taking breathers mid-shift. He kept turning around and saying in an incredulous tone: "Is this uphill? It feels uphill."

It was beginning to look as though we were going to have to walk out of this snow, because it was not changing for the better with time. We hoped it would not be too far.

The temperature was in the teens, but we were generally comfortable in single thermals and no windproofs as we slogged through the drifts. This did pose a risk because it left us with no protection if the slightest breeze sprang up. On Peter's lead Keith was in the rear, and I heard him yelling about something. This was unusual, so I stopped and turned to catch his words. He was still hauling, but looked distracted. "Bloody hell it's cold!," he blurted out as he came closer. "I'm going to lose it!"

"Lose what?" I yelled back.

"I've got to put a sock down where it counts or I'm going to lose it!"

It dawned on me. I had suffered cold arms, a cold belly and cold thighs at various times, but my intimate parts had always felt warm. Perhaps I'm insensitive in that area.

In a panic, Keith tossed his stocks down, stumbled to his sled and began rummaging in the depths.

"It feels like it's going to come off," he said.

He pulled something out, stuffed it down his pants, then relaxed. We had all been concerned about the possibility of losing digits in Antarctica, but not that digit!

We pulled into camp disconsolate. Peter was sure we had achieved our 25 km, but when the GPS indicated only 23, his disappointment was palpable.

Blizzard gives way to a burst of weak sunshine near the top of the "John Leece Pass" pass, as Peter stops to adjust his clothing and survey our ascent route. Heavy fresh snow made the climb even more arduous.

151

"…go straight for the white wall, and then close to the mountain…" was Børge Ousland's cryptic advice on the route he'd pioneered up Wujek Ridge, but falling snow cut visibility and made route-finding difficult. Gradually gaining height below massive cliffs, Keith leads the way through a snowstorm.

Once we'd crested Wujek Ridge the flat, 1200 m high expanse of the Sallee
Snowfield led us through the mountains. The icefalls on the back side of the
Dufek Massif climb another 600 m into the clouds.

In swirling snow below the steepest pinch of the pass,
we stopped for a food break. Peter puts on his down
jacket as the wind strengthens.

A sled-hauler's view of the world. In the frequent
white-outs, the only points of orientation were the
compass and our own skis pointing the way, we hoped!

Keith sights the compass in good visibility on the Sallee Snowfield, where we could use the mountains ahead as targets. It was a relief to have features on the horizon by which we could gauge our slow but inexorable progress.

*The mountains were a delight after the monotony of the lowlands. The view
of the ever-present but diminishing symmetry of the Dufek Massif (top) holds
our gaze, making it hard to rise from our rests. Keith and I were thrilled to
unexpectedly come across a rock outcrop below the Forrestal Range (above).
Like kids at Christmas we fondled the sun-warmed stones and pocketed a few
treasures, but this was to cause intense friction with Peter, who had gone ahead.*

*Evenings in the warmth of the tent were spent yarning, marking up maps,
cooking, making repairs and writing up the expedition log and our diaries.
Keith (top) takes just a few minutes to complete his diary; mine sometimes
took up to an hour. The vestibule of the tent was perfect for preparing breakfast.
Before settling in for the "night", Peter (above) arranged the vacuum flasks,
billies and stoves (under the billies) for a flying start in the morning.*

Morning sun on 3 December highlights the cornices of Ray Nunatak, one of the last peaks of the Forrestal Range, as Peter, front, and Keith head into the 700 km vastness of the Polar Plateau.

CHAPTER 7

TRIAL *by* SASTRUGI

At times, during the long hours of steady tramping
across the trackless snow-fields, one's thoughts flow
in a clear and limpid stream ...

DOUGLAS MAWSON, THE HOME OF THE BLIZZARD (1915)

4 DECEMBER

I had begun the course of anti-inflammatories on the night I talked to Kate, and this morning I bound my wrist with an elastic bandage and a splint made from a piece of foam I'd cut from our tent-floor insulation.

After breakfast Peter said: "I hope this snow gives out soon. It's really blowing our averages out of the water."

I couldn't help thinking how sensitive he was to quite minor threats to the schedule. Sure, if we continued to have soft snow, the impact would become significant, but the fact was that we had fallen a total of just 3 km behind the 25 km a day target in two days of heavy hauling.

We packed our sleds under a lightly overcast sky. Keith, who was leading the first shift, jerked his sled into motion. Peter glanced at a dark pall of stratus sitting on the Forrestal Range. "Look how ugly it is out there," he said.

I followed his gaze across the steely plain to the black clouds, then leftwards to where a glorious band of sunlight lifted two nunataks from the gloom.

"Those nunataks are magnificent," I said.

He returned to strapping his sled. "The sooner we lose sight of them the better," he said.

It didn't take us long to catch up with Keith as he veered this way and that in the difficult light. He stopped frequently to check the compass and adjust it

As we gained height on the Polar Plateau and conditions became colder, our stops became even more unpleasant and perfunctory. We rarely used our cameras.

161

on his chest, then he would move on, muttering. Even though we had not been aiming for them directly, the mountains had given us some idea of direction over the past few days. Now there was nothing. Nevertheless, Keith seemed to be having an unusually hard time of it, and his exasperation grew.

He suddenly stopped, stomped back to his sled and rummaged through it.

"What are you looking for?" I asked.

"You'll see."

When Keith got a bee in his bonnet about something, he became very focused. He pulled out his rolled-up foam mat and strapped it to his chest under the compass mount. This pushed the compass forwards. We all found it hard to keep an eye on the horizon and the compass at the same time in bad light. Peter dealt with this by watching his feet and the compass and ignoring the horizon. I usually switched from one to the other.

Keith skied on for a few minutes before stopping again. He pulled the compass harness off, took his multi-tool out of its pouch and attacked the bolts of the compass bracket. Peter and I waited nervously but dared not say anything until it became obvious that Keith intended to remount the compass further out on the bracket. This was a vital piece of equipment with 700 km of navigation ahead of it, and we feared for its wellbeing. Peter pleaded with Keith to let him take over the lead so we could adjust the compass in the tent later. But Keith was determined. He dropped one of the screws in the snow and had to use strapping tape to lash the compass to the front of the bracket. Luckily, he found the screw soon afterwards and put it in his pouch. After that he seemed satisfied and continued more steadily.

Soon the cloud cleared. It turned into a great day but the soft snow dogged us still. I opened a conversation with Peter about the ice scarp incident. Peter said he had got over his anger. He insisted he and Keith did not need to talk it through because they understood each other, and their way of doing things complemented each other. I said I preferred to discuss such things and clear the air. However, Peter did not seem to want to pursue the matter. I moved on to the issue of our speed. "Why are you so fixed on 60 days?" I asked.

"So we compare favourably with other teams and have a good margin of safety," he replied.

"You realise no-one back in Australia will give a damn?" I said.

"I know. But still, if I was really pushing, I'd be trying to finish in 50 days. We waste a lot of time during the day, like an hour at those rocks."

I let the exaggeration pass but focused on the principle: "I call it achieving our other objectives. I don't call it waste."

"I do," Peter retorted.

"I know, and that's a problem we should talk about."

But we never did.

We seemed to disagree not about our main objective (reaching the Pole) but rather his unilaterally determined subsidiary aim of doing it fast and sacrificing other possible outcomes in the process. If it took us a few more days to get there because we enjoyed ourselves, climbed a peak or took better photographs, I reckoned it would be time well spent.

Peter, for his part, must have been exasperated by Keith's and my apparent lack of commitment. Perhaps he felt that by trying to enjoy the experience we were jeopardising the main objective. I couldn't help feeling that the reasons he had given me for a rapid trip merely rationalised his desire to connect A and B as quickly as possible.

I decided the tension arose out of two fundamental differences. First, Peter placed value only on completing the journey, whereas I also valued the quality of the experience and our ability to communicate that experience later. Second, Peter was constantly worried that we faced failure and that time spent doing anything other than furthering progress added to the risk of failure, whereas I was more sanguine about the risk. To Peter my attitude might have appeared reckless. For me there was not a lot of merit in merely reaching the Pole. If all we could say afterwards was "Yes, we did it, and it was bloody awful", I would expect people to ask why we'd bothered. Peter would perhaps answer that question by speaking of overcoming difficulty, demonstrating the value of commitment, accepting a challenge and meeting it.

At the heart of the conflict lay the normal human conviction that what inspires oneself must also inspire others. I was more inspired by beauty and meaning; Peter was more inspired by achievement, especially when it could mean something. These differences in purpose and approach were to remain unreconciled throughout the journey, posing a threat to all our objectives.

We all worked hard when leading our shifts today. Peter and Keith even complimented me on mine, Peter saying he had found it hard to keep up. However, in no way could I keep up with Peter when he led the third shift, coming in seven minutes behind him.

On the fourth shift Keith led powerfully up a long incline that provided a superb view back to the Forrestal Range. In such a subtle landscape even small heights can provide spectacular sights. We were probably only 100 m above the surrounding plain. It became apparent that yesterday we had descended into a huge basin and were doomed to spend most of today climbing out of it.

Peter stayed close behind Keith on the ascent but I fell behind. As it was the last shift, it would not matter much if I was a little late, I reasoned. Climbing was killing my feet. From the top we descended again and spent the rest of the evening wandering through a weird landscape of basins and domes, each perhaps 1 km across and up to 100 m deep or high.

As I followed the others at some distance, I saw we were about to enter the deepest basin yet. They tried to skirt the rim at first, but their sleds wanted to slip sideways down the slope. So they gave up and made straight for the depths.

It was much further than it looked, and after a while I stopped for a routine hit of chocolate to push me through the last hour. The others stopped just after me, and although they were perhaps 500 m away, it was so peaceful I could hear them talking. I could almost make out their individual words.

The long descent continued. Keith and Peter stopped in the bottom, and since our time was up, I expected to see the cheery green tent being pitched. But then I saw them start climbing the other side, strongly at first, then more slowly, then fitfully, with many stops, as the concave slope gradually became steeper. It looked like hell. Why hadn't they stopped? I cursed their decision as I trudged across the bottom of the basin.

When I started climbing, they soon disappeared. The slope steepened, my skins began losing their grip and I was grunting and swearing. When my skis slipped, my stocks took all the weight, plunging in to a quarter of their length. I had to use both hands to extract them. It was all disturbingly familiar.

I was at the limit of my powers and immensely relieved when the slope eased. What a bastard of a way to finish the day! As I crept over the top, the half-pitched tent appeared. I lugged the sled the last few metres and parked it beside the tent. The view was magnificent. To the north the mountains were faded and distant. To the east, the plateau fell away to the Support Force Glacier, lost in haze and brightness. Peering, I thought I could see some hills on the far side – but you could never be sure in this land of illusions.

"We thought it would be too depressing to camp in the hole and have to face the climb first up in the morning," Keith said.

I agreed it was a good move but probably one I wouldn't have had the strength to make. It was a pleasant surprise to discover that, because they had pushed our travelling time to 10 hours, and despite the horrible conditions, we had managed 27 km. For a net gain of 130 m of altitude over the day, we must have climbed at least 300 m through the hollows. We had all worked at it, and Keith in particular had put in a big effort during his two shifts.

There had been no frost in the tent for many nights. The tent was always pitched on a north-south axis; it was delightfully warm on my side in the evening and on Keith's in the morning. That night the temperature rose to a sweltering 14°C inside, and I had trouble sleeping until the sun moved around.

Keith's diary: "Great but hard day again. Fantastic weather, lousy soft snow. Right ankle ligaments very sore."

5 DECEMBER

Our desperate haul out of the pit had extricated us from the torturous ups and downs. The terrain beyond was relatively flat. Even better, before the end of the first shift the soft snow quite abruptly gave out. Our rejoicing was moderated by the sandy texture and slight bumpiness of the surface. The going was reasonably firm and flat but still not fast. Either we were impossible to please or it was the norm to have some form of surface difficulty.

Keith and I were weary from yesterday's exertions, but Peter seemed none the worse for them. I felt sluggardly and uninspired; the psychological pressure of another 700 km of more of the same weighed heavily. We all had some sort of affliction; Keith's neck was very painful and his ankle still hurt. Peter and I had sore feet, and goggle-fogging was a major hassle for us. Peter's calf was also still bothering him. On the bright side, the weather was sunny and clear, even sweaty. We were back on the crest of the divide, and the steep chocolate-brown peaks of the Neptune Range were again visible in the western distance, providing inspiration to the mountaineers in all of us.

Keith gave me some advice: "If you try and keep up with Peter all the time, you'll hurt yourself."

"Do you mean you can't keep up with him either?" I asked.

"Oh, I can burn him off if I want to, like in the desert or on this trip, but day after day, you've got to hand it to him, he's good."

He was referring to a tale he had told me earlier about a day when he got really livid during the Simpson Desert crossing. He just took off, leaving Peter trailing in his wake. I had no intention of competing against Peter because I knew we were in different leagues. Still, it would have been nice to be able to keep up with him more consistently. Peter never openly acknowledged his superior ability, which was a problem because the corollary was that he expected us be able to move as quickly. I suspected he was capable of pulling a lot faster even than he already was when leading; he was restraining himself. Peter's diary confirmed this:

This was a day that Ian and Keith struggled. In fact I stopped 15 minutes early so as to "not flog a dead horse". Ian in particular stopped and got diarrhoea towards the end of the day. For some time now, Keith and I have got to camp, set up the tent before Ian has arrived. Today, Keith also struggled all day …

I'm concerned to keep Ian and Keith going. I'm feeling fine and could have kept moving … tonight.

The mood tonight is high as we did 26 km and passed half way. The 26 km was mainly a result of my pushes. In the first lead I was 20 minutes ahead of the others. The last lead saw me at least a further 20 minutes ahead. Hope I can keep them going. I want to finish this trip within 60 days and by 31/12/97.

Snowquakes continue by the hundreds.

We decided to keep to 10 hours a day. This made our shifts two and a half hours each, a long time without stopping, at least for me. At the end of the last shift I had to stop three times because of my inexplicable diarrhoea and was left feeling weak and shaky. The others were not far ahead and, realising I was in trouble, stopped early. When I caught up, Peter was unusually cheery. "I thought we could justify an early mark for half way."

HALF WAY! This was fantastic, and encouraging too. The 84th parallel had also passed under our skis during the day. We had accomplished the most difficult half of the journey in 34 days – 32 not counting the first day (when we'd hauled for an hour) and our day confined to the tent. Peter's schedule aside, we would have no problem achieving the easier second half in our 69 food days, barring bad weather or human disaster.

We set up the video to record the landmark evening in the tent. Peter put down his diary and calculator and said: "We've used 34 days, 32 food days, and based on food days, our average has climbed to 20.5 km for the trip so far."

Keith pounced on this: "So we've only got to average 20 kays a day - great!"

"No, no," Peter said. "That's average to date. We've got 26 days remaining at 655 [km] to go, that's 25 km a day."

I asked Peter to clarify: "That's to do it in 60 days?"

Peter concurred.

Keith interjected: "But whether the body can get there in 60 days is another story."

I laughed at this and threw some sarcasm at Peter: "Does your calculator tell us that?"

Keith chuckled and said: "That's one thing you haven't factored in, Pete, whether the old body will actually stand the punishment of your schedule."

While pretending to work this out on the calculator, I suggested that Peter's body probably could cope with the schedule, and the conversation died. Keith and I attended to the soup; Peter flicked through his diary. The tension that had been building was eased when we moved to more mundane topics.

I was carrying a little present of chocolate fudge for each of us. I originally intended to bring it out on Christmas Day, but I decided half way was a more fitting occasion. We celebrated with gusto.

6 DECEMBER

My double shift day. They always seemed to come around more quickly than the day we each got rid of a food bag – also every third day. As I strapped on the compass I glanced at the horizon and experienced a moment of near panic. It was so far and so featureless! Usually in the wilderness there is something to fear, but here the only thing to fear was nothing. I concentrated on fixing my bearing on a beacon of sunlit snow. One step at a time; one beacon at a time; one shift at a time; one day at a time: that was the only way to beat the void.

The snow continued to improve but displayed a great variety of surfaces. That evening Peter explained his hopes for better progress to the video:

> *Rather than grunting away all day, achieving our 25 kays and being pretty tired, we can do 28 kays and feel fairly reasonable. What we're trying to do is ... more than 25 km a day because we know that further on in the trip we've got a 200 kilometre belt of sastrugi that's going to slow us down, and our averages are probably going to drop.*

Keith's ankle was giving him hell. He never said much but his demeanour betrayed the pain, and he made vague references to breakdown. He was wearing the ankle brace he'd brought. "I'd be crippled without it," he said.

On the third shift Peter tore off like a greyhound from the starting gate with Keith in hot pursuit. Although he worked hard and produced some valiant sprints, Keith kept falling behind. I managed to stay with Keith until I began to wonder how wise it was. Then for some reason Peter stopped, and when we pulled up alongside, Keith actually asked him to slow down.

"It was either hurt something or goodbye," he said. "I felt like I was on a 5 km run!"

Peter completed the shift more slowly. I took over for the last shift. I always found this one the hardest physically because I was weary by then, but psychologically it was often the easiest because the end of the day was close.

I was chugging along feeling happy with the day's progress when Keith called from close behind: "This is a good pace, Ian. Don't go any faster." It was a request I was happy to grant.

In his diary Peter emphasised that we needed to do more than 25 km a day in case we slowed later. This was not his only worry:

The other looming problem is Keith's ligaments which are causing him some problems. Very similar to the Simpson Desert trip. He asked me this morning how many days rest would be allowed before we call in the plane for an evacuation. I said a max of 2 days. We need every day we can get as our safety allowance is very thin.

Hopefully, the better snow will continue or get better and the boys will hold together. It's my continual worry that they will fall to bits.

I feel strong and good, as I have from the start. I always want to go faster and further on every shift, but hold myself back for the benefit of the team.

I was a little disappointed with the day's 27 km tally because progress had seemed better. Still, it was another 2 km in the bank over our 25 km a day target. I felt satisfied that I had maintained a reasonable pace during my two leads. As he stirred the dinner pot, Keith patiently explained to Peter that the purpose of increasing our travel time to 10 hours a day was to achieve our quota of kilometres, or a little more, without pushing ourselves too much. Peter listened and then said: "I had no idea I was going fast. I was worried I was holding you guys up."

7 DECEMBER

Every day seemed to pass so slowly, but once over, it seemed to occupy so little space in the memory, banished to the land of the past in the same way that our tracks became lost in the whiteness.

Day 36 went smoothly for me. By loosening the laces on my boots, I was able to reduce the pain in my feet. And it was my turn to finish a food bag! I reached the end of the day feeling stronger than usual. I kept my mouth covered all day because my tongue had been sore for several days and, as bizarre as it might seem, I suspected sunburn.

As well, I had been aware of a superficial soreness on my belly for some days, but despite a vague sense of déjà vu, I couldn't figure out a cause. In calm conditions earlier in the day I had been skiing along without my parka when a slight breeze had sprung up. My belly suddenly began to hurt, so I emulated Keith and stuck a glove inside my shirt. This worked well. In the tent this evening I found a few small bruise-like marks within larger areas of red in a line above my navel. To my dismay, I realised I had a frostnipped belly. This possibly went back to a few days earlier when sweat had frozen in my thermals.

The other guys fared worse than I today. Keith's ankle was no better and Peter had an assortment of afflictions.

I found today hard going. The snow, while harder, was frozen into waves of sastrugi which made pulling and navigating the sled very difficult. Added to this was my bum was chafed, my feet hurt, my back hurt from all the jarring and I knocked over my water at the first stop and was without water for the rest of the day. I also tried Keith's vapour barrier socks and found that they were a bit small and left my foot very moist. I'll persevere with them.

Keith and Ian found the going better than me and did good shifts. If we achieve a good mileage today it will be because of their shifts.

The only liquid Keith and I had to offer Peter was tomato soup – which always made him gag. I was concerned about dehydration, and suggested we take 15 minutes to melt some snow on the stove. Peter dismissed this out of hand and kept going. I remembered Keith once telling me Peter had a very high pain threshold. Certainly he seemed able to rise above most ordinary discomforts and, despite his afflictions, was still going strong.

The surface continued to harden and we had some quite fast travelling for a while. But it didn't last long. The ground became increasingly bumpy and then the first sastrugi appeared. Soon we were weaving between breaking waves of ice, with dolphin shapes leaping from the frozen sea around us, their arching backs reaching as high as half a metre above the surface. They often came in family groups, pods of adults and young together. We had to skirt the largest obstacles, adding to the distance we had to haul.

Børge had warned us about a field of rugged sastrugi between 85.5°S and 88°S, amounting to more than 200 km of difficult travel. "It is unavoidable," he had told us. We were still a whole degree short of 85.5°S and wondered if this was another field (perhaps insignificant compared with the main one) or if the extent of sastrugi varied from year to year and we were going to be unlucky. Either way it was not good news, however beautiful the formations.

Bumpy sled movements punctuated our erratic course through the sastrugi. As in the sastrugi we'd encountered before the mountains, the sleds would descend a rise and stop abruptly while we kept going unawares until the ropes pulled us up short. By the time we were out of the sastrugi and in better travelling conditions, we were all sick of being jerked by our sleds like dogs on a chain. I suggested it was time to switch from the ropes to the rigid titanium hauling shafts we had brought. I theorised that with the shafts we would not only be able to tell exactly what the sleds were doing behind us, but we might also get a little push when they slid off a bump.

Keith had another overdose of chocolate late in the afternoon. He was going so powerfully at the end of the allotted time that we couldn't catch him to stop him. As a result, we did an extra half hour. Because of this and some good surfaces, we covered 30 km during the day. Six hundred to go.

Before retiring, we tackled the fiddly chore of changing the hauling systems. As the manufacturer had warned us, it was not a task we would want to do too often. By the time we had finished we were all glad to leap into the tent.

8 December

My hand was much better. I could get it functioning earlier in the day, and this evening, the first in many, I could write my diary without pain. It no longer woke me in the night. It was eating that caused me distress tonight: the cayenne in the rice pasta and curry made my sore tongue suffer. I also seemed to be having a recurrence of the chafing at the tops of my thighs that struck me on Berkner Island. Areas on both legs felt tender and slightly bruised and were faintly purpled, with a reddish fringe. All strangely familiar.

As we shovelled our dinner away, Fran came on the radio from Patriot Hills with news of the Trekathon back in Australia. John had sent a message that 4000 Scouts marched on 14 November in Sydney in support of our journey and to raise money for the medical charities. The event received good coverage in the media. Home at times seemed like another lifetime, but this report reminded us again of all the people backing our efforts, following our progress in the newspaper and willing us to succeed and return safely. We all felt boosted and hoped that a lot of money had been raised.

Fran reported that the Belgians were going slowly and had 1200 m yet to climb. They had not been able to use their sails much and had travelled less than 500 km from the Queen Maud Land coast. It seemed impossible that they could complete their goal.

At the end of the radio sched, the accented but perfect English of a member of the Icelandic team broke in, asking if he could talk to us direct. It was good to compare experiences with our companions of the ice. The Icelanders reported that sastrugi had plagued them for most of their journey from Patriot Hills, but no soft snow, and they laughingly said their biggest problem was the sun overheating their tent, making sleep difficult. Both our teams were very close to 85°S and we joked that we would arrive at the Pole together.

The day had begun sunny and warm, with low scud blotting out a last view of the stark peaks of the Neptune Range behind. The cloud advanced upon us from the north-west. Soon it deepened to white-out and snow began to fall. The snow and cloud kept up all day even though the wind shifted several times. We had become used to abrupt and unexpected wind shifts through 90° and even 180°, but generally they were accompanied by weather changes.

We entered a zone of sastrugi and struggled through it for most of the day. The lumps, bumps and gullies rose and fell in the greyness ahead of our ski tips. Occasional snow flurries even obscured our bright red parkas, which would re-emerge wraith-like when the mire parted. It was like wandering over the surface of a cloud through a pall of smoke. Only the weight of my sled – and the hardness of the sastrugi when I bumped into it – seemed to have any substance.

Keith found using the compass difficult in the fog. On top of that, his ankle ligament was giving him a hard time. He gave up his lead and Peter and I took two each. Peter showed an uncanny ability to weave rapidly through the sastrugi in the lead. We all had stumbles and tumbles. As tough as it was, the day was also challenging and engrossing and the surface excellent. The hauling shafts proved a real boon. Instead of being jerked back by the sled on the ropes we got a kick in the backside whenever the sled spurted downhill.

We stopped a little early on the last shift because of Keith's obvious but quiet suffering and the difficult conditions.

Remarkably, despite our erratic course, the GPS advised us that we had deviated only 2° from our bearing during the day. With the worst yet to come, it seemed we had better grit our teeth. The trial by sastrugi was the final rite of passage we must endure.

9 December

Peter's diary:
Dawned clear, which was what we needed to navigate after the white out, snow conditions of the day before. It was very cold, however, –20 [°C] and a wind of approx 15 kph. We wore our double thermals and goretexes all day … All of [us] led good sessions, particularly Ian who had the double lead. We are hopeful of reasonable mileage, but are not confident of making 25 km. Time will tell. We expect much more of this slow and difficult going for at least another 10 days. We also climbed considerably today, about 120 m to 1700 m.

I wrote of the sastrugi:

Welcome to my nightmare! Fields of sastrugi with soft snow between. Yesterday's snowfall has been blown into long drifts, settling in the troughs and extending as wind shadows behind the larger swells, sand dunes up to one or even two metres high that block the passage of our sleds like mashed potato. Again the elements seem to have conspired to snatch a firm surface away.

Slogging the slugs through the sludge. I take my two shifts in the lead, finding the dunes more wearing than even the quite tortured belts of sastrugi, always diagonally across our path from the east-south-east. One patch extends for about three kilometres, complex knots of arching spines, bombs and torpedoes on pedestals and dolphins rearing in the sun, all burnished to an opaline, absorbent sheen. More like whales, some of them, whales and dolphins surfing with their heads and backs leaping from the breaking waves of ice. Or old American limos with their grand streamlined bonnets sculpted in fins and voluptuous curves. Others are more random and fantastic, like gargoyles and surreal creatures of myth. There are miniature sculptures in crystal, as small as a hand or a bird. These protruding forms can usually be avoided, and then it is like roaming through a garden of organic sculpture, individual creations placed randomly by the path for our appreciation.

There is another quite different form that is harder to avoid and therefore more difficult to traverse – mazes of interlocking wind-sharpened ridges, up to half a metre high. We walk on tip-toe, trying not to slip between the knives into the gaps between.

This sculpted landscape was strange and wondrous, fierce and unassailable. A product of natural forces and the laws of physics, it existed for years, perhaps millennia, through darkness and light without an eye to see it, a mind to marvel at it. Mute and barely known, its radiant beauty reaches to the heart of what it means to be human – sentient and responsive – in a mysterious and insentient universe.

When confronted with chaos, it was easy to despair. We could see no end to it, no escape. There was indeed only one way. Ahead.

My diary:
Directly south, I look for a shining beacon, a sculpture brighter than the rest because it catches the sun just so, three or four hundred metres ahead. Finding one, I memorise its appearance and survey the intervening ground for a path of least resistance. Then I set off, ducking and weaving towards the beacon as directly as possible but avoiding the roughest ground. Keith and Peter follow, sometimes opting for a slightly different attack when they see me struggling to get my skis over a ridge or my sled

jammed into an overhang. It takes me ten or fifteen minutes to get there, then I do it again ... Eventually the wave of complexity passes behind us, and we escape into more straghtforward terrain of flattish ground with scattered, friendly dolphins watching.

Since leaving Berkner Island we had been using a cut-down 1:2,000,000 scale Jet Navigation Chart to plot our course. Every day we moved just over a centimetre, leaving a trail of red dots with blue numbers for each camp, connected by spidery red lines. Every night it was satisfying to view the extending line and our inexorable march towards the edge of the map, until the moment arrived when I needed to re-fold the map and reveal more of the Polar Plateau. In an instant, soaring satisfaction was grounded by the realisation of how much paper had yet to be traversed.

As Peter punched numbers, calculator and notebook on his lap, he compared abstract notions of the journey with another, more personal reality.

"You know, if we finish in 60 days, we'll be the slowest group ever on this route."

Almost in unison, Keith and I reacted with the same question: "Does that bother you?"

"No, no. Just stating a fact, that's all," Peter replied.

Keith was not going to let this pass. "There's only been two others who've done it without sailing, and they had lighter sleds ..."

Peter chose not to prolong the discussion, and I was left contemplating the merit of comparisons. Personally, I cared little if we were the slowest, the second slowest or twice as slow, as long as we made it. I would be no less satisfied. Not Peter. He does his utmost on any journey and typically overcomes all possible reasons for not reaching his goal. His idea of success is to leave the competition sprawling in the starting blocks. It is many years since anyone, except Peter himself, has tried to beat one of his records. He knew he could be doing this traverse much more quickly alone, and this must have caused him great frustration. Sixty days seemed to be the minimum he could accept.

10 DECEMBER

My diary:
Neptune's legs were lagging, causing dunes of diurnal diarrhoea and spoiling the shellite.

Such is the mnemonic I construct as I sledge along, to try and remember all the subjects I wanted to write about in my diary tonight.

I must admit that I quite enjoy having Keith operating at a slower pace than I, and invoking a very conservative attitude to issues of pace. This somewhat unworthy thought does not extend to wanting his predicament to continue.

Unfortunately for Keith, it was his day for a double shift. He led the first, looking glum as his ankle began to ache earlier in the day than usual. I began to consider options if it did not improve. With more than 500 km and at least 20 days to go, I thought it had better not get worse. Keith was as aware of the implications as I was, but if he was worried he was not showing it.

We traversed solid sastrugi for most of the day, although there were some intervening flatter sections. I found my leg muscles were slightly sore each morning, probably from the extra strain of pulling through all the bumps. Our sleds should have been approaching 110 kg; I was grateful they didn't still weigh 170 kg. As I pulled away from a rest stop, I was alarmed to feel a short-ness of breath, and my legs felt weak and oxygen-starved. Moving carefully and breathing deeply, I slowly recovered. The sensation was familiar, and when it happened again I knew I was feeling the effects of altitude. However, we were still not even at 1800 m, so I was puzzled. I wondered if I was so weak that I had become more susceptible to the effects. I didn't mention it to the others.

It was cold and breezy. The sastrugi inhabit a zone of wind that circles the Pole in a counter-clockwise direction. The engine that drives these winds and carves the sastrugi is an almost permanent high-pressure system that sits above the Polar Plateau. In summer it is in a languid mood; in winter ferocious winds sweep across the darkened ice beneath the stars.

My diary:
I would love to linger for hours and photograph the rich and bizarre wildlife of ice forms that inhabit the sastrugi gardens – if it was warm and there was time! I am saddened that so much goes unphotographed. Today I can only manage a single frame before my hands must beat a retreat into fleece gloves.

The rest stops were cold and unpleasant. The wads of ice that glued up our moustaches and balaclavas made it difficult to eat. I unscrewed the lid of my vacuum flask and forced my moustache over the opening, allowing the steam to loosen the lumps of nose ice so that I could pick them off. To free my lower lip I carefully plucked at the ice goatee, several centimetres thick, that had formed beneath my mouth, attaching itself to the balaclava as well as to the beard. I could then drink from my flask and push biscuits into my mouth. Early in the journey, all our fingertips had gone numb. The more benign conditions of the ice shelf and mountains had allowed us to recover full feeling, but now the fingertips of my right hand were going numb again. This hand was always colder; perhaps the carpal tunnel problem had impeded the circulation.

At the end of the second shift Keith was some distance behind. Peter and I sat on our sleds and watched him coming towards us. It was the first chance to observe how he was moving. The small climbs onto the sastrugi ridges were difficult for him. I watched as he shuffled up, favouring his good leg. The trouble with this sort of injury, I thought, was that it put more strain on uninjured parts. I voiced my disquiet to Peter. "If Keith's ankle is getting worse we'll have to consider taking some action," I said.

"Yeah, but what?"

"Several things come to mind," I said. However, I wanted to hear Peter's thoughts before I revealed my own.

"Like taking some load?" he asked.

"That's one of them," I replied.

"I'm happy to consider all of those things," he said.

I sensed resignation in his voice. I wondered if there were some options he would not countenance and whether resting was one of them.

Keith pulled in, looking tired and unhappy. We decided Peter should take the final lead, in the interests of speed and kilometres. During the shift, Peter turned to Keith and asked: "Is the pace okay? I can go a bit faster if you like."

I couldn't help thinking that Peter would not consider rest or a slower pace and that Keith would be sacrificed if he fell by the wayside. A brother in uncertainty, I felt just as exposed and vulnerable. We were all expendable in pursuit of the higher cause. I had no doubt that Peter would go on alone if necessary, and I wondered whether I would do the same if for some reason Peter and Keith had to pull out.

In fact Peter was prepared to consider limited rest. His diary:

A cold and clear day. −20[°C] and a 20 kph wind made travelling initially very unpleasant … As usual my hands were the biggest problem, especially after each stop. Sometimes it would take 30-60 minutes to warm them up …

Keith was the main worry today. His foot is getting worse and he lagged behind a fair bit. It was his double lead today, but I did it for him so that we could keep up our speed and he could rest his foot. … His injury is a constant worry for me. How to manage this? If necessary,

175

whilst I don't like it, we may have to have a day of rest. I am not prepared to have 2 days rest as it cuts into our safety margin.

The insurance policy drawn up for us by Commonwealth Connect, the insurance arm of the Commonwealth Bank, one of our major sponsors, provided for the extraction of one, two or all of us in an emergency. The definition of emergency included being unable to proceed safely. Any extraction terminated the policy based on the premium we had paid. Since ANI required rescue insurance to be in place for the expedition at all times, additional coverage would have to be arranged before any remaining members could go on. In the absence of such coverage, our contract with ANI allowed them to terminate our expedition unilaterally and extract us all forthwith.

Such are the rules of the game in the modern age of Antarctic adventure. They are there to protect lives, reputations and balance sheets. ANI had a plane and crew in constant readiness to fly to the assistance of any ANI-supported expedition in the field. This is not just a professional responsibility. The continued presence of ANI as the only independent and private adventure operator on the continent depends on the goodwill, even sufferance, of the Antarctic nations. Generally these nations, and especially the United States, dislike private expeditions. One disaster or botched rescue, with a subsequent call upon a government for help, might be enough to confirm their worst fears.

As we drew ahead of Keith, Peter told me that the same situation had arisen in the Simpson Desert. "His body just started breaking down. I didn't think he was going to make it," Peter said.

Both Peter and Keith had told me at different times about the trials of their desert venture. There had been tension between them about the hours walked and the speed of travel on that intense journey, during which they hauled their carts – carrying all their food and water – 550 km in just 21 days. They were ahead of schedule based on the amount of water that remained, and Keith wanted to slow down. But Peter would not consider it, fearing the unknown part of the desert ahead. He feared failure.

"No-one had ever done what we were trying to do," Peter said. "We had no idea if it was even possible or what might still go wrong."

As we struggled through the sastrugi, much as he and Keith had done through the Simpson's dunes, all the memories of that desert walk came back to Peter. With a sense of foreboding he could see it all happening again: he, so desperate to finish and succeed; his companions' physical condition deteriorating, raising the spectre of failure through forces beyond his control. It must be so much simpler on a solo expedition, when it's all up to him.

Peter in fact set a good pace during the last shift. I, still reasonably sound in body if not brimming with energy, could keep up only because he stopped to get his bearings possibly more often than he needed to. At one point, having checked the compass, he turned to me as I pulled up behind him. "If he falls too far behind, we might have an early mark," he said.

The terrain flattened out and Keith kept up pretty well. If I'd been in his boots I would have been worrying that I wasn't going to be able to continue, or about the weeks of pain ahead if I did. Peter said to me that Keith was, psychologically, the toughest person he'd ever known. When we got to camp, Keith was his usual cheerful self and undaunted.

During the day I had finally worked out why the thigh "chafing" and belly "bruising" were familiar. It was frostbite. I wondered why I hadn't realised it before. I tried to remember when my thighs might have frozen. There had been no pain either when they froze or when they thawed, and I could still hardly believe it. But in the tent my thighs stung in the warmth. Examining the areas, I found confirmation: a small blister on my right leg. Perhaps it had happened a couple of days earlier when I was wearing just thermals and a wind sprang up. I remembered getting slightly cold before I pulled on overpants. I was amazed that frostbite could be so insidious. The 'chafing' on Berkner had obviously been frostnip. It had gone away but no doubt had predisposed the area to further damage. I hoped this latest injury would also go away.

Keith was also frostnipped in the same place. I cleaned the affected areas on both my thighs with alcohol and applied some friar's balsam. Then I covered the worst bits with plastic skin. I was very conscious of the fact that Børge had been forced to abandon his first crossing attempt and been evacuated after similar frostbite wounds had become infected.

11 DECEMBER

Keith's diary:
"Not as rough today. Clear but windy 25 km southerly into face at −20 to −18°C. COLD. Ankle not as sore today, thank heavens. −10°C in tent writing this."

It was not a good day for me:

Keith is a born-again hauler today, pulling strongly over better terrain than yesterday. We pass through some large but scattered sastrugi with little extra effort. Both of the gazelles are going well, and I slog in their wake, hot and bothered. Sometimes I hate those buggers when they get in front and thrash it! Stewing in my sweat, I only curse them until the end of the shift, because I know I would do the same. Overall I go pretty well, except when it comes my turn to lead [and] I feel like a tired old man. The others say I went all right.

Or for Peter:

Keith was feeling better today and did his double lead for yesterday instead of me having to do two. We are now back in sequence. I'm hopeful of a good total today as it felt like we covered quite a few kilometres. I was feeling generally low on energy all day and was glad to complete the 10 hours stint.

The harsh weather was very unpleasant and demanded constant attention to the management of our clothing. A blistering wind blew in our faces all day, whipping spindrift around our legs in the afternoon. It was as if the plateau was in a hurry to move somewhere else, grain by grain. Swaddled against the furies, it was like being in a Saharan sandstorm. I finally used the neoprene face-mask that I'd been keeping as my last resort against the cold. It covered my nose, cheeks, mouth and chin, just about everything left unprotected by goggles, and created a cosy little space behind it. Warmed by the air from my mouth, the ventilation holes over the mouth didn't ice up too badly. The mask warmed the outside air slightly before I inhaled it.

The blister on my right leg had grown by this evening, and both areas stung and hurt, as if burnt. I extended the dressing to improve protection. I decided to swab the surrounding skin with alcohol every night to keep infection at bay.

By the time I'd finished with my wounds and diary, it was 11 o'clock. Seven hours of sleep a night was the most we were getting. This was not enough, although I could not point to any obvious impact on my condition or performance. We passed another invisible landmark during the day: 500 km to go.

My diary:
I wonder if I'll make it, or whether physical collapse or frostbite will do me in. One day at a time, take great care and do everything right.

12 DECEMBER

My first lead was a hard grind through quicksand, and it was impossible to develop a rhythm, even a slow one. Fortunately the rest of the day was better.

Sand still lurked in the hollows and wind rows, but the ridges protruded and we rode over most of it. Although we were well into Børge's sastrugi zone, the ridges and lumps were mild and easily negotiated. Sastrugi surfaces are always hard and slick – great sledging material. Pity it never comes in the flat model.

During the day we reached a height of 2000 m, almost as high as Mt Kosciuszko, in our slow and steady climb to the Pole. Only 834 m left to climb. I was relieved to know that Peter and Keith were both feeling breathless at times. Reinhold Messner, who had climbed the world's highest mountains without oxygen, reckoned that the South Pole's 2834 m felt like 4500 m in the Himalayas. Although this may have been an exaggeration – the official increase in effective altitude, due to the generally lower air pressure over the Poles, is somewhat less – it was some consolation.

Peter's diary:

A very similar day to yesterday. Clear sky, –21. 25 kph wind. Snow conditions were also similar as was the sastrugi. The sastrugi, however, was more sustained and large, up to one metre in height. The thought of doing another 150 km in it is not a pleasant one ... We are now at about 2000 m and the bodies are finding it more difficult to do the strenuous work and provide the warmth we require. This I think is the main reason we are all feeling the cold more.

On the radio sched Doug held the satellite phone to the microphone in Patriot Hills so that John could join us on the radio.

"The media coverage has been great," John said. "Interest is growing because they can smell success now."

Such news from home never failed to raise our spirits. Less inspiring news was that the Trekathon had not been as successful as we'd hoped.

Reception faded after that but Doug relayed for us: "John says that you were pushed off the front pages for a while by big fires around Sydney, but they're all out now. He said to tell Ian that all the people in National Parks are okay."

The brief message threw me. Where had the fires been? Were some people not okay? In this icy land, where we had a hard time getting petrol to burn, it was too great a leap of the imagination to picture flames consuming the Australian bush. We knew it was going to be a bad year for fires, so I had been grateful for the encouragement from my colleagues as I'd left. Along with a hint of guilt at the news, I also felt some relief: I had worked through the dramatic 1994 fires and was not quite ready for another dose of the extreme stress that surrounds such events. I hoped all my friends had fared reasonably well.

13 DECEMBER

Severe pain from the frostbite on my thighs kept me awake for part of the night, and I slept only erratically for the rest. By the second shift of the day my thighs were hurting intermittently and by the third they were really bad. It felt as if red-hot screwdrivers were being pushed into them. I suffered the indignity of having to give up my lead.

Keith led the third shift, with Peter tail-gating him. Keith's ankle was much better. Even though he took it easy, I fell behind, halting occasionally to allow the pain to subside. When Keith stopped to relieve himself I pulled up a little way behind the others so that they couldn't see me grimacing. As we started off again, Peter turned and looked at me. "How's it going?" he asked. "You're getting along there like an old man."

That was exactly how I felt. I was gritting my teeth and so close to crying out at the stabs of pain that I could not answer. The frostbite dejected me. I knew it had the potential to keep me from the Pole. I suspected it was now six days since it had happened, so I hoped it might have reached its worst and would begin to heal.

The magnificence of the weather partly compensated for my discomfort. It was cold but windless. On days like this Antarctica felt like an old friend.

In camp I examined the damage while waiting for dinner. More blisters had risen beneath the dressings. The area affected was disturbingly large, covering about 150 sq. cm, and I was concerned that if the pain increased I might not be able to move at all. I must have appeared to be fussing, because Peter said: "Just ignore it. No point in worrying about it." Such an approach seemed to have worked for his cheek, which had healed into a scab the size of a 50c piece. But the frostbite on my thighs covered an area the size of a $20 note plus a handful of small change. He probably thought I was a bit of a softie, and maybe he was right. I dislike injuries, the feeling of not being whole.

Peter had some afflictions of his own to worry about, as he explained to the video:

I've lost a couple of fillings over the last couple of days, split a couple of teeth and I've got a not too pleasant job tonight of trying to fill them in. The dentist that I went to told me how to fill them in and gave me some putty and stuff, so I'm going to see if we can fill them in. I'm not sure if it's the best thing to do or not. In some ways I'm inclined to leave it and hope like hell that I don't get any pain. On the other hand there's food going in and out of it, so it might be better to plug it up. So tonight's the night I'm going to try to plug the holes.

Peter's diary:

Keith's first shift was slow because of the soft snow. I had the second shift and whilst very sastrugified (some very large) the snow was hard and we moved pretty well. That is, Keith and I moved well. It's good to see Keith moving well in view of his leg. Ian, however, was moving very slowly and took 20 minutes to catch us at the end of the shift. Keith decided to then do his second shift and Ian lagged so far behind that we could barely see him. Apparently the frost nip on the front of his thighs is very sore.

I decided to do Ian's shift straight after the third shift. I did not have a rest and went straight into the shift which we decided to make 2 hours [instead of two and a half] on account of Ian ... I had the tent up by the time Keith arrived and he had the stove going by the time Ian arrived …

We made 24 km. If we had proceeded for another 1/2 hour we would have made the 25 for sure.

It was the first time we had slipped below 25 km mark in a week and a half.

14 DECEMBER

I was leading the first shift and decided to start as early as possible to try to make up some of the lost distance. Again it was cold and clear, perfect for travel. But when I pulled away from the tent at 6.30 my skis met quicksand, sustained and unrelenting, an absolute drag. I made for a bright area of snow on the horizon that offered the promise of light sastrugi. Strange to be wishing for sastrugi! Not long ago I was cursing it.

After an hour I reached the bright area. As I had hoped, it turned out to be a swath of firm, low-amplitude sastrugi, a godsend after the quicksand. I'd applied protective pads to my thighs and they were only slightly sore by then. I seemed to go reasonably well over the better ground. Peter and Keith, who had started 15 minutes after me, caught up with me at the end of the shift.

Peter continued to feel the cold, especially in his hands, as a result of the wind and the consistently low temperatures we were experiencing – in the high teens and 20s. During breaks he cooled down faster than Keith or I and often suffered pain when his hands thawed out during the subsequent half hour. The sight of Peter standing and shaking his hands whenever he was not eating was becoming very familiar.

Peter took the second lead. He moved off while Keith was still drinking his soup. At the end of the shift Peter had been waiting for nearly 15 minutes by the time we arrived. Almost before we sat down he was stamping his feet and beating his hands. Keith ate uncharacteristically quickly and then prepared to take the lead. With stocks planted wide, he made an announcement, directed at no-one in particular, simulating a bus driver briefing his passengers: "Okay, folks. This lead will be more relaxed because there's no plane to catch and I won't be pushing it quite so much."

Peter looked away and muttered under his breath: "Pushing it? If I was going any slower I'd fall asleep!" I didn't think Keith heard the remark, or was meant to.

I continued with only mild pain until near the end of the third shift, when one of the pads came adrift. Fortunately the "cone of silence" was in my sled. I sat down with it over me, pulled down my pants and did a makeshift repair job. Peter and Keith were waiting for me at the end of the shift and I offered to lead on the last to repay Peter for taking my lead the day before.

Half an hour later I was in such pain and limping so badly that I reluctantly relinquished the lead again. Peter and Keith became small in the distance. Near the end of the shift the tracks led upwards through mild but sustained sastrugi. The extra workload lifted the pain to agony. I hobbled into camp just before 7 p.m., hardly able to move. At least we had travelled for the full 10 hours (and I more than 11) and moved another 27 km towards the Pole.

I was beginning to understand the pain. It was proportional to the strain of hauling and increased through the day. If more effort meant more pain, I wondered whether forcing myself on was counter-productive. I suggested to Keith and Peter that it might be better next time to halt if my pain was getting bad. We decided Peter would do my double lead the next day.

Peter's diary:

... I ran the second section and at the end of it had to wait 20 min for Ian and Keith to catch up. Keith's third session was so slow I thought I was going to go to sleep. He seems lethargic.

Ian tried to pay me back for the session I led for him yesterday, but only lasted about 10 minutes. I took over and pushed the session hard, very hard. At the end Ian was about 1.15 hr behind. By which time I had the tent up and the billy was on the boil ... I hope my pushing today made up for lack of mileage yesterday.

15 DECEMBER

My legs were sore all night. I slept for four hours and fitfully for another two, waking at five o'clock to very tender thighs and the roaring of the stove. Peter had moved the wake-up time to 4.45 a.m. As we prepared for the day, I raised our options for discussion.

It emerged that Peter had always been working to a 60-day schedule, with the additional food as insurance against bad weather only, not human problems. This was different from Keith's and my understanding. Peter reckoned we needed to have enough spare food to see us through a week-long blizzard right up to the end. This meant we could allow only two days for injury without jeopardising the expedition. I was less hungry, having only just started to eat my two packets of biscuits a day, and was more confident about surviving on short rations if slowed by bad weather (which I considered an unlikely event anyway, given the experience of previous travellers on the plateau). Keith asked the obvious question: What if we used only our spare biscuit rations for rest days? Peter admitted this would leave our food reserve intact.

I viewed Peter's stance on the food reserve as unnecessarily conservative but at least rational. However, some of his other arguments for reaching the Pole by 31 December were flabbergasting. He suggested that if we were late we'd face the blizzards that start in January, that finishing in 1997 would be good for the sponsors. He told me later that he knew these arguments were irrational but that he must have been desperate.

If he hadn't been so serious and the situation so tense, I would have laughed aloud. Instead, I wondered what sort of fools he thought we were and whether he was becoming unbalanced. Being focused on success and feeling stressed by the pressure were understandable, but irrational thinking could be downright dangerous. Not that I was in a serene and objective state of mind myself. My predicament and the interpersonal tensions were placing great pressure on me. Perhaps I was the one not seeing things clearly.

I suggested that stopping rather than aggravating the injury by continuing might maximise the distance we covered in the long run. Peter accepted this.

It was Keith's turn to take the first lead. I limped behind, already in pain, with Peter following. This was not good; the frost-burns had never been so sore early in the day. Pain aggravated by movement often eases once you warm up and get into a rhythm. This wasn't happening; in fact it was getting worse. I would be lucky to make it through the first shift. Keith was a considerable distance ahead after little more than an hour. In agony, I stopped and hung in my stocks, head bowed. Peter came up alongside. "How's it going?" he asked.

I choked down a sob, overcome not only by the pain but also the emotions stirred by my situation. "Terrible," I said. "I don't know if I can even finish this shift. We'll have to stop and camp."

Peter was quiet for a moment. Then he said: "Okay. I'll go ahead and catch Keith. We can't just hang around. We'll set up the radio and try to contact Patriot Hills."

I said: "I know, I know. I don't want to stuff up the expedition."

He pulled away. When he was a few lengths in front I followed. He went slowly, then stopped and turned to me.

"What about two slow shifts?" he asked.

"No. It will be better to stop."

He skied on. I hoped he would catch Keith before the end of the shift, but he didn't. The travelling was good over firm snow with small bumps, but still my legs protested at every movement. I crept slowly on, wincing with pain and trying to come to terms with the crisis. If I couldn't go on, there were only two options: either I died or we used our rescue insurance to fly me back to Patriot Hills. It was an easy choice!

The contrast with the "Heroic Age" of Antarctic exploration could not have been greater. On journeys into the interior, the explorers of old had no hope of rescue. If someone was sick or injured, the members of an expedition worked together to overcome the situation, or they waited until the person succumbed, or they all died together. Another option, exercised by Lawrence Oates – who, lamed by frostbite, walked out into a blizzard in 1912 and sacrificed his life in the hope of saving Scott's doomed expedition – would never have been contemplated for him by his companions. I wondered if I would be prepared to subject myself to such an expedition with no chance of rescue.

I tried to steel myself for either a prolonged struggle – assuming I could survive the worst of the injury and keep moving – or the shattering disappointment of failure and evacuation and seeing Peter and Keith go on to the Pole without me. For the next hour I swung between despair and determination. I was furious that it had come to this after two years of hard work and nearly 900 km of hauling. Had I slogged across Berkner Island and up Wujek Ridge just to experience the shame of not being good enough?

I wrestled with the possible outcomes. One minute I was reconciled to the idea of evacuation, seeing the good side of going home early. Next minute I was determined to reach the Pole. However, even though I knew the importance of being positive, it was hard to be resolute, much easier to lapse into despondency. The pain was such that I could hardly contemplate going on.

Keith told me later what happened at the end of the shift. After seven kilometres, he looked back at my distant shape. Peter drew up beside him.

"Looks like we've got a problem," Keith said.

"Yeah. Let's get the tent up and try the radio."

I reached them more than an hour later. Peter was in the tent attempting to get through to Patriot Hills on the radio. I limped around the tent under Keith's gaze, reinforcing the anchor system with the ice axe and spare stocks from my sled as I usually did. I was afraid to meet his eyes.

"Hurts pretty bad, eh?" he said.

I nodded. He went into the tent and I crawled awkwardly through the doorway after him, ready to do battle with my parka and boots. Every movement was excruciating. Overcome with pain, frustration and disappointment while trying to get into my sleeping bag, I blurted out my summary of the situation: "I think I might be f ... ed."

Then I burst into tears. Keith and Peter remained silent and tried not to look in my direction.

Outside it was a perfect day for sledging. I took a couple of painkillers and tried to sleep between sharp stabs and rippling waves of pain. Keith also took the opportunity to rest. Peter fixed his tooth again, fiddled with his gear and kept trying to raise Patriot Hills, repeating the call on each of the four frequencies every half hour: "Patriot Hills, Patriot Hills, this is Aussies."

It was not our usual sched night, but someone should have been listening all the same. Occasionally Keith reminded Peter of the battery power he was using with the repeated calls, but Peter persisted. We agreed it was necessary to get the approval process in train for evacuation in case it was needed. Maybe the best course for all of us was for me to opt out now and let the others get on with it. I was almost resigned to extraction because I thought the pain would be too severe to allow further hauling. It would be better to end it quickly. Peter agreed, but not necessarily for the same reasons.

"If we're going to fly you out, we need to make the decision quickly and get it done quickly. That will help us and it's best for you," he said.

We went onto spare rations of biscuits and soup. I set the Argos off on Code 3 ("rest day"). At 8.45 p.m. Steve Pinfield finally answered the radio. After Peter explained the situation and the need to consider rescue, Steve sounded a little annoyed that we had not told him about the problem before. He agreed to contact John in Sydney and get approval to extract me if required. There was also the not inconsequential matter for John of finding the cost of additional cover if Peter and Keith were to continue. We stressed that the media and our families were not to be told because there was no need to raise fears until the matter was resolved and there was no real danger.

Peter explained to Steve in detail the need to keep moving to reach the Pole by 31 December and then he talked to Steve King, the Twin Otter pilot, about landing requirements. It was apparent that the sastrugi might cause difficulties. Peter arranged to contact Patriot Hills at noon the next day if a rescue was required. Dr Kate came on the line and Peter passed the mike over to me to describe my wounds and how I was treating them.

"The blistering is a good sign," she said. "It sounds like a superficial injury and it should be okay. Take some antibiotics as a prophylactic and some anti-inflammatories to control the pain. Use painkillers if you need to, and keep the wounds clean."

"How long do you think the pain might last?" I asked.

"Anything from days to weeks, depending on the injury," Dr Kate said.

I normally avoid drugs and have gone for decades without taking an aspirin, but I was happy to take anything to help at this stage. In a slightly more positive frame of mind (I had not thought of anti-inflammatories) I began taking the medication immediately.

Peter gave our situation a good airing in his diary, going over his calculations again. He wrote that he aimed to cover the remaining 400 km to the Pole in 16 days, averaging 25 km a day. There was enough food for 27 days, which would allow for bad weather.

I hope we can do it in 16 [he wrote] but what if I'm wrong and it takes the full 27 days [of] food left? We had always planned on a 60 day trip with 9 days back up of food. This is why we can't wait indefinitely for Ian's legs to heal. If it takes us the full 69 days to complete the trip we will have exhausted all our food. The safety margins are too thin.

Keith says we should wait longer, but I'm not prepared to given the risks involved. I hope it will be finished in 16 days, but how do I know? As harsh as it now sounds 2 days max will be allowed for recuperation. It will probably take another day to arrange a plane in any event. Hopefully, we'll talk to the doctor tonight and set another sched for tomorrow morning. If Ian's leg is still no good then maybe we'll need to arrange a pick up tomorrow or the day after.

A foul wind was rising and continued to howl around the tent all night.

16 DECEMBER

I slept very well, with no pain, and in the morning my legs felt much better. We were all in a sombre mood as Peter prepared breakfast at the usual hour. We talked awkwardly about the options before us. I was torn between taking another day's rest (in the hope of promoting faster recovery) and pushing on, with the risk of exacerbating the injury and perhaps having to stop early again. If Peter was going to stick to his limit of two rest days, it might be better to go on now and save a day for later. Peter said it was my call, adding that we would have to be back at full speed tomorrow.

Peter had not looked at my wounds. Until I was forced to stop, he kept saying he couldn't understand how I could have been frostbitten in that area and suggested it was just chafing. Not once did he say it was important for us all to reach the Pole, and I felt I was getting no support from him, only pressure. I was appalled by his attitude and felt betrayed. Where did this fit in with the ideals of the expedition?

My diary:
I see no imperative to get to the pole in 60 days other than that manufactured in Peter's own mind. It is his preference, and it would be nice and neat – fine, leave it at that but don't try and justify it with any other bullshit. There is no way in the whole of Antarctica I will hop on a plane to satisfy what I regard as a someone else's personal obsession. I will not sacrifice myself unnecessarily, but neither will I wantonly jeopardise the chance of Peter and Keith to reach the Pole just to save myself.

Keith was very supportive, telling me my injury was fixable and that I had come too far to get sent out on a plane. After all, we had only 400 km to go! His encouragement meant a lot to me. He felt my best course was to keep covering ground. However, I suspected that, even if he disagreed with Peter's motives, he would defer to his desire for speed. I had no doubt that if just Keith and I were in the same situation, we would have waited a couple of days before pushing on. We'd have reached the Pole well within our food margin, no worries, and perhaps with a lot less aggravation.

Keith's ankle was still bothering him, and perhaps he identified with my situation. As for Peter, on top of his cheek, tooth, calf and foot problems and his constant battle to keep his hands warm, his thigh was still hurting after a fall in sastrugi a few days ago. He asks no favours even of himself.

After delaying my decision and weighing the possible outcomes, I took a deep breath and said: "I suggest we move on, but I can't guarantee how far. And we have to accept the risk of another early stop."

Peter concurred. Keith bustled around, making positive noises. "I reckon we should just move steadily but make the breaks as short as possible so we can get as far as we can before Ian's painkillers wear off," he said.

I agreed, though I felt uncomfortable about being so drug-dependent. No-one needed to say that Peter and Keith would take all the leads, and they made a pact to keep me between them while hauling. As we prepared to move off, I asked Peter why he hadn't slept yesterday afternoon instead of trying to raise Patriot Hills on the radio. His reply was abrupt: "I didn't want to sleep.

I wanted to get this thing sorted out. I didn't want to be stuffing around here!"

His unsympathetic frustration hurt me at the time, but with hindsight I realised that to embark on a journey like this with Peter and expect any other reaction was naive. I also later understood his view better. As soon as one potential nightmare – Keith's injury – was out of the way, I produced another one. Keith's support and fellowship were an important counterweight to Peter's hostility at the time. Later that day, as we skied along, I stopped to thank Keith.

"That's okay," he replied. "I don't want him to send you home. That's how I feel about it."

Slowly but steadily I reached the end of the first shift. My legs were sore but the pain was bearable. I dared to hope that the worst had passed.

Peter walked across to me. "Can you go another shift?" he asked.

I nodded.

"Good on you," he said, and slapped me on the shoulder.

Fortunately the snow surface was good and the sastrugi negligible. It was cold and windy, but I hardly noticed the weather. I lived in a very small part of my goggles and rarely lifted my eyes from the tracks a metre in front, walking tentatively, waiting for the agony to strike. I composed a positive mantra and endlessly exhorted my legs with it: "You will stop hurting and heal quickly, and I WILL get to the Pole!"

Noon passed with no suggestion that the plane be called. The others kept their speed down and I stayed with them. The soreness in my thighs increased to severe stinging in the last hour, but was nothing like the burning and stabbing of the past few days. With a sense of joy, I pulled up after 10 hours and 24 km. I hoped I would go even better tomorrow and would escape the plane.

Peter stressed the need to return to our normal daily tally as soon as possible. As long as I kept moving, he would not be able to justify an evacuation on safety or any other grounds. My main concern was that we were now in what Børge had indicated was the worst sastrugi. My legs hated the ups and downs and manoeuvring, but I hoped that after another 50 km we would be through it. "I think I'll get there," I told myself. I was determined to reach the Pole if I could, pushed by the collective will of all our helpers.

That night on our regular radio sched we could hear the relief in Steve's voice when Peter cancelled the rescue. Some days earlier Peter had ordered bangers and mash from Fran for a New Year dinner on our return. Now Steve joked that she made bangers and mash only for groups of three and there would be no celebration unless all of us were there. It was nice to feel that the Patriot Hills crew were rooting for me too.

Peter, left, and Keith take a windless spell in the bleak and powerful landscape of the plateau icecap, which occupies most of Antarctica and is up to 4 km thick. Altitude 2500 m; just 300 km from the Pole.

Keith strains to haul his load over the bumps of a moderate sastrugi field, his skis making minimal snow contact. Through some sastrugi fields we struggled to cover 22 km in a day. My frostbite injury made me particularly slow.

It was my task was to keep track of our progress and route, marking up the maps every night (above) after Keith's interrogation of the GPS. On the featureless white expanse, the relentless dotted line provided abstract confirmation that we were indeed closing in on the Pole. A field of sharply ridged sastrugi (right) stretches ahead. Hauling a sled through such terrain tested both our strength and our resolve.

Large sastrugi up to a metre and more high (top) resembled dolphins or whales leaping from a ruffled sea. The undercut snouts, formed when fierce winds sand-blast ice grains into packed layers of snow, gradually subside under their own weight. The accoutrements of sledging (above) at one of our camps on the Polar Plateau. Rigid hauling shafts were a boon in the rough sastrugi.

85°S, −20°C. Keith, in front, and Peter follow through mild sastrugi interspersed with open flats. For 10 hours every day we hauled in our own private worlds, communication made difficult by separation and the noise of the sleds.

Like waves breaking on a frozen sea, wind-carved sastrugi (above) were beautiful to behold but daunting to traverse. Occurring intermittently for more than 400 km, this chaotic landscape seemed never-ending.

197

Chapter 8

The FINAL CIRCLE

Great God! this is an awful place …

CAPTAIN ROBERT SCOTT, JOURNAL ENTRY AT THE SOUTH POLE, 17 JANUARY 1912

The plateau is at its loveliest between 88 and 90 degrees.

BØRGE OUSLAND, ALONE ACROSS ANTARCTICA (1997)

17 DECEMBER

Today we travelled in our coldest conditions yet. There was little sunshine; the wind blew constantly from the east at up to 25 km/h; and the temperature fell to −24°C. Keith's fingers were frostnipped again. Belt after belt of sastrugi lay across our path. We climbed innumerable ridges, one rising at least 2.5 m, and once passed what looked like a humpback whale nearly 3 m high. Beyond my iced-up goggles, these magnificent formations wafted by as in a thick fog.

My legs were sorer than yesterday but bearable until the sastrugi of the last hour. Then the strenuous step-ups and stretching plucked at the destroyed skin and dressings. It was becoming more difficult to arrange the bandages so that they protected the damaged areas without adding to the aggravation.

We managed 24 km again. Since we had crossed difficult sastrugi, this meant we had improved on yesterday's performance. I was sure the others were finding my slowness frustrating, especially Peter, because he suffered so much from the cold. But what could I do? They did all the leads; I was grateful for that and told them so.

Peter's diary confirmed my perception:

I had instant problems with my hands, they were cold for most of the day, sometimes seriously. Again the problem was Ian who was walking better

---

So close to the Pole, but still so far to go. His hours filled only with mind-numbing monotony, Keith moves his aching ankle across the endless, shining snowfields.

199

than yesterday but still very slow. Keith and I got cold constantly trying to wait for him...

The differential in pace is excruciating in that Keith and I would easily walk 30 km a day if he could, but we can't. We have to be patient, hoping we can get ahead in some sessions.

The sastrugi seemed to inhabit the steepest inclines (which were still quite gentle), on which we gained more than 200 m in altitude during the day, though our yoyoing through the lumps masked this climb. In the last hour of the day we traversed some of the steepest and roughest sastrugi we had encountered on the expedition. Peter and Keith went ahead to erect the tent. Arriving 20 minutes after them, I attempted some bravado. "Crikey!" I exclaimed. "There was certainly some blister-splitting action back there, eh?"

The landscape was unmoved, and I don't even know if the others heard me in the tent, but it meant something to me that I could still try to laugh.

18 DECEMBER

The wind shook the tent all night. Luckily it was the quietest tent I had ever slept in, taut as a drum and prone to flapping little. A wildly flapping tent can exaggerate the severity of the weather outside; but in a quiet tent the opposite can happen. I crawled out of the tent first.

"How is it out there?" Peter called.

"Bloody horrible! Snowing and no visibility. The sleds are buried!" I yelled back above the wind.

Keith came out next. As we dug out the gear I expressed my disquiet.

"If this was any worse I'd suggest we stay put. It's going to be a tough day."

The sun broke through occasionally, allowing us to see the ground and a head-high blizzard of spindrift flying past. It was this rather than low cloud that was the main threat to visibility. We agreed to stick together, so I set off in the lead. The white-out cleared but I was hampered by the ice in my goggles. Unable to see my way through the bumps, I handed over to Keith.

It is common for people to want to travel quickly through unpleasant conditions, and Keith and Peter were no different. I hastened to follow, weaving through the most amazing ice sculptures: shoulder-high complexes of wings, flanges and turrets, wind-sharpened and fragile as glass. The wind buffeted our bodies in waves of raw force. Suddenly the sun burst through the rampaging clouds to shine on two red-clad figures tracking between gleaming monuments of sastrugi. The figures leaned into the wind, bright in the sunshine and lashed by spindrift, spectres striding through a gorgeous wasteland. This remains with me as one of the most striking images of the journey, perhaps because it was so fleeting, lost in an instant to a flurry of mist and cloud-shadow.

The ice-filled air streamed past at 20–30 km/h, gusting to twice that speed, bringing occasional snow-squalls and white-outs. The thermometer stayed at around −24°C. In these conditions the windchill factor gave an equivalent air temperature of below −100°C. We were deep in the zone where exposed flesh freezes almost instantly.

Our bowels had adapted to our daily routine by usually becoming active when we emerged from the tent each morning. But today the miserable weather upset my timid system, and soon after we left camp I had to stop and expose my tender parts to the howling laughter of the tempest.

To paraphrase Shakespeare, if it is to be done, it is best done quickly. The unsavoury chore was completed with damage only to my dignity, and I managed to catch the others just before the inky clouds and furious snow squall of the next white-out arrived.

It caught us in a field of complex ridges. In just a few minutes both Keith's and my ski skins came adrift. Then I blundered into an ice overhang just as my sled came careering off a vertical step behind me, ramming me forwards. My sorest thigh slammed into the ledge while my upper body sprawled over the top. It just wasn't my day. I was jammed there like a ferry under a wharf, unable to back out because of the weight of the sled. I had yelled on impact and Peter turned around and saw my predicament. By the time he had shaken off his harness and skied back to help, I had managed to force the sled back slightly and wiggle my skis out sideways. The worst damage seemed to be a bent stock.

Slip-sliding through a maze of ice-ridges on flapping skins was no fun. My thighs protested against all the strain and stretching. Stepping forwards at one point, I caught the back of my left skin with the heel of my right ski, cleanly snapping the velcro strap that kept the rear end of the skin in place. A flapping skin is awkward enough, but when attached only by a loop at the ski-tip it becomes a hindrance. In a fit of pique I ripped the skin off the ski and stuffed it into my pocket, mindful that most wilderness disasters begin with minor errors. The skinless ski provided no traction on the polished névé; it was like trying to walk over glass with a bar of soap under one foot. More havoc was wrought upon my legs. I hobbled after my disappearing companions, occasionally waving a stock in the hope they might see I wanted them to stop.

They did stop, because they could see I was falling behind. They must have been tiring of my misadventures. We each carried a pair of wider skins, and when I reached the others I quickly dug one out of my sled and fitted it.

It was excellent. It stayed on the ski and felt very secure on steep steps.

However, the damage had been done to my thighs, and by the third shift I was slowing markedly. I didn't think I'd manage a reasonable pace in the fourth shift, and if we travelled too slowly in such conditions we risked hypothermia or frostbite. I wondered if it would be best to abandon the last shift and camp.

Keith was in the lead and Peter was right behind me. He must have been feeling the slackening pace because he overtook me. "I'm moving on to get warm," he said as he passed.

I couldn't blame him, and I decided to recommend a halt at the next break. I never got the chance. Peter caught Keith easily and they moved on together, always a long way ahead of me, a pair of black ants in the distance. Hour after hour I followed, ever more slowly. Sometimes the ants grew larger and I thought they were waiting, so I put my head down and forced myself to go harder. The next time I looked up they were smaller again, obviously moving. I didn't dare stop for fear of losing them altogether. I waved my stock but they didn't see. I suspected it must be well past break time and wondered why they weren't stopping. I feared they had decided to eliminate the break.

I was in a nightmare. All I could see in the greyness were a few metres of intermittent ski track rapidly being erased by the wind and, on looking up, two tiny insects in the distance. All I could feel was the pain in my legs and growing hunger and thirst. I began to weaken from lack of energy.

I experienced bouts of exasperation and anger, until it struck me that perhaps they were pushing ahead to establish camp early. Squinting, I thought I could see them setting up the tent. Then they got smaller again. I was bursting for a pee and my hands were growing colder as my energy output fell. I had thicker gloves keeping warm next to my chest, but I wasn't game to stop and put them on for fear of losing them to the wind. My shadow told me it was after 5 o'clock. I was furious at their behaviour. My mind began to wander, drafting newspaper headlines, such as "Polar explorers leave mate to die".

Could I bivvy on my own if I had to? If I lost my companions I would have to. Mentally reviewing the gear in my sled, I decided I would survive. This made me less anxious. But I couldn't put my pee off any longer, so I stopped to relieve myself. Then I hunkered down behind my sled and pulled out my thicker gloves. When I stood up I saw that the others had stopped. With renewed energy I gritted my teeth and hauled on. I caught up about 10 minutes later and gave them an angry serve: "What the hell is going on? I've been waving to you and trying to catch up all afternoon! Why didn't you stop?"

Keith tried to explain. "We had you in sight all the time," he said. "We kept checking to make sure you weren't too far behind. We were going slower and slower so you could catch up but you never did. It wasn't planned. Peter kept saying he was freezing, so we kept moving. We haven't had a break either."

I calmed down in the face of Keith's obvious contrition. I said: "That's why I wanted to talk to you – to say it was too dangerous to keep going and we should camp. I'm really sore and have to stop. It must be nearly time anyway."

Peter remained quiet, hunched over his stocks looking miserable. After a moment he said: "Come on, let's go. I'm bloody freezing!"

Keith led and soon found a suitably flat spot. It was 6 p.m. For nearly 11 hours we had been battling the worst blizzard we had experienced on our journey. The tent bucked and ballooned in the gale as we wrestled it down with numb hands. Peter crawled inside and yelled to me as I passed in the poles: "We've got to do something about your pace – it's killing us!"

When we were all safely inside I tried to explain that I'd wanted to call a halt because of the danger to all of us, but Peter made no comment. Keith appeared to realise that I had felt threatened and he continued to stress that the situation had developed entirely unintentionally. I couldn't decide if this made it better or worse, but in the end I concluded that the whole incident had been wilfully perilous. I knew Peter was feeling the cold; but if I couldn't go any faster, what was I to do? He was obviously annoyed with my slowness, but I couldn't understand why he didn't put on more clothes. None of this was debated openly, and I could only guess what he was thinking.

We discussed the issue of pace more fully. I suggested the severe terrain and weather were causing my speed to fall and adding to the risk of separation. Peter accepted that we must hope such a combination did not occur too often and that we must try to deal with it better next time. The safest option – of staying put when it became dangerous to travel – was not raised, and I felt our underlying incompatibilities remained unresolved and would surface again in difficult circumstances. Peter suggested taking some weight off my sled by swapping his two empty fuel cans for two of my full ones. This would reduce my load by 8 kg and increase Peter's by the same amount.

"But I want it to make a difference," Peter said. "I don't want to be slogging up ahead and have you still miles behind."

Pride made me reluctant to let someone else take some of the load I had dragged so far, especially since he had made his offer unwillingly and had attached conditions. If I wasn't pulling my weight in the chores, at least I would do so with the kilos. I thought an 8 kg reduction was unlikely to make a great difference to my speed, so felt I could make no promises. I suggested we reserve that option and act according to the conditions the next day.

The dark side in everyone emerges in times of stress. While outwardly I tried to remain reasonable, a sensitivity to hostility led the emotional part of me to dwell darkly on Peter's attitude. The more objective self that seems to inhabit a higher place recognised his dilemma. It must be hard to cope when one's personal ambition is threatened by the weakness of others. The same remarkable qualities that had enabled Peter to achieve the near-impossible when alone, and even to pull this expedition together, might not easily adapt to a situation where his own powerful will was no longer enough. My simmering but submerged hostility was cooled by the understanding that Peter's stubbornness stemmed from everything that made him unique. Besides, he was partly right. Instead of allowing my anger to surface, I poured vitriol into my diary. "I wonder if he will turn back into a human being when we get to the Pole?" I wrote.

Peter's diary:
An absolutely terrible day. Ian was going like a slug, the weather was overcast and white out, the ground was huge sastrugi, the temperature was –25 [°C] and the wind was gusting up to 50 kph. The main problem was Ian again. He was moving so slow that we all had to slow down to his pace, through the heavy sastrugi. The other major problem was that Keith and I were getting very cold, especially the hands, when we waited for Ian.

With the weather so bad the pace differential is a major problem. Ian had other problems, he fell in the sastrugi and bent his stock and then broke his [ski] skin. We took time to fix it under very unpleasant conditions.

We discussed the problem and there's not much that Ian can do except I offered to take some of his weight. I'll take two of his full fuel cans and give him my empty cans. I don't want Keith to take any weight as this might hurt his leg.

Only 13 days to go, if we can keep Ian going.

The atmosphere in the tent remained tense. After entering his thoughts and the day's reduced progress of 22 km in his diary, Peter worked on his calculations and announced the bottom line: "We have to do 26 km a day to get there on the 31st."

Keith, who was making dinner, asked: "And what's wrong with getting there a day later?"

"I'm just stating the facts," Peter retorted.

"And I'm just asking the question: what if we get there a day later?"

Peter offered no response.

I spent the evening sewing the velcro tail back on my ski skin. After dinner we re-attached the skins to our skis. During the radio sched we spoke with Doug, Kate, Jennifer Foreshew from *The Australian* and the Icelanders. Peter described the lousy conditions of the day in strong terms and Doug replied laughingly: "Sounds like Antarctica all over again. You guys have had it easy!"

Peter explained to Doug that we would have to increase our daily distance to 26 km to make the 31 December deadline. I could not understand why he thought the people at Patriot Hills would be interested. In my twisted mental state I visualised Doug having a great time reporting the latest hilarious transmission from the crazed Aussies to the Patriot Hills crew. I imagined them scratching their heads and musing: "They have 22 days' food left, a little over 300 km to go, an injured party member … and he's still setting deadlines?"

In such ways did I bolster my own determination.

Kate advised me to change dressings every five days. I'd had the artificial skin on for seven. When we had settled into our sleeping positions, I set to work on the left leg, slowly peeling away the plastic skin. The nerve endings were exposed so it was like ripping off real skin. Afraid that pulling too quickly would cause more damage, I carefully snipped each stuck hair with scissors.

A soggy, smelly mess of raw meat was revealed, white and blotched with red and purple. The blistering seemed to have reached its full extent and most blisters had burst. Peter was asleep, but Keith was very interested and made suggestions on treatment. I cleaned the wound with sterile swabs, added some vitamin A cream and re-bandaged it, with non-stick dressings this time. In spite of the full hour of stop-start agony, the wound felt more comfortable afterwards. By then it was nearly midnight and I could not face any more. The other leg would have to wait another day.

19 December

I slept for five blissful hours, painless and painkiller-free, before Peter started hassling us at 5 a.m. He was a force of nature, irresistible.

It was a clear, sunny day. A light north-easterly puffed at our backs as we travelled. However, the terrain was not so friendly: we sailed into a quartering sea of large sastrugi ridges that crossed our path at 45°. All day we hauled over the breaking waves, gaining and losing hundreds of metres in endless ups and downs. When Keith was in the lead, plugging steadily, I was able to keep up.

During the last shift, Peter went ahead to set up camp. He stopped at 6 p.m. Keith arrived 25 minutes later, and I turned up 15 minutes after that. Although I was very sore and exhausted, I'd had a day of relatively low pain and steady progress. I could hear the stove purring comfortingly inside the tent. In the benign weather, I indulged in some stress relief by taking a few photos around camp, the first in many days. This added to my positive mood. The extreme pain seemed to be over and I was travelling reasonably well until later in the day. I hated feeling like a passenger, but I knew I could keep going. I knew I could make it as long as the strength of my companions kept going as well.

Peter agreed this had been one of our toughest days: 23 km of lumps and bumps. I sensed his disappointment with our score but nothing was said.

I stayed up late again, on the warm side of the tent, to change the dressing on my right leg. There was no sign of infection (my main concern), and I felt that if I looked after the injuries I would be able to keep them healthy. I would not be able to relax my guard until we reached the Pole.

Only three degrees to go. We had already passed the point where, according to Børge, the worst sastrugi ended.

My diary: "I will be glad to finish; to make an end of the pain and worry of the frostbites, the tedium, the pressure, the driven routine and rushing all the time."

Peter's diary:
A much better day than yesterday ... Sastrugi all day. I led the first shift, Keith the next two, and me the last. I led the last so that we could cover the ground ... By the time Keith arrived [at camp] I had the tent up and some of my things inside.

Ian's pace seems to have improved as he kept up most of the day except for the last shift. Keith's shifts were fairly slow. Neither of them kept up with me on my first shift even, arriving 15 mins later.

20 DECEMBER

The weather was all over the place: a clear morning, then patchy cloud, followed by complete cloud cover with snow showers, then clear again. Another slow day of rough sastrugi and poor visibility. We were all sick of sastrugi and wanted it to end. Børge's records showed that he sailed 100 km in a day from 87.45°, and we hitched our hopes to this. We imagined a vast plain of hard snow that would take us to the Pole; we spoke of it as the Promised Land.

I had a go at leading through white-out, since we were all forced to travel slowly. It was good to be contributing again. Peering ahead, straining to pluck detail from the shrouded void, I found it was easy for the mind to play tricks. On one occasion I saw a blurred shape moving across the gloom ahead of us, a woolly creature of some sort. I even followed it with my eyes. I knew it was impossible. I shook my head, turned away and looked again, but it was still there. I ignored it and walked on, emerging from the sastrugi onto a flat plain of sandy snow.

The going was slow and painful and, with the light improving, I handed over to Peter. Keith found the going hard too, but Peter strode away. If anything, he seemed to be getting stronger as we progressed, while Keith and I were being worn down.

Peter seemed more relaxed and cheerful tonight. We talked more freely about my legs and our pace. Perhaps he accepted delays caused by sastrugi and fog more easily than a slow companion and had come to terms with the possibility of not reaching the Pole until 1 or 2 January. I figured that once beyond the sastrugi we might still make 27 or 28 km a day and beat the New Year.

Peter's diary:

I led the second shift with Ian and Keith about 20 minutes behind at the end. I again got very cold waiting for them.

Ian tried to lead the last session in the white out. We figured the speed didn't matter and as soon as the sun came back out I took over the last 45 min and in this time ended up 20 mins ahead of them. They are very slow. I had the tent up by the time they arrived.

All through the slow stages I found it very difficult to keep warm, probably because I had sweated during my strenuous sessions and this became frozen.

Ian is still very slow, as he has been throughout the whole trip, and this dictates our daily progress.

21 DECEMBER

Summer solstice; the longest day of the year, an odd concept on the ice, where the sun would not set for another two months or more.

The day certainly felt like a long one to me, however. The surf reared up during the last shift, a horror show of huge waves, a great rolling sea with a 2–3 m swell. A whole landscape of complex ridges and gullies spread around us. The endless stretching and straining over the ridges gave my legs hell.

The further I went, the higher and mightier grew the waves, until they reached a crescendo in a great white whale, perhaps 4 m high. Beyond it, the mountainous ridges gave way abruptly to a smooth plain. The black specks that were Peter and Keith had grown quickly more distant, so I knew the travelling was faster ahead. I hoped the sastrugi had finished for good. If so, it finished in grand style with the Great White Whale. Peter and Keith dubbed the whale "Big White", after "Big Red", a notorious sand dune on the edge of the

Simpson Desert. Glancing back later, I could still see the sharp termination of the great lumps, with "Big White" bulging above a crinkled horizon.

A continuing matter of regret for me is that all the sastrugi action went unphotographed. Words can do full justice to neither the beauty of the terrain nor our effort in traversing it. It was difficult enough to take photos when lashed to the sled for 10 hours and trying not to "waste time" (in Peter's words), without being the slowest and injured one as well. We had all been preoccupied and had shot no video footage for several days.

Keith went well today: the altitude, his tiredness and his ankle seem to be bothering him less. I began the day with a burden of lethargy and legs already sore, feeling quite alone in the face of my companions' strength. As I trudged along, my body just wanted to sleep. Occasionally I swayed and nearly fell over.

Peter was relaxed and cheerful. I took this to mean that he had accepted we were going to get to the Pole and had perhaps discarded the 60-day deadline. We had reached a practical agreement whereby he could go ahead without waiting for me, and he was probably finding daily travel less stressful. He said to me: "When we get to the Pole, three years of focus will end."

Keith's report to the video:

> It's been quite a good day, from the point of view of getting a few miles done. Hopefully we've done about 24 or 25 kays, which means that we've now gone 1070 kilometres or thereabouts and we've got about 270 kilometres to go. The most amazing thing about today is that we hope we've come out of the worst of the sastrugi... We've done about 300–400 kilometres of sastrugi and we've all had enough of sastrugi at the moment and looking forward to nice flat snow...

We were all at the stage then of wishing we could wake up in the morning to find that we had travelled the remaining distance in our sleep. We talked about everything that would happen after we reached the Pole and what we would do between there and home.

It was pleasantly calm outside this evening and the warm glow of the sun filled the tent. Midsummer's day night: as bright and strong as it would get. The slow retreat to winter had already begun. The occasional sting in my legs was not enough to keep me awake. After packing away my diary, I snuggled into my bag, relishing its comforting security. Tomorrow was a long way away.

22 DECEMBER

The whole world was ice. It was becoming difficult to imagine that anything else existed. Only the radio sched confirmed that there were other realms elsewhere. Beneath our feet the ice was nearly 3 km thick and so heavy that it pushed the Antarctic continent deep into the Earth's crust.

Before the end of the first shift we ran into another nasty belt of sastrugi. We had been traversing those barriers for nearly 400 km; thank heavens we hadn't known they would go on for so long when we began.

Peter's diary:

The weather is great for travelling – what we need is an end to the sastrugi and flat plastic snow. On my calculations (31/12) we have 9 days left. However, on present progress we will not finish the trip for 10 days 1/1/98.

On my last lead of the day Keith was 20 minutes behind and Ian 1 hr. I had the tent up by the time they arrived. Ian whilst still very slow is improving. He is still not doing any leads. Keith and I are sharing them.

23 December

My diary:

The mind struggle has begun.

Each day is an eternity; every hour an ordeal. I am tired of this icy waste and this journey. I want to be there, at the Pole. I want to be at Patriot, at Punta, at home with the family. I want this to end. An end to the drudgery and pain of dragging a f...ing reluctant sled for 10 and more hours a day, every day, without respite, through humps and soft snow, with no reward other than the day comes to an end, and we camp. Another day closer, nine more to go: it is too many...

This journey has become stupid. Where is the joy, where is the magic? Perhaps it will return when it is all over. When I leave this Polar Plateau I never want to see it again – leave it to the winter blizzards and the darkness of space.

I had no idea the ground conditions would be so constantly perverse. Almost the entire journey has been over either slow snow or sastrugi, all of it bumpy. We are all heartily sick of it...

I had a poor day, lacking in energy and very sore. The dressings felt as if they were pulling on damaged skin on the edge of the wounds.

Peter hated leading the last session into camp. This evening he shook off his harness at 6.45 p.m. and had the tent up before Keith arrived at 7.20. I crept in at 8.25. We had consigned another 26 km to the country of the past.

My diary:

I hope I feel better tomorrow! I've got to work harder to psych myself into this. I've been carrying the pain for 12 days now, another nine to go to success and safety. Of course I can do it! At least the weather is being helpful at present.

Before falling asleep I wallowed in the pain of another matter. When following Keith on the first lead, I'd found myself on an appallingly slow surface. It was as if we'd been transported back to Berkner Island during the night and my sled had regained its original weight. Keith was going so slowly that even I caught him up easily. As I got close, I could see he was really struggling. "Hey, Keith, is this bloody awful or what?" I said.

He looked back in despair. "Yeah, it's just like Berkner Island. It might go like this all the way to the Pole. I've got to say I've been thinking of desperate measures."

My spirits sank. I realised what he meant and how close he was to acting on the idea. I said nothing as we plodded on slowly. There was no let-up in the appalling surface.

When Peter caught us up, a similar conversation ensued, except that Peter greeted the suggestion with enthusiasm. Faced with their combined resolve, I knew there was little chance, but I tried to dissuade them from taking what I saw as an unjustified and hasty action. I wanted no part in something that went against everything I stood for and against what I believed to be the ethic of our expedition. But I was a part of it. As the slowest and injured member of the team, I felt it was not possible for me to go against the majority – and by doing so reduce my comparative speed even more.

"This is all very rash," I said, arguing for the sake of my own soul. "I know it's really disappointing to strike this lousy snow again, but it's very unlikely to go all the way to the Pole. It might improve soon, and then how would we feel? Why don't we go on for a while and see how it goes, and think about it some more?"

If I could fend off the decision for a while, maybe the conditions would improve and they would realise the action was unnecessary. Keith's response was abrupt.

"This is survival. I can't pull for 250 km of this!" he said.

He told me later that his thighs and ankle were hurting him badly and he was convinced he could not finish the journey. To reach the Pole within Peter's deadline, something would have to give: if not his body, it would have to be something else.

Keith and Peter were determined to do the deed then and there; I could not prevail. Peter tried to convince me they were right. "I know you don't like it, but every ounce counts and it'll make a big difference to our pace," he said.

I doubted his assessment of the benefit, but I also knew there was some truth in what he said. I was already part of the conspiracy. Standing my ground might have led to an unseemly fight, all for the sake of my integrity. I gave in.

The deed done, we moved on. I hardly noticed the lighter sled, but my heart was a whole lot heavier. The small mound in the snow, concealing our little load of rubbish and superfluous gear, hung like a dark cloud in my mind. The snow surface improved soon afterwards.

It was a drop in the ocean, perhaps. There are many wrecked aircraft gradually sinking into the Antarctic ice, all containing many times the poison of our small monument. The government bases on the coast until recently used to dump their waste into the sea. And the US Amundsen-Scott base at the South Pole still pumps its sewage and other muck deep into the icecap. It was acting against our stated principles and my personal ethics that weighed heaviest.

I wondered what I would do if anyone asked me about it. Would I have to keep a guilty secret? Would I cover up just to protect myself? Would I have joined the expedition at all if I had known this was going to happen? I wondered how much more quickly we would reach the Pole. How many saved days would it take to justify the act? I would have gladly extended our ordeal of hauling to have avoided it, yet part of me also wanted to finish as quickly as possible. I must admit to some duplicity. We were all under a lot of strain in a threatening and complex situation. Although Peter was finding the going easy, he may have felt that Keith and I desperately needed the relief of lighter sleds.

I spent most of the day stewing about our crime. It was to have a lasting effect on my feelings about the expedition. The mound of our guilt rests alone on the ice, now part of the irrevocable past. It will have begun its slow descent into the ice, and its glacial journey to the sea. That trip will take many tens of thousands of years. I wonder if after that time it will have any impact.

24 December

My diary:

It is the "graveyard shift". I try to confine myself within the orbit of my parka hood. Then, as I plod along, I am not confronted by the vast horizon, now even more distant, even frightening, since we left the bumps and ridges of high sastrugi behind. I also avoid being confronted constantly by the image of Peter and Keith growing smaller in the distance ahead, pushing on towards camp. Instead, focusing downwards, I see a few square metres of bright snow, encompassing the tracks I am following, my own deep blue shadow, and the infernal shadow of my right ski stock. I can judge the time by this shadow as the sun circles the sky. When it falls perpendicularly across the ski tracks, the sun is due west and I know it is 6 p.m., the allotted hour for Peter and Keith to complete their 10 hours of skiing and camp for the "night". At that point I feel relief, because then the distance between myself and our camp begins to decrease, instead of steadily increasing as the others pull away ...

I am so bored I am running out of things to think about ... Peter apparently spends his time re-arranging his garage, piece by piece, and designing a deck for his house. I could not command the recall of such detail, which must take a certain type of mind. Keith manages to drift off completely to somewhere else, "communing with the fourth dimension", and keeps walking as an automaton. This is more like an option for me, but I can only manage it for short bursts before reality intrudes in the form of pain ...

I expect to arrive at camp about half an hour after the others, which equates to nearly a kilometre and a half, but sometimes I am an hour or more behind. With any luck, the tent will be pitched and Keith will have soup and dinner on the stove. We have a radio sched tonight, and I have volunteered to erect the aerial when I get there, a fiddly, unpleasant task usually done by Keith. That way he is freed up to establish his kitchen in the tent and get dinner moving, and I make some contribution ...

I watch the rhythmic slide of the skis, as if they belong to somebody else, and listen to the pain in my thighs, which are definitely my own. It is always there, pulsing with each step, growing slowly through the day. Moving each leg forwards about 25,000 times every day is significant aggravation. Occasionally there is a stab of intensity, and today, an odd itch in places. I hope nothing bad is going on down there.

I walk like a zombie this evening. I was up until midnight last night changing the dressings, back to synthetic skin. The wounds had gone dry and scabby black under the cloth dressings. I need to manage them carefully and walk carefully, to ensure that my legs do not grow too sore to complete a full day or to carry on the next ...

My reverie is interrupted by a growing discomfort in the gut. Quite suddenly I have to stop and make an undignified trackside squat on my skis, baring my bottom to the wide Antarctic sky, the greatest wilderness on earth ... It is easier in the morning straight from a warm tent, but we are eating so much that we sometimes need to go twice a day. At least the antibiotics have not caused diarrhoea, a common side effect when the good gut flora are killed along with the baddies.

When I have finished, the others are noticeably smaller and further ahead. This is disappointing, for although the strategy of separation is essential, I do not enjoy being so far behind. I spend more than half of the travelling day alone.

Moving on, I come across a confusion of ski tracks. This must be where Peter and Keith stopped to swap the compass and change leads. They are sharing the graveyard shift now. There are two yellow stains on the snow where they have urinated. I figure it would have taken them five minutes and I know they intended to split the shift at 4.45 p.m. I calculate I am 20 minutes behind. Depending how fast Peter wants to push the final section to make distance, I will probably arrive at camp half an hour after him.

I return to my parka hood and plod on. The shadow stick says I have about another hour before they stop. So close to the solstice and so near the earth's axis of rotation at the geographic pole, each hour is represented by a 15° movement of the shadow. The sun circles 20° above the horizon.

I realise that back in Australia it is already Christmas Day. It will be about 7 in the morning and my two children will be up and opening their stockings and other presents. Cale no longer believes in Santa Claus, but does not break the faith for Holly's sake – and I suspect because the idea still holds an appeal he does not want to give up. I wish I was there. For the first Christmas of their lives I will not be there to pack their stockings.

The day had some pleasures. An overcast sky and ice-fog early in the day deposited rime everywhere, including all over us as we moved. Fine crystals of frost grew out of thin air on the coldest parts of our clothes, spreading along the seams of our parkas, around our faces and on our outer gloves. The red covers of our sleds were decorated in lace as well. The ground conditions continued to improve, with only a small amount of sastrugi and some very flat plains of good firm snow.

The haphazard and subtle changes to the surface continued to bemuse us. We had no explanations. The sastrugi made some sense: yesterday we seemed to climb through a series of benches, each several kilometres wide and separated by slopes of sastrugi. When the climbing eased, we were less than 200 m below the altitude of the Pole, and at last the sastrugi appeared to be letting go.

My diary:

Just before last night's camp we crossed the 88th parallel, and this morning our 1100th kilometre ticked over. We expect to do another 26 kilometres, which will mean that sometime during the final shift we will pass under 200 kilometres left. This still seems like a very long way, but soon we will enter the final circle of 89°. With 100 to go, then I might feel like we are on the home straight. Objectively, there is now little doubt that we will get there, it is just a matter of when.

The sundial shadow tells me the lads have stopped now and will be pitching the tent. There is now an end point to the day, and as long as I keep placing one foot in front of the other, I will get there.

We had a wonderful surprise on the radio this evening. Not only did John and Jennifer call on the satphone to wish us a happy Christmas, but so did Beth, Leanne and Marianne. Reception was poor, but it was so moving to hear the voices of my family and to know that they were all okay and thinking of me that a tear came to my eye.

25 DECEMBER

Christmas Day, but it was no holiday for us, just another day in the straps.

As had become customary, I got away early and led the first shift, but it was very slow and the others soon caught up. Peter and Keith then each took a lead before sharing the last one of the day. I caught them briefly as they finished their second break, then watched them pull away into the distance as I sat eating my biscuits. We had no further contact until I reached camp, although we could see each other on the horizon. At one point as I tramped through the lonely afternoon, I had to fight a sudden urge just to stop and sit down. It all seemed too much. We ended the day with another swag of sastrugi. Nothing gives up easily in Antarctica. I wrote: "It seems that our vision of striding the last degree or two to the Pole over flat, wind-polished plastic snow, the sleds skipping along behind, will be forlorn. Every step will have to be won."

After our regular dinner, we celebrated Christmas with a small pack of honeyed cashews and a special block of chocolate.

26 DECEMBER

My diary:

Perhaps the dark days are coming to an end. The ground has really flattened out and the snow texture is quite good. Pleasant travelling at last!

Have we reached the Promised Land? I can imagine Børge flying across these plains into the Pole, way ahead of schedule and with a big smile on his face.

The weather was calm and balmy. I was able to sit on my sled at the last break, hands bare and pants around my knees, making running repairs to the bandages. I discovered why my legs had been particularly sore all day: plasma was leaking from the wounds, caking on the outer bandages and abrading tender, slightly frost-damaged skin beyond the main wounds. I taped the spots up.

Kate advised me by radio to keep the wounds dry with cloth dressings.

27 DECEMBER.

A harrowing day of −21°C and wind in our faces. Because our supply of bandages was dwindling, I decided to leave the leaking dressings for another day before changing them. I soon regretted the parsimony. The synthetic skin began to come adrift as a result of all the fluid, and the dried plasma chewed into the skin with every step. I had to stop three times to fix the problem.

During the second shift I got into the "cone of silence" to do a proper job while the others, somewhere ahead, cooled their heels at their rest stop for 40 minutes, growing miserable. It was a choice between losing time solving the problem or hobbling on, getting lamer and slower and maybe not finishing the day. I decided not to let the bandages get bad again. As I approached the others, Peter skied back without his sled to find out what was wrong. He asked if it was okay if they moved off straight away and kept going until it was time to camp. I said it was. He turned to go but then looked back.

"Are your legs going to be okay for the rest of the trip?" he asked.

What could I say except that I hoped the problem would not recur? Before I reached the rest stop the others had begun moving ahead to get warm.

It was a long slog through the afternoon. I focused on my ski-tips, wishing my skis, like Børge's, had pictures painted on them by my children. At 6.30 p.m. I looked ahead but could see nothing breaking the white horizon: no people, no tent. I must have a long way to go. I knew the extra time that Peter and Keith had spent waiting for me earlier would be added to the last shift in order to make the full 10 hours. To avoid being disheartened by the distance to the tent, I resolved not to look up again until the tracks led me into it. Slide, slide, slide, slide. I concentrated on planning a complete refit of my dressings, which I would carry out in the tent.

Nearly an hour later, for no apparent reason, I lifted my eyes to discover the tent just 10 m away.

Peter's diary:

I woke up with a toothache in the bottom back molar. It's the tooth that I lost the filling in and have tried before to fill. This morning I filled it again and have eaten with the side of the mouth ... The only problem is that there is a hole in this side as well. The tooth remains very painful and I cannot chew on it as it hurts too much.

I found sledging today slow and tiring and was glad to find that we had done 26 km again. This leaves us on target for a 1/1/98 finish. There was some uphill on today's course and with temp of –21[°C] and breeze up to 25 kph straight in the face it was very cold.

Ian again proved to be a problem. At the second break we had to wait 50 min. We got very cold. From then on we didn't wait for him. He was over 1 hour late for camp. Keith and I had the camp up by the time he arrived.

I worked till midnight on my surgical masterpiece, cleaning away all the crystallised fluid from my wounds and constructing a durable bandage system that I hoped would withstand the rigours of hauling. I took a calculated risk and used nearly all the remaining dressings, reasoning that the next few days would be critical and, if I had to, I could limp to the end with any sort of bodgied arrangement. I put a frame of synthetic skin around the tender outside and cloth dressings over the raw areas and then secured the whole thing with strapping tape. It felt firm and healthy, once the hot pain of disturbance passed away.

Keith and Peter were asleep; it was quiet, and warm on the sunny side. I spent 10 minutes writing my diary and chewing on a chocolate reward. It was my own small time of peace and retreat.

28 DECEMBER

My legs enjoyed the new dressings, giving me little pain early on and suffering no collateral damage from bandage problems. But I just could not summon up any energy, and by the end of the day I felt totally flogged, my legs as sore as ever. Maybe my battery was simply running down. Unrelenting sand dogged our path, begrudging our every step. We had the wind in our faces all day, and for the first time my toes felt slightly cold after each stop.

We passed many milestones: 1200 km done; under 100 to go; and the final circle at 89°. Three more days to go before the final shift. The first of January was a sure thing on current progress. If we could push it at the end, a New Year's Eve finish might even be possible.

One problem was that part of our minds had already reached the Pole. The resulting psychological situation was unique and perilous: because we did not dwell fully in the present, unforeseen setbacks could throw us.

Some days earlier Peter had revealed, to our amazement, that he had been wearing a cotton T-shirt next to his skin ever since we had arrived in Antarctica. We persuaded him that it might be affecting his ability to keep warm, especially when sweating, and he decided to remove it. I was shocked when he took it off but didn't say anything to him. The smeared brown colour of the offending article was one surprise in the cleanest land on Earth. Another was the absence of the expected stink. But the real shock was Peter's body: his chest was thin and his arms scrawny and wasted. He was not quite emaciated enough to fit into a Burma Railway work crew, but he was well on the way.

We were all experiencing slight numbness in our fingers due to mild frost-bite, with two of Keith's being worse than the others and quite sore. Peter was still trying to mend his teeth in vain. Temporary fillings they certainly were: none lasted more than a day. One of his teeth had begun to hurt. Today I broke a tooth. We were the walking wounded. We needed to get to the Pole before any of those problems intensified.

Tonight the Icelanders were about 7 km closer to the Pole than we were. In the Australian camp, we said how funny it would be to arrive at the same time, having slowly converged on that special point. Both teams had originally planned to fly out in the Cessna, possibly leaving some equipment behind temporarily. If we were all there at the same time, ANI could send the Twin Otter and we could depart with all our gear. Both we and ANI were in contact with the US base at the Pole, and the staff there were aware we were coming.

29 DECEMBER

Keith's diary:
Good snow at long long long last.

The weather was benign and my first shift went well, the other guys catching up only at the end of it. I felt re-energised: my legs were less sore and my sled was lighter by another 4 kg (it was my food bag day). But for the rest of the day I lagged behind in my usual way, shuffling into camp more than an hour late. Keith and Peter had some time ago eliminated all mid-shift breaks unless unavoidable. I could not emulate them, although my stops by now were always brief. We did 28 km today over some very good silky snow, even some plastic. We were homing in on that spinning axis at the end of the world.

Peter's diary:

We had 4 good sessions with even Ian's session going faster...We are having daily schedules with the radio so that PH [Patriot Hills] can monitor our progress against the Icelanders so that a pick up can be arranged.

I lost yet another filling at lunch time. This makes 4 in all. I'm not sure if it can be filled or not. I hope that a toothache does not develop. I intend to change my eating habits ... for lunch I'll use my bowl and add the biscuits to the water and add the chocolate to this.

30 DECEMBER

Late in the afternoon the terrain became almost flat, but for some reason I could not see the tent. With less than an hour to go to the end of the hauling day, it should have been visible. I theorised there was some slight intervening bumpiness. The dull overcast sky had spawned a rising crosswind. Spindrift blew over my skis and the tracks were beginning to drift over. I was tending to get hungry late in the day – from not spending enough time eating – and more susceptible to the cold. My hands were cooling, so I hoped I would reach camp soon.

Strange rumblings in my abdomen suddenly turned into cramps. My gut was in turmoil and I was forced by the worst pangs to stop and double up. My speed dropped another notch, along with heat production. I suspected the foul wind I was emitting was the result of the antibiotics upsetting my digestion. Perhaps I should not have had the second course. If I was not digesting food properly, I would also not be harvesting all of the energy from our diet.

Still no sight of camp. I was becoming slightly alarmed, and again I thought about bivvying in my sled. If I did, the other guys' tracks would be swept away and I would have to set the Argos off to indicate my position to Sydney. Keith and Peter could then get the coordinates through Patriot Hills and use the GPS to navigate to my position when the weather cleared. A risky option.

Fortunately it didn't come to that. I looked up to see the tent hovering above the drift like a black limpet on a silver rock. Its size told me I was about half an hour away. In spite of the debilitating cramps in my fermenting bowels, I went faster.

The last shift took me more than three hours. At exactly 7.45 p.m. my sled creaked to a halt and I wasted no time accomplishing the unpleasant task of erecting the radio aerial before crawling into the shelter.

We did 28 km again. Only 35 to go. My diary: "The lads are talking about putting in a big day and walking right through, but it will depend on me – who wants so much to be there but maybe cannot do it!"

Peter was so keen to finish. In his diary he noted that we were now ahead of the Icelanders. He mentioned that we had discussed the possibility of walking the last 35 km tomorrow or, alternatively, walking most of it, camping and then finishing on 1 January.

> The guys appear to be very lethargic [Peter wrote] ... Ian's lead was very slow and I couldn't get warm. Hands and feet cold ... I hope we go all the way tomorrow, but Ian as usual is very slow and came into camp tonight 1½ [hours] after us complaining of stomach upset. There's always something wrong!

31 DECEMBER

New Year's Eve (Chile time). Peter's diary:

> There was some discussion in relation to how far we would go. I wanted to ski the 35 km to the pole. Ian didn't know if he could make it.
> We used the GPS at the end of each shift to ensure that we were on the right bearing. At the end of Ian's lead we had completed 6 km leaving 29 to go. Keith then took over and covered 7.5 km. During my shift which reduced the outstanding distance to 14 km, I saw the SP [South Pole] station about 22 km out. I was then more determined than ever to reach the station that day. This would mean a 59-day trip and an expedition completed within 1997.

We started the day under a clear sky with little wind, the thermometers fixed on −23°C again. Although my spirit was keen to make it all the way to the Pole, my body was already feeling weak by the first break. I expressed my doubts to the others. They went ahead, saying they would pitch the tent and cook dinner at the end of the fourth shift while waiting for me. Then we'd decide whether to push on.

During the second shift I began to struggle, suffering gut pains and sore legs and needing a toilet stop. The prospects of completing the journey without another camp did not look good. But as the day wore on, my afflictions eased and I was able to plug steadily, growing ever more confident as the kilometres passed under my skis. My muscles were still doing fine. I'd be okay if only I could keep the frostbite pain at bay.

The terrain dipped and rose gently, and I often lost sight of the others. I had long ago given up trying to wear glasses inside my goggles, so when a smudge appeared on the horizon and then quickly disappeared, I dismissed it as an illusion. Ice crystals were drifting down from the stunningly blue sky as if by magic, sparkling in the sun. More shapes appeared on the horizon. And stayed there. And grew larger. Peter's and Keith's tracks led straight towards them. I had no idea what the buildings of the US base would look like, and with no reference point to indicate scale, I thought I was seeing the tents of an out lying camp. Cold cloud darkened the sky and brought a light, frigid wind.

Near the expected end of the fourth shift I was feeling hungry and cooling down. Rather than stop and don more clothes, I decided to push on to the tent, where I could revive in comfort. By then I was sure that after a rest we would continue – to complete the greatest journey of my life.

I couldn't work out why the tent was not visible, until my brain suddenly made sense of the visual signals. Two of the odd shapes I'd been seeing turned out to be much closer than the others. They were Peter and Keith with their sleds. Bloody hell! They haven't put the tent up, I thought.

Drawing closer, I could see them huddling over the stove, sheltering from the wind behind their sleds under the metal-grey sky. It was 7 p.m. and they'd been waiting more than an hour. I realised then that no power on Earth was going to stop Peter from going on. I was happy to do likewise but dismayed that I would have to change clothes in the open.

"Why the hell didn't you put the tent up?" I screamed over the roar of the stove, ripping off my parka and putting on my down jacket. Gesturing at the fuzzy, grey shapes ahead, I said: "What the hell is that over there anyway?"

Peter answered excitedly: "It's the base, just seven kay away!"

I pulled some extra cooking gear from my sled and joined them over the stove. Keith was calmly stirring the pot as Peter danced around waving his arms to get them warm.

Peter's diary:

Our main problem was Ian who, as usual, was very slow. At the end of the 4th shift we had 7 km to go and could quite clearly see the SP. It was cold and blowing by this stage and Keith and I had to wait 11/2 hours for Ian to catch up. We had already determined that we wanted to push on to the pole that day. The wait for Ian was one of the coldest we had had…Ian was also agreeable to go for the pole that day so when we completed our meal I led the last section very fast in an attempt to warm myself up. My hands and feet had gone.

As Peter tore off, Keith and I packed up the gear and moved together towards the end of the Earth. I went slowly, contemplating success at last – and safety. Finally, the sense of disbelief that had accompanied me from Australia was ebbing – I would take those last joyous steps! I felt everyone who had backed our crazy dream was walking with us. A pride in succeeding after so many difficulties began to grow in me. We were indeed privileged: we were about to become the first people from our country to walk to the South Pole from the edge of the continent and only the fifth or sixth team in history to complete such a trek unaided by machines or the wind.

Keith and I spoke of the journey, recalling our joy in the mountains and the unearthly radiance of the wind sculptures. Though the hardships of the long trudge were already fading from memory, the beauty remained.

Keith occasionally drew ahead but then slowed to let me catch up. The snow in those last kilometres was perfect, some of the best of the entire journey. The tracks of snowmobiles began to appear. Having warmed up, we stopped to remove our extra clothing. Colours and shapes filled the horizon: the base was far more extensive than I expected. We were not sure which building we should be heading for. It seemed an inappropriate place to end a journey across the cleanest and emptiest part of our planet. An empty expanse of snow would have been more fitting.

We could see Peter approaching the first outbuildings and someone walking out to meet him. He filmed the base with the video and spoke into the camera, his excitement bubbling over at the culmination of a dream, of years of work and commitment:

> *I'm about half an hour to an hour out from the Amundsen-Scott Base at the South Pole. I'm just waiting for the other guys to catch up. They're about half an hour behind me. Half an hour to the South Pole! Wow! Three years worth of work and we're almost there. It's about 9 o'clock at night at the moment and if we do it today we'll finish in 1997 – the 31st of December 1997.*

Peter was cooling down. He left his sled and skied back to brief us. "Rodney, the Australian astronomer, came out to meet me and showed me where to go," he said. "There's heaps of people coming out!"

We could see them now. They were appearing from everywhere, on foot, ski, skidoo and even bicycles! At least 50 were coming towards us.

A kilometre from the base we met the first. They shook our hands and their cameras clicked. They'd been watching for hours as we crept across the windswept plain. I could hardly speak. As they swarmed around us and escorted us to the Pole, I tried to hold back tears, touched by the unexpected warmth of the reception.

At the Amundsen-Scott Base, which ran on New Zealand time, it was the small hours of New Year's Day. I had joked earlier that we would probably arrive unnoticed in the middle of the "night", knock on the back door of the dome and maybe rouse a nightwatchman and ask him to show us a spot in the snow where we could camp. I was almost totally wrong.

I found it hard going on the slippery, machine-packed ice of the airstrip. Peter and Keith waited for me for the last time, huge grins shining through their goggles. We entered the ceremonial circle of Antarctic nation flags, with all the colours of the rainbow whipping in the wind on bamboo poles, and stopped at last. The smiling throng, swaddled in thick jackets, gave us three rowdy cheers. I was profoundly conscious of the bond beyond words that linked people who chose to be in such a place. We shook hands and posed for the cameras. I was numbed by relief and satisfaction. My head swam with confused thoughts and emotions: the intoxicating sweetness of victory, the nearness of failure; the immensity of the journey we had completed; the difficulties we had confronted; the prospect of going home.

The nightmare was over – but so was the dream.

The visiting representative of the US National Science Foundation, Hilleary Everist, and station manager Dave Fischer gave us a warm official greeting. A woman stepped forward and produced a bottle of champagne from inside her jacket – where she had been keeping it to stop it from freezing. Since none of us drink, we didn't know what to do with it.

Still in a daze, the three of us were led to the main dome, down a tunnel to the interior – and to more shocks. Without skis, we tottered down the hard, sloping surface. We entered the mess room through a massive door like that of a walk-in freezer. The warmth hit us like a mammoth's breath. The timber and metal room was crowded, noisy and full of the smells of food, drink and humanity. I was reminded of a scene in the movie *Star Wars*, in which Han Solo visits an interstellar bar bustling with bizarre alien life forms. Everyone in the room turned to look at us and burst into spontaneous applause. Peter wrote in his diary that I was crying. I can't remember if I was, but I'm not surprised. I must have been smiling too.

His mouth encased in icicles of frozen breath, Keith sometimes couldn't get biscuits into his mouth. Temperatures constantly in the −20s and altitudes of nearly 3000 m made it a battle just to survive the final weeks.

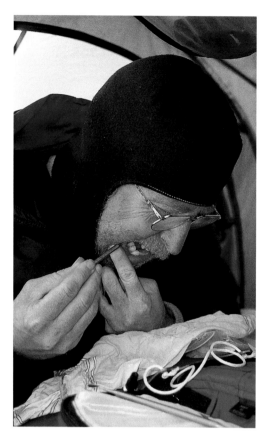

Worried a painful tooth abscess could develop, Peter
(above) repeatedly used a special dental kit to repair
fillings broken by rock-like frozen chocolate, but
the temporary cement always fell out again. It was
like a frozen carnival when we arrived at the US
Amundsen-Scott South Pole base (right) after walking
for 1317 km and 59 days. The Antarctic Treaty
nation flags flapped in the wind as a large crowd of
polar workers came out to escort us in from the cold.

226

*Satisfaction shines on our faces. Despite all the trials of the journey, Keith (left),
Peter (right) and I became the first Australians to walk to the South Pole, and
perhaps only the fifth team in history to get there on foot without any
physical assistance.*

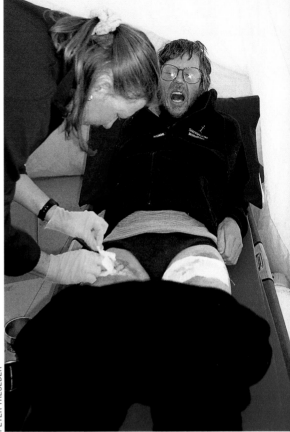

Pilot Steve King landed the Twin Otter at the Pole (left) on 3 January to collect the Icelanders and us. Under a solar parhelion, formed by ice particles diffracting the sun's rays, we haul our sleds for the last time. "You're a sight for sore thighs," I declared to ANI's doctor Kate Brown when we landed at Patriot Hills. In the medical tent (above), she painfully strips off stuck bandages and decaying skin killed by the frostbite.

EPILOGUE

The applause in the mess room reminded me that we had done something amazing. We'd ventured across a mighty land with nothing but what we carried – in our sleds and in ourselves. Three glowing embers on an ocean of coldness.

We weren't heroes, just ordinary people looking for the strength that waits in all of us. We weren't alone, a great wave of goodwill carried us forward. And we were a long way from flawless. The dream could have failed, if Antarctica had thrown more than a few hard times in our way, if we had been just a little less committed. Success was so much sweeter for the nearness of failure.

Reaching our goal and finding ourselves so suddenly in such a different world left us in a state of shock. We waited for nearly three days of bad weather for the ANI plane, enjoying the hospitality of the polar workers and copious quantities of cake and hot chocolate in the mess room. It was hard to return to our tent to sleep: the Polar Plateau had become a painfully uncomfortable place. I could understand how the intentions of past teams to walk the return journey had been demolished.

We found that Keith now weighed 61 kg (down 4 kg), I weighed 65 kg (down 9 kg, the skinniest I had been for decades) and Peter 67 kg (more than 6 kg down). We'd suffered other physical effects. When climbing the stairs to an observation lounge, we could hardly lift our legs. Despite our hard work in the sastrugi, our bodies must have sacrificed unnecessary muscles under caloric stress. My knees remained weak and wobbly for months.

Will Silva, base doctor and experienced mountaineer, attended to Peter's broken fillings and frostbitten cheek, and my frostbite. I had lost 150 sq. cm of skin from my thighs. Will diagnosed second- and third-degree (full depth) frostbite but was optimisitic the worst areas would regenerate without skin grafts. A month later they did, leaving scars as the only permanent damage.

The day after we reached the Pole, an announcement came over the public address system that the Icelanders were in sight. We rushed out to greet them. The shaggy, happy faces of Olafur, his son Haraldur and friend Ingthor were blistered and scabbed by frostbite.

The physical effects of our exertions were obvious, but the psychological impacts less so. The monotonous landscape we had crossed contrasted with the complex internal terrain that I was only just beginning to penetrate. Lying in our sleeping bags one "morning", Peter and I yarned about our roles and attitudes during the journey.

My diary:
Peter said that the pressure he put on me and my injury was deliberate, but he was never sure if it was right. He found the whole thing difficult because of the impact on our travel and the waiting. Overall he is much more relaxed and pretty satisfied with our achievement in 59 days. He said the doctor had congratulated us on holding it all together … he has seen other expeditions fall apart either because the injured person falls apart or the others can't handle the impact [of the injury].

It was a nice compliment, but the truth is we'd had no choice. I was still bitter about Peter's approach to the problem and told him that putting more pressure on me had not been useful. He said that at the peak of the crisis, when we had been contemplating evacuation, he had already decided I could have as much time as I needed to recover. I could not see how this attitude squared with his actions.

Peter said later he would adopt the same attitude again. Because at the end of the day we got there, he seems confident that he handled the situation well. I could not deny that Peter's drive had been an important component of our success. My concern was more with the way in which he had exerted his will.

There can be no right or wrong in something like this. Even with hindsight it is difficult to judge what level of Peter's focus – or pushing, as he calls it – was essential to our success. Three people had lived together for two months in a small tent, working all day, every day to achieve a difficult task in demanding physical and mental conditions. It would have been remarkable if we had been in complete harmony. Three individuals had struggled to operate in the way that was best for them. Perhaps it was the only way each of us had been able to cope with the journey's stresses. I can see that Peter might need to set himself immutable deadlines in order to harness his incredible energy. Such a strategy may be less effective when he is travelling with others less capable.

On one point I have no doubt: without Peter's relentless drive and commitment, and John Leece's efforts, we would never have even started.

On 3 January the two Belgians blew in on the wind, having walked and parasailed more than 2000 km from Queen Maud Land. In a remarkable conjunction, all three successful South Pole expeditions of the 1997-98 season met at the Pole. The next day the Belgians continued towards the Ross Sea, where, on 10 February, they completed the sixth crossing of Antarctica and the longest ever on foot, a total of 3499 km.

Just as the Belgians were arriving at the Pole, the ANI plane touched down to collect us and the Iceland team. At Patriot Hills we had a joyful reunion with the ANI staffers; they were delighted with our success. As we left the plane, the sun was warm on my back. Next day a week of blizzards struck, confining us when we wanted to be home. It was a time to think of the future.

Peter had been planning his next expedition even before we reached the Pole. We had done it in 59 days, but Peter knew he could do it faster. He wanted to attempt something closer to the impossible: a trek right across Antarctica, with no support or parasail. No-one has come close to walking so far without assistance. It is twice the distance of the longest manhauling journeys ever achieved (of which ours was one).

I was thinking of a less arduous journey than our polar walk but one with the elements of challenge, discovery and scenic richness. I hope to have time for photography and contemplation, and fewer financial pressures. Sledging is an effective way to travel and I might try it again, but in the Arctic. Keith might join me, although he has other ideas, for the Himalaya and elsewhere. It is vital to have a feast of dreams waiting on the shelves.

On 11 January the storms calmed sufficiently to allow the Hercules to reach Patriot Hills. A hectic schedule then gave us only 12 hours in Punta Arenas to sort out our freight and other matters, then three days of flying to Sydney.

There, after running the gauntlet of the arrival lounge and hugging our families, we faced a media barrage. All the questions were straightforward, our answers almost banal. The videotape shows the three of us looking cheerful and healthy, but I felt diminished under the withering gaze of the public eye.

We had completed the journey, the second stage of the expedition. The third and last phase was just beginning: promoting the ideals and the positive outcomes we had embraced at the start by taking our story to the nation.

Following an initial presentation to members of the Federal Government at Thredbo in February 1998, Peter has taken his inspirational, polished expedition show on national tour (supported by Paddy Pallin Adventure Equipment and Peter's employer, the Commonwealth Bank). By April 1999, 121 audiences, totalling more than 41,000 people, all over Australia had heard his message of adventure, commitment, perseverance and responsible risk-taking.

These talks have raised more than $310,000 – to be distributed among the beneficiary charities, mainly the Victor Chang Cardiac Research Institute and

Tired but full of joy, Peter (left), Keith (right) and I waited out a week of bad weather at Patriot Hills before going home to the third stage of the expedition – and to dream of new journeys.

St Vincents Hospital Transplant Unit – as well as additional funds to help repay expedition debts. The expedition has been used as a major vehicle for promoting the values and benefits of scouting, with some activities raising more funds for Scouts Australia.

The third phase of our journey continues.

There will always be some regrets, over aims and ideals not achieved as we had hoped and about circumstances that we wished might have been otherwise. But we did, with the greater team, complete a wonderful journey, taking many people with us in spirit. We'll never know how many people smiled when they heard that we had reached the Pole or have been encouaged to grow just a little by our story. It is said that the only thing you can really do for another person is to inspire them. I hope we have brought a little inspiration into the world. In this way we may be able to offer some return on all those inspirations, great and small, that carried us across the white emptiness.

APPENDICES

EQUIPMENT

Anyone undertaking a long journey must balance weight against the risk of equipment failure. Everything carried must be essential, durable and as light as possible.

Our understanding of the potential demands of the journey was limited, so we adopted a wide safety margin. We took advice from experienced polar expeditioners. We carried replacements for any item that was either critical to success, unlikely to last the distance or prone to sudden failure or loss, such as stove, skis, poles, gloves and hats. For any item not duplicated, we took repair equipment and spare parts. We might have overdone the spares in some respects. More significantly, we could have eliminated some gear entirely, including most of the climbing equipment we carried for crevasse travel and rescue.

There was room for small improvements but all the key equipment – skis, sleds, tent, sleeping bags, stoves, GPS – performed almost perfectly. The prize for the most valuable piece of gear, gram for gram, goes jointly to our 10 g spoons and 32 g neoprene face-masks. Though on the heavy side, the huddle bag ("cone of silence") was almost a life-saver. I owe a personal debt to Keith's excellent medical kit. The booby prize has to go to the heavy radio and its batteries.

We obtained as much equipment as possible from Australian manufacturers and suppliers, with only the sleds, boots and maps coming directly from overseas. We owe special thanks to Paddy Pallin Adventure Equipment stores, which made or supplied most of our clothing, camping and climbing gear and gave valuable advice and support. Thanks also to Eveready Australia for camera and GPS batteries, Snowgum, which supplied other equipment, Rottefella for ski bindings and Mobex for help with the Casio watch-altimeters.

Item	details	no.	item weight	total weight
PERSONAL EQUIPMENT				
Sledging				
sled	2.3m Kevlar, nylon cover, titanium, ropes	1	16 kg	16 kg
hauling harness	shoulder/waist, padded nylon webbing	1	632 g	632 g
skis	Black Diamond Synchro X, 191cm,			
	Rottefella Super Telemark bindings	1 pr	2.64 kg	2.64 kg
binding cables	for Rottefella	1 pr	112 g	112 g
ski straps	safety attachment	1 pr	28 g	28 g
ski skins	50mm & 35mm Montana self-adhesive, nylon	2 pr	502 g	*(total)* 502 g
ski poles	Black Diamond adjustable probe	1 pr	584 g	584 g
crampons	Black Diamond Sabretooth	1 pr	962 g	962 g
bumbag	Macpac module	1	184 g	184 g
Sleeping				
sleeping bag	Paddy Pallin, custom Twynam + stuff bag	1	2.1 kg	2.1 kg
sleeping bag liner	vapour barrier - proofed nylon	1	250 g	250 g
sleeping bag liner	silk	1	130 g	130 g
sleeping mattress	self-inflating, 3/4 standard	1	724 g	724 g

Item	details	no.	item weight	total weight
sleeping mat	full-length closed cell foam	1	336 g	336 g
sleeping mask	black	1	6 g	6 g

Safety

karabiner	Black Diamond Big Easy Screw	1	58 g	58 g
karabiner	Black Diamond Hotwire	3	45 g	135 g
Prussik slings	5mm kermantle	1 pr	150 g	150 g
tape sling, long	Black Diamond spectra ,44"	1	58 g	58 g
sit harness	Black Diamond Alpine Bod	1	364 g	364 g
multi-tool	Leatherman PST II	1	190 g	190 g
whistle	plastic pealess	1	8 g	8 g

Clothing

boots	Alfa Arctic	1 pr	2.41 kg	2.41 kg
inner boots	Harjo wool felt	2 pr	300 g	600 g
overboots/gaiters	knee-length, insulated foot	1 pr	580 g	580 g
inner soles	various	var.		200 g
down jacket	Macpac Sundowner reflex, large	1	480 g	480 g
windproof jacket	Paddy Pallin custom, full zip, mid-length, 3 layer Taslan Gore-Tex, u/arm zips	1	890 g	890 g
windproof pants	Paddy Pallin Vortex, full leg zips, braces, 3 layer Gore-Tex	1	685 g	685 g
fleece jacket	Paddy Pallin custom, full zip, Polartech 300, u/arm zips	1	550 g	550 g
fleece pants	Paddy Pallin custom, full leg zips, Polartech 300	1	600 g	600 g
thermal top 1	Paddy Pallin Techcrew, Malden bipolar	2	225 g	450 g
thermal top 2	Paddy Pallin custom Techzip, Hivoid Grid	1	240 g	240 g
thermal pants 1	Paddy Pallin Techpants, Malden bipolar	1	280 g	280 g
thermal pants 2	Paddy Pallin custom Techpants, Hivoid Grid	1	178 g	178 g
socks, thin	Thermastat	10 pr	42 g	420 g
socks, thick	thermal/wool	2 pr	100 g	200 g
gloves, thin inner	Thermastat	3 pr	36 g	108 g
gloves, light	Black Diamond Windstopper	1 pr	94 g	94 g
gloves, heavy	Black Diamond AC GTX, fleece-lined Gore-tex	1 pr	328 g	328 g
balaclava, light	silk (IB and KW only)	1	20 g	20 g
balaclava, medium	Thermastat	2	78 g	156 g
bomber hat	fleece-lined Gore-tex	1	118 g	118 g
face mask	neoprene	1	32 g	32 g
goggles	Smith, double lens (OTG for PT/IB)	1	126 g	126 g
sunglasses	various	1	50 g	50 g
briefs	thermal	2	44 g	88 g
briefs	cotton, various	4	44 g	172 g
briefs	paper	25	7 g	175 g

General

vacuum flask	stainless steel 1 litre	2	700 g	1.4 kg
spoon	plastic	1	10 g	10 g
bowl	plastic 1 litre	1	58 g	58 g
watch/alti-meter	Casio G-Shock Riseman	1	66 g	66 g
neck-pouch	fleece, for battery-warming	1	22 g	22 g

Item	details	no.	item weight	total weight
diary, pens, etc	various	1	330 g	330 g
vitamin pills	various	many	800 g	800 g
face cream	30+ UV filter	1	126 g	126 g
lip balm	30+ UV filter	1	32 g	32 g
foot kit	anti-bacterial powder, alcohol swabs, etc	1	250 g	250 g
personal items	toothbrush, medications, etc	var.	170 g	170 g
		TOTAL FOR EACH PERSON		**39.65 kg**

GROUP EQUIPMENT

Camping

tent	Bibler Bombshelter + attic + mesh pkts	1	4.15 kg	4.15 kg
tent stakes	44cm aluminium	8	60 g	480 g
tent pole	Spare	1	244 g	244 g
tent floor insulation.	4 sq. m. x 3mm foam	1	600 g	600 g
snow brush	plastic	1	100 g	100 g
huddle bag	poly-tarp	1	900 g	900 g
snow shovel	Black Diamond	1	378 g	378 g
snow saw	pruning saw	1	200 g	200 g
pee bottle	Nalgene wide mouth	1	102 g	102 g

Cooking

large pot	aluminium 7.6 litre, + bag	1	754 g	754 g
medium pot	aluminium 4.5 litre, + bag	1	534 g	534 g
small pot	coated steel 2.2 litre + bag	1	472 g	472 g
pot stand	19cm aluminium, home-made	1	220 g	220 g
pot lifter	aluminium	1	70 g	70 g
stove Kit 1	MSR XGK-II Shaker, 1 litre bottle, 2 x fluid lighters	1	650 g	650 g
stove kit 2	MSR XGK-II Shaker, 1 litre bottle, 2 x fluid lighters (+ spares-pump, parts, cleaning)	1	730 g	730 g
fuel bottle	1 litre aluminium	2	216 g	432 g
heat exchanger	to fit medium pot	1	162 g	162 g
stove boards	plywood, home-made	2	206 g	412 g
cooking accessories	plastic funnels for fuel and water, wooden spoon, measuring spoon, plastic mug bailer, 100ml plastic oil jar	1 of each	144 g	144 g
stove fuel	1 US gallon (3.78 litre) can gasoline	12	4 kg	48 kg

Navigation, communication, weather

spherical compass	Silva 70UN	1	256 g	256 g
compass mount	chest, modified Silva	1	330 g	330 g
sighting compass	Silva 54	2	43 g	86 g
GPS navigator	Garmin 12XL, case, batteries	2	288 g	576 g
GPS manual	for Garmin 12XL	1	68 g	68 g
spare batteries	Eveready AA lithium	10	12 g	120 g
binoculars	Compact 8x20	1	178 g	178 g
Argos transmitter	TAT-3, + batteries	1	1.2 kg	1.2 kg

Item	details	no.	item weight	total weight
HF radio	Spilsbury SBX-11 (10 watts) + batteries, spare batteries, aerial	1	7.5 kg	7.5 kg
calculator	solar	1	70 g	70 g
expedition log	A5 notebook	1	308 g	308 g
map kit	maps, case, pens	set	800 g	800 g
anemometer	digital	1	180 g	180 g
thermometer	-30°C	2	15 g	15 g

Safety

Item	details	no.	item weight	total weight
ice-axe	Black Diamon Alpamayo 70cm + twist leash	2	940 g	1.88 kg
ice screw	Black Diamond 22cm/17cm	2	150+186 g	336 g
climbing rope	9mm x 50m kernmantel, dry	1	2.8 kg	2.8 kg
medical kit	bandages, drugs, dental, etc	1	3 kg	3 kg
alcohol	250 ml medicinal	2	250 g	500 g

Photographic

Item	details	no.	item weight	total weight
compact camera	Olympus mju-II + case	2	186 g	372 g
SLR camera body	Olympus OM1 & OM1N + straps	2	602+558 g	1.16 kg
SLR lenses	Zuiko 21mm, 50mm, 28mm, 35–70mm, 75–150mm	5	1.45 kg	total 1.45 kg
bags and pouches	for SLR equipment	var.	828 g	total 828 g
accessories	instruction book, light meter, spare batteries, flash unit, filters, lens caps, cleaning, etc	var.	802 g	total 802 g
tripod	mini-strap to ice axe	1	120 g	120 g
35mm film	Fuji Velvia and Provia 100	58	30 g	1.75 kg
video camera	Sony Digital Handycam DCR-VX100DE, + carry case + battery	2	1.9 kg	3.8 kg
video batteries	spare, rechargeable	4	180 g	720 g
video tapes	60 minute	25	40 g	1 kg
video battery charger	11 watt flexible solar panel + leads + charger	1	1.2 kg	1.2 kg
video accessories	various	var.	400 g	400 g

General

Item	details	no.	item weight	total weight
mementos	Mawson balaclava, Amundsen charm, etc.	var.	400 g	400 g
flag	Australian Geographic	1	54 g	54 g
sponsor logos	spare – cloth, adhesive	var.	90 g	90 g

Spares

Item	details	no.	item weight	total weight
skis	as above, with bindings	1 pr	2.64 kg	2.64 kg
ski poles	as above	1 pr	584 g	584 g
gloves, light	as above	1 pr	94 g	94 g
gloves, heavy	as above	1 pr	328 g	328 g
bomber hat	as above	1	118 g	118 g
goggles	as above	1	126 g	126 g
sunglasses	various	2	50 g	100 g
spare skin glue	Montana, tube	2	80 g	160 g
repair kit	general – ski, sled, clothes, small spares, etc	1	1.4 kg	1.4 kg

			Total group gear	99.63 kg
			Total for each person	33.21 kg

FOOD

The amount of fuel a human body needs for hauling a heavy sled for two months in extreme cold is substantial. It is a critical factor on such a journey. After much research, including looking at the experience of previous expeditions, Keith recommended a daily intake of 25,000 kJ per person to avoid substantial loss of body weight. Keith and Peter had needed almost 17,000 kJ a day to cross the Simpson Desert in 1996 without weight loss.

We also needed to keep the total mass of food to a minimum. This we did by excluding foods with water in them and including plenty of fats and oils, which yield the most energy per unit of weight. We had to be able to cook breakfast and dinner efficiently, and our daily sledging food had to be easily handled. After considering all this, Keith devised a diet of 17 food items. It proved very successful, being nutritious, balanced, tasty, efficient and simple to manage and prepare.

We lost a total of nearly 20 kg between us, which was significant but bearable. Weight loss varied between 4 and 9 kg per person as a result of physiological factors and of not eating the full allocation of food, especially in the early stages of the trek, when appetites were not up to consuming 25,203 kJ every day. Some expeditions plan for this with a reduced diet for the early weeks and more kilojoules for higher altitudes.

The food remained tasty throughout. Even the cravings normal on long treks were absent. The high olive oil content of all three meals caused no observable problems. Arnott's low-moisture, high-energy biscuits formed a major part of the diet. They contained the finest ingredients and continued to appeal after the expedition.

Health specialists at Blackmores checked the diet and supplied a range of supplementary vitamins and minerals, including vitamin C and E to help with iron absorption and body repair, Bioace Excell multi-vitamin complex, fish oil and ginseng for endurance. We took these, as well as

DAILY RATION ROUTINE

For one person for one day

breakfast: 1 1/2 cups muesli with 6 spoons milk and 41.6ml olive oil.
bowl of Milo: 20g sachet with 3 spoons milk.
vitamin/mineral tablets.

daytime snacks: 2 litres soup + 83.2 ml oil + 2 pkts biscuits (400g).

dinner: cup of soup, then one of;
a) macaroni (100g) and cheese (33g) + veg (23g) + 41.6ml oil.
b) rice pasta curry (83g) and noodles (28g) + nuts (30g) + sultanas (60g) + 41.6ml oil.
c) potato (114g) and soya grits or salami (30g) + veg (23g) + 41.6ml oil.

Each evening meal was supplemented with herbs and spices, plus more vitamins/minerals.
It was followed by a 50g fruit biscuit and bowl of Milo (20g) with 3 spoons milk.

total weight = 1217 grams per person per day x 70 days = 85.2 kg total each.
(comprising 151 g protein, 289 g fat and 646 g carbohydrate – plus fibre, moisture and ash.)
Total weight of food for three people for 70 days = approx. 280 kg (including packaging).

These rations provide an average daily energy supply of 25,203 kJ per person.
10% of this energy is derived from protein, 45% from fat and 45% from carbohydrate.
One gram of food provides on average 20.7 kJ. This compares well to other teams.

iron, in the weeks before the trek and during it.

We packaged food into daily portions, a laborious task that proved worthwhile. We needed special packaging for some items, in particular plastic pouches for the olive oil, which remained frozen throughout our time in Antarctica. We carried 45 litres of stove fuel but used only 30 litres. This worked out at 500 ml per day, which was quite efficient. Most cooking time was spent melting snow and heating water. We maximised

efficiency by using a pot with a wide base and placing shields around the stove to contain heat.

Many manufacturers generously supplied complimentary foods. We bought the rest from supermarkets. We owe thanks to Arnott's, Nestlé, Cadbury's, Continental, Blackmores, Meadow Lea and Unifoods for providing food items; South Corp Packaging and Arrowpak for packing the oil; and Leanne Williams for help with food planning and packing.

COMPARISONS TO OTHER SOUTH POLE EXPEDITIONS:

party	year	weight per person per day	x 70 days	energy	yield kJ/g
Scott	1911/12	980 g	68.6 kg	18,543 kJ	18.9
Amundsen	1911/12	975 g	68.3 kg	19,087 kJ	19.6
Swan	1986/7	970 g	67.9 kg	20,966 kJ	21.6
Stroud	1992/3	1092 g	76.4 kg	21,766 kJ	19.9
Australians	1997/8	1217 g	85.2 kg	25,203 kJ	20.7

RATION LIST

item	grams per person per day*	kj per person per day*	grams x 3 persons	grams x 70 days
muesli	150	2260	450 g	3.15 kg
powdered milk – Nestlé Instant Full Cream	100	2021	300 g	2.1 kg
biscuits – Arnott's custom made	400	7953	1.2 kg	8.4 kg
chocolate – Cadbury	100	2202	300 g	2.1 kg
hot Drink – Nestlé Milo	40	695	120 g	8.4 kg
soup – Continental Cup-a-Soup	52.5	976	157.5 g	11.03 kg
*wheat pasta – Maggi 3-min	33	515	100 g	7 kg
*rice pasta	27.7	406	83.3 g	583.1 g
*noodles – Maggi 2-min	9.4	147	28.2 g	1.97 kg
*potato flakes	38	532	114 g	770 g
*cheese – Parmesan	11	205	33 g	2.31 kg
*dried vegetables – mixed	15.5	188	46.5 g	3.25 kg
*sultanas	20	251	60 g	4.2 kg
*roasted cashews	10	243	30 g	2.1 kg
*soya grits or salami	10	188	30 g	2.1 kg
fruit bar	50	762	150 g	10.5 kg
olive oil – Meadow Lea cold-pressed	150. 2	5659	450 g	33.75 kg
TOTALS	**1.21 kg**	**25203 kJ**	**3.65 kg**	**245.57 kg**

Note: * Items not eaten every day are averaged over the whole period.

ROUTE AND NAVIGATION

In theory a straight southerly line would be ideal for a walk from the Weddell Sea to the South Pole, but in practice a number of direction changes are needed. After Berkner Island we took a more directly southerly route across the Ronne Ice Shelf to the Antarctic mainland and up the Ford Ice Piedmont to the escarpment of the Dufek Massif, part of the Pensacola Mountains. We breached the mountains at "John Leece Pass", beside Wujek Ridge. On the Sallee Snowfield, a plateau separating the Dufek Massif and Neptune Range on one side from the Forrestal Range on the other, we made several direction changes to avoid crevasses. On the Median Snowfield, at the end of the mountains, we took a straight line for the last 730 km.

The straight line from our starting point to the South Pole is 1290 km long. Our route totalled 1312 km, so even with direction changes it was very efficient. It was also remarkably safe, with few crevasses and only one very steep slope ("John Leece Pass"). Our total height gain, including height lost descending from the southern end of Berkner Island and from the Sallee Snowfield, was close to 4000 m. We wore crampons on only three sections, and we never felt the need to rope up for crevasse travel.

We navigated by GPS receiver and compass. From the GPS we got the position (latitude and longitude) of each night's camp and the bearing to be followed to the next entered waypoint, usually where the next direction change was required. The GPS also computed the distance travelled from the previous camp (in a straight line) and the distance to the next waypoint. Antarctica is well serviced with GPS satellites, and our receiver could access up to eight in under a minute, giving a high level of accuracy.

While travelling, we used a magnetic compass to follow the GPS's bearing. The compass needle became sluggish as we neared the geographic and magnetic Poles but did not cause difficulty. Mounting the spherical marine compass on his chest enabled the leader to maintain the straightest and most efficient course possible.

At each camp we activated an Argos TAT-3 transmitter to communicate our position (as well as the temperature and a simple coded message) by satellite to the support team in Australia. This information was then sent by phone and radio to the ANI base camp at Patriot Hills. Dead reckoning was a useful check, coupled with plotting our positions on the map.

Map coverage of the area we traversed was poor. Jet Navigation Chart JNC 121, at a scale of 1:2,000,000, covered our route but was topographically inaccurate. A German glaciological map at the same scale gave more accurate coverage of Berkner Island and the Ronne Ice Shelf, indicating areas of ice disturbance. The mountain areas were covered by several 1:250,000 sheets from the US Geological Survey, which seemed quite accurate within their scale limitations.

Our thanks go to GME Electrophone for the Garmin 12XL GPS navigators, Argos SIT in Melbourne for helping with the Argos transmitter and data acquisition, Macson Trading for helping with the Silva compasses and Professor George Bennett for navigation advice.

PHOTOGRAPHY

We recorded the expedition through still and video photography. Opportunities for photography on the journey were restricted by lack of time, cold that threatened frostbite to the hands, photographers being lashed to sleds, and restricted subject matter (the landscape, though often complex in detail, could be monotonous on a wider scale).

We carried two video cameras, in case one failed and also to allow for variation in viewpoint: Peter carried one and Keith the other, and all three of us filmed at various times. John shot both video and still pictures at Patriot Hills and Berkner Island. All of us were inexperienced video photographers and relied on the cameras' automatic exposure meters. An in-built neutral-density filter reduced the harshness of the light on bright sunny days. Both video cameras had identical zoom lenses that went from long telephoto to moderately wide-angle. On the long telephoto setting, camera shake was a problem because of the cold. It might have been better to carry two lenses, one with wider capacity, especially for scenes inside the tent. We strapped a small tripod to an ice-axe rammed into the snow to shoot some scenes inside the tent and take outside shots of the three of us. All cameras, video and still, had to be slowly warmed inside the tent to prevent lens fogging and frosting.

The digital video cameras and tapes delivered broadcast-quality results in a very light package. We recharged spent batteries within 12 hours with a flexible 11 W solar panel. Batteries lasted quite well provided we warmed them against our bodies before use. With the amount of filming we did – up to an hour a day – we never had more than one flat battery at a time.

For still photography we had four cameras – two Olympus SLRs and two Olympus mju-11

compact cameras Keith and Ian carried one of each. We used older mechanical SLRs with manual exposure metering to maximise reliability in the cold. Both the OM1 and OM1N performed perfectly, with only one battery change required for the internal light meters. We used 21–150 mm zoom lenses. These minimised lens changes and reduced the need to move around (towing a sled) when framing and composing.

The compact cameras performed well provided we kept them warm against our bodies, as all functions are battery-driven. The compacts could be kept handy, whereas we generally carried the SLRs in the sleds. Although we used some print film at Patriot Hills so that John could take photos back to Australia for the media, transparency film was used exclusively during the expedition: Fuji Velvia (ISO 50) in the SLRs and Provia (ISO 100) in the compacts. These films were very effective within the limitations of exposure latitude. It is always tricky to avoid burnout or loss of texture in snow exposures.

Thanks to Hanimex for providing all our Fuji still film, R Gunz Photographic for supplying the Olympus compact cameras, equipment servicing and various accessories, Showboat Entertainment and Sony for providing the video cameras and film and Colormaster for processing still films.

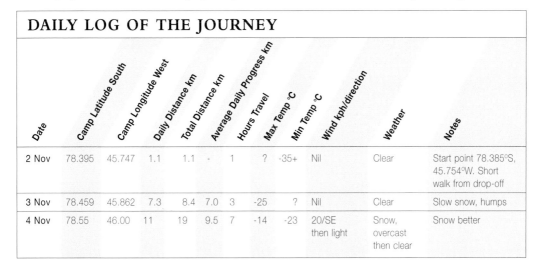

DAILY LOG OF THE JOURNEY

Date	Camp Latitude South	Camp Longitude West	Daily Distance km	Total Distance km	Average Daily Progress km	Hours Travel	Max Temp °C	Min Temp °C	Wind kph/direction	Weather	Notes
2 Nov	78.395	45.747	1.1	1.1	-	1	?	-35+	Nil	Clear	Start point 78.385°S, 45.754°W. Short walk from drop-off
3 Nov	78.459	45.862	7.3	8.4	7.0	3	-25	?	Nil	Clear	Slow snow, humps
4 Nov	78.55	46.00	11	19	9.5	7	-14	-23	20/SE then light	Snow, overcast then clear	Snow better

Date	Camp Latitude South	Camp Longitude West	Daily Distance km	Total Distance km	Average Daily Progress km	Hours Travel	Max Temp °C	Min Temp °C	Wind kph/direction	Weather	Notes
5 Nov	78.68	46.20	15	34	11.3	8	-12	-14	Light SE-calm 10/E	Overcast -clear-snow	Undulations, downhill
6 Nov	78.68	46.20	0	34	8.5	0	-12	-14	40/E	Whiteout, snowing	Weather day in tent
7 Nov	78.784	46.340	11	45	9.0	8	-15	-20	Light E	Overcast, snowing	Good snow, uphill
8 Nov	78.880	46.454	11	56	9.3	8	-13	-20	Nil	Clear then late overcast	Very uphill and humpy
9 Nov	78.992	46.631	13	69	9.9	8	-16	-20	20/SE	Clear then overcast	Uphill, cold, better snow
10 Nov	79.124	46.826	15	84	10.5	8.5	-16	-24	Nil	Clear	Uphill
11 Nov	79.272	47.080	17	101	11.2	8.5	-16	-24	Light NE-N-NW	Clear then fog	Beautiful fog
12 Nov	79.412	47.347	17	118	11.8	8.67	-19	-25	Light N	Clear	Slow snow, first snowquake
13 Nov	79.592	47.594	21	139	12.6	8.67	-14	-25	30/SW in a.m.	Snow overnight	Fresh snow, feet problems
14 Nov	79.766	47.955	21	160	13.3	8.67	-11	-15	20/SE in a.m.	Clear-overcast	Snowquakes
15 Nov	79.941	48.271	20	180	13.8	8.67	-15	-18	Slight	Clear	Uphill
16 Nov	80.115	48.617	21	201	14.4	8.67	-11	-18	Slight	Clear	Passed 80° and 200 km
17 Nov	80.308	48.971	23	224	14.9	9	-10	-15	Nil	Clear	Very warm
18 Nov	80.503	49.338	23	247	15.4	8.67	-3	-11	Nil	Clear-overcast	Downhill, very warm
19 Nov	80.705	49.774	24	271	15.9	9	-6	-6	Nil	Overcast-clear	Downhill
20 Nov	80.898	49.991	22	293	16.3	9	-5	-8	20/W in a.m.	Clear	Crossed Berkner coast c.1230 hrs
21 Nov	81.096	50.151	22	315	16.6	9	-10	-10	Light N	Clear-overcast	Passed 81° and 300 km. Sighted Transantarctic Mtns
22 Nov	81.306	50.269	24	339	17.0	9	-1	-10	Nil	Overcast-clear	Reached 1/4 distance
23 Nov	81.517	50.377	24	363	17.3	9	-10	-18	5-10/N-NW	Clear	Many snowquakes
24 Nov	81.700	50.448	20	383	17.4	9	-15	-18	20/W	Clear-ice haze	Very slow snow
25 Nov	81.914	50.565	24	407	17.7	9	-10	-15	15/ENE-10/W	Low cloud then high	Unpleasant wind in a.m.

Date	Camp Latitude South	Camp Longitude West	Daily Distance km	Total Distance km	Average Daily Progress km	Hours Travel	Max Temp °C	Min Temp °C	Wind kph/direction	Weather	Notes
26 Nov	82.149	50.753	26	433	18.0	9.25	-14	-18	15/SW	Clear	Crossed Antarctic coast 1000 hrs. Passed 82°. Uphill. Alt. c.370 m
27 Nov	82.428	50.838	31	464	18.6	9.5	-7	-12	Nil	Fine-overcast, snow	Great day, bare ice below pass. Alt. c.575 m. Passed 1/3 distance
28 Nov	82.539	50.893	12	476	18.3	9	-3	-8	10/E	Snow and cloud	Ascended pass 500 m. Alt. c.1175 m
29 Nov	82.787	51.203	28	505	18.7	9.33	-7	-10	5-20/NE	Cloudy, light snow	Passed 500 km. Snowquakes. Alt.c.1080 m
30 Nov	83.021	51.547	26	531	19.0	9.33	-10	-13	0-12/NE	Overcast-clear	Snowquakes. Gained 240 m alt. to c.1320 m. Passed 83°
1 Dec	83.245	51.830	26	557	19.2	9.5	-6	-14	Nil	Clear -overcast	Very poor light, up and down, snowquakes. Alt. Alt. c.1405 m
2 Dec	83.455	52.045	24	581	19.4	9.5	-10	-14	20/S-nil	Clear	Camp by last nunataks. Snowquakes. Alt. c.1500 m
3 Dec	83.664	52.065	23	604	19.5	9.33	-12	-16	Nil	Clear	Soft slow snow, downhill, snowquakes. Alt. c.1300 m. Passed 600 km
4 Dec	83.902	52.166	27	631	19.7	10	-10	-12	0-10/SW-S	Overcast-clear	Slow snow, up and down, a few snowquakes. Alt. c.1390 m
5 Dec	84.139	52.200	26	657	19.9	10	-10	-14	Nil	Clear	Sandy snow, snowquakes. Alt. c.1390 m. Passed 84° and halfway!
6 Dec	84.383	52.207	27	684	20.1	10	-16	-19	0-10/SE	Clear	Better snow, few snowquakes. Alt. 1430 m
7 Dec	84.654	52.253	30	714	20.4	10.5	-13	-17	0-5/SE	Clear	Good snow, sastrugi. Alt c. 1480 m. Passed 700 km and 600 to go

Date	Camp Latitude South	Camp Longitude West	Daily Distance km	Total Distance km	Average Daily Progress km	Hours Travel	Max Temp °C	Min Temp °C	Wind kph/direction	Weather	Notes
8 Dec	84.879	52.337	25	739	20.5	9.5	-13	-17	10-20/ NW-E-NE	Low cloud-whiteout. Snow	Good snow, sastrugi. Alt c.1600 m
9 Dec	85.109	52.328	26	765	20.7	10	-16	-20	5-15/NE-ESE	Clear	Slow snow, big sastrugi. Alt. c. 1700 m. Passed 85°
10 Dec	85.338	52.208	26	791	20.8	10	-18	-20	10-20/ESE	Clear	Some slow snow, sustained sastrugi. Alt. c.1750 m
11 Dec	85.575	52.154	26	817	20.9	10	-18	-20	5-25/SE	Clear	Better snow, avoidable sastrugi. Alt. c.1900 m. Passed 800 km and 500 to go
12 Dec	85.816	52.001	27	844	21.1	10	-19	-21	5-20/ESE-SE	Clear	Sastrugi belts. Alt. c. 2000 m
13 Dec	86.031	51.853	24	868	21.2	9.5	-16	-21	Nil	Clear	Much sastrugi, some slow snow. Alt. c. 2080 m. Passed 86°
14 Dec	86.276	51.784	27	895	21.3	10	-19	-21	10-15/SE	Clear	Open plains, some sastrugi. Alt. c. 2100 m. Passed 2/3
15 Dec	86.340	51.800	7	902	21.0	2.5	-20	-22	0-15/SE	Clear	Stopped by IB injury. Alt. c.2100 m. Passed 900 km
16 Dec	86.557	51.827	24	926	21.0	10	-20	-23	15-25/SE	Clear-overcast	Good going, slowed by IB. Ground blizzard. Alt. c.2075 m. Passed 400 km to go
17 Dec	86.770	51.904	24	952	21.2	10	-20	-24	15-25/ENE	Cloudy	Major sastrugi. Ground blizzard. Alt. c.2300 m
18 Dec	86.963	51 0971	22	974	21.2	9	-20	-24	15-30/NE-E	Cloudy, snow squalls	Some sastrugi, 'sand'. Ground blizzard. Alt. c.2400 m
19 Dec	87.169	51.990	23	997	21.2	10	-18	-22	5-15/NE	Clear	Sustained sastrugi, 'sand'. Alt. c.2450 m. Passed 87°
20 Dec	87.367	52.077	22	1019	21.2	10	-15	-21	5-20/E-NE	Cloudy then overcast then clear.	Sustained sastrugi. Alt. c.2450 m. Passed 1000 km

Date	Camp Latitude South	Camp Longitude West	Daily Distance km	Total Distance km	Average Daily Progress km	Hours Travel	Max Temp °C	Min Temp °C	Wind kph/direction	Weather	Notes
										snow showers	and 300 to go
21 Dec	87.586	52.227	24	1043	21.3	10	-16	-21	0-10/NE-SE	Cloudy then clear	Huge sastrugi. Alt. c.2450 m
22 Dec	87.796	52.316	23	1066	21.3	10.25	-20	-21	0-10/SE	Clear	Sastrugi belts. Alt. c.2550 m
23 Dec	88.027	52.387	26	1092	21.4	10.25	-22	-22	0-10/E	Clear	Mixed ground, undulations. Alt. c.2650 m. Passed 88°
24 Dec	8.261	52.568	26	1118	21.5	10.24	-16	-16	0-10/E	Overcast then clear	Better ground. Alt. c.2650 m. Passed 200 km to go
25 Dec	88.490	52.556	26	1144	21.6	10.33	-23	-23	0-10/E	Clear	Mixed ground. Alt. c.2750 m. Christmas!
26 Dec	88.728	52.481	26	1170	21.7	10	-12	-21	Nil-light/NE	Clear then overcast	Improving ground. Alt.c.2800 m
27 Dec	88.958	52.945	26	1196	21.7	10	-21	-21	0-25/SE-SSE	Overcast then cloudy	Some sastrugi, undulations. Alt. c.2800 m
28 Dec	89.182	53.334	25	1221	21.8	10	-21	-21	10-20/SE	Clear	Bumpy and sandy. Hard and windy. Alt. c.2880 m. Passed 89° and 100 km to go
29 Dec	89.436	54.030	28	1249	21.9	10	-22	-22	5-10/NE	Clear then overcast	Flat, improving snow. Alt. c.2900 m
30 Dec	89.687	52.207	28	1277	22.0	10	-18	-21	10-20/SE-NE	Overcast then clear Snow	Flat. Alt. c.2980 m
31 Dec	90.000	-	35	1312	22.2	12.5	-21	-25	0-10, E	Clear then overcast. Snow	Big day - S. POLE REACHED 10 p.m.!

Notes:
1. First day of journey (1 hour travelled) was not counted as a travel day.
2. Camp positions are as given by the GPS.
3. 'Hours travel' includes only time spent moving, excluding breaks - sum of leader's time for each hauling session.
4. The GPS computation of total distance travelled was 1317 km, due to rounding-off anomalies.
5. "Average Daily Progress" is averaged over whole journey to date (excluding 1 hour on 2 November).
6. Altitudes were derived from wristwatch barometric altimeters with minimal calibration by map. The true altitude of the South Pole is 2834 m.

FINANCE AND SPONSORSHIP

The expedition cost about $600,000, a staggering sum but less than many Australian entertainers and footballers earn in a year. Most of the money went on the flights to and in Antarctica provided by Adventure Network International. The flights from Patriot Hills to Berkner Island and from the Pole back to Patriot Hills were particularly costly because of the expense of delivering fuel to such remote places. Other major costs included insurance, equipment (especially sleds), commercial airfares to Punta Arenas and airfreight.

Raising this amount of money for a risky venture of uncertain outcome was an enormous task achieved only by two years of hard work coupled with strategic use of contacts and networks. The sheer size of the sum was a major hurdle in itself because people thought we could never raise it. Success depended on establishing credibility and gaining the support of key individuals, especially Prime Minister John Howard. We could not have achieved this without Peter Treseder and John Leece effectively articulating the expedition's aims – raising funds for charity and promoting a positive image of striving for success through inspiration and commitment. Also crucial was the special place Antarctica and Antarctic exploration hold in the Australian psyche.

We struck up key partnerships, with Scouts Australia in particular, that greatly helped us gain further support. As our credibility grew and momentum increased, each step forward rested upon previous wins. Despite a very slow start and numerous setbacks, the struggle to raise the funds progressed steadily after we got the support of key community leaders and the first significant offer of sponsorship. Once the expedition looked a going concern, it became easier to attract the many smaller supporters and product sponsors we

needed. Still there was not enough cash, and a benefactor who wished to remain anonymous stepped in at the last minute to help.

Three major corporate sponsors contributed most of the money, with others giving smaller amounts. Many more companies and individuals provided goods or services at no or minimal cost. Others have helped the expedition's achievements since the journey. One of the challenges resulting from the number of sponsors and the diversity of contributions was to deliver the exposure and other outcomes expected by each sponsor. The ability of the expedition to provide media coverage, a public speaking tour, a magazine story, a video and a book helped to meet these requirements. The level of support achieved and the amount of post-expedition activity would not have been possible if this had not been the first Australian expedition to attempt and succeed at such a journey.

MAJOR FINANCIAL SPONSORS

MAJOR FINANCIAL SPONSORS AND PARTNERS

Arnott's Adventures, Commonwealth Bank of Australia Ltd, *The Australian* newspaper, Scouts Australia.

OTHER FINANCIAL SPONSORS

Australian Geographic, Coles Myer, Roche Products Pty Ltd, KPMG, Boeringer Mannheim Pty Ltd.

PRODUCT SPONSORS and OTHER ASSISTANCE PROVIDERS

Paddy Pallin Pty Ltd, Snowgum, Argos Satellite Information Technology Pty Ltd, Arrowpak Packaging Pty Ltd, Blackmores Ltd, Borough Mazars, Cadbury Confectionery Pty Ltd, Colormaster, Continental Foods, Eveready

Australia, Foxtel, GME Electrophone (Garmin GPS), Hanimex Pty Ltd (Fuji film), Leo Burnett Connaghan & May, Lolly Pops (QVB) Pty Ltd Macson Trading Company Pty Ltd, Meadow Lea Foods Ltd, Mobex Pty Ltd (Casio watches), Nestlé Australia Pty Ltd, NSW Department of Sport and Recreation, NSW National Parks and Wildlife Service, Paterson & Associates Event Management Pty Ltd, R. Gunz Photographic Pty Ltd (Olympus equipment), Rottefella A.S., Rover Australia Pty Ltd, South Corp Packaging.

SOUTH POLE SLEDGING JOURNEYS

After Roald Amundsen and Captain Robert Scott led the historic first journeys to the South Pole in 1911-12, three-quarters of a century passed before anyone else tried to reach the southernmost point of our planet on foot. In the intervening years, machines came to dominate polar exploration, first in the air, then on the ground.

In 1957-58 the Commonwealth Trans-Antarctic Expedition made the first crossing of Antarctica via the South Pole, employing over-snow vehicles, dog teams and aerial reconnaissance. In 1980-81 Sir Ranulph Fiennes, Charles Burton and Oliver Shepard drove skidoos from Queen Maud Land to the Ross Sea to achieve the second crossing of the continent. As Antarctic frontiers were pushed back and it became obvious that vehicles were capable of almost any oversnow traverse, adventurers returned to the challenge of unmechanised journeys.

The new Muscle Age began abruptly in 1985-86 when Robert Swan, Roger Mear and Gareth Wood retraced Scott's route from McMurdo Sound to the South Pole. In 70 days they man-hauled all their food and equipment 1450 km, reaching the South Pole 74 years after Scott's team left there and died. They travelled without air or ground support, food dumps, sails, or even a radio. They had maps but navigated by the traditional compass and sextant. The purity of their approach set the standard by which all future journeys could be judged.

In the past 23 summers a remarkable series of mostly non-government expeditions has built upon these historic foundations. The following table summarises every known attempt at a major adventurous journey, but the bare statistics do not to do justice to the human spirit and sheer effort embodied in every one of them. As in all fields of adventure, the concept of the impossible has been steadily redefined by progressive advances in technique, equipment and, most important of all, boldness.

In 1988/89 the first women walked to the South Pole from Patriot Hills, as part of a commercial expedition resupplied by air - which also laid the foundations for Adventure Network International's support of most private expeditions since. Four years later an American all-women team completed a similar trek, and two years after that Norwegian Liv Arneson became the first woman to walk alone and unsupported to the Pole. Only one other woman has repeated this feat. Remaining challenges for women include the application of parasails, a journey to the Pole from the edge of the continent and a complete crossing.

For men, progress has been faster. Børge Ousland achieved a full crossing of Antarctica alone and unsupported in 1996/97, with a parasail. Two even longer (but supported) parasail crossings have been made since. A muscle-only crossing may yet be attainable, but wind-power offers the greatest potential for further advances. The last great journeys by dogsled were completed in 1990 and 1991, before dogs were permanently banned from Antarctica in 1994. Many of the greatest challenges in South Polar journeys have been achieved but, as ever, others wait beyond the white horizon.

MAJOR NON-GOVERNMENT ANTARCTIC JOURNEYS

1957/58	**Name**	*"Commonwealh Trans-Antarctic" (UK/NZ)*
	Route	Vahsel Bay (Filchner Ice Shelf) – McMurdo via S. Pole
	Dates	29 Nov – 2 Mar (99 days) **Distance** 3472 km
	Details	Large, complex expedition with govt funding. Ground vehicles, dogsleds and air support. Main traverse party (including 1st Australian, Jon Stephenson) led by Vivian Fuchs reached S. Pole 19 Jan and McMurdo 2 March. Route Vahsel-South Ice prepared 1956/7 summer. McMurdo–Pole route prepared by Edmund Hillary and party 1957/58, who reached Pole 3 Jan. 1st crossing of Antarctica and 2nd dog team to reach Pole

1980/81	**Name**	*Fiennes/Burton/Shepard"Transglobe"(UK)*
	Route	Sanae – Scott Base via Pole
	Dates	29 Oct – 11 Jan (67 days) **Distance** c.3600 km
	Details	Party of 3 – Ranulph Fiennes, Charles Burton, Oliver Shepard. Travel by snowmobile with air support. S. Pole 15 Dec 2nd crossing of Antarctica, longest at the time, 1st one-way journey.

1985/86	**Name**	*Swan/Mear/Woods "In the Footsteps of Scott" (UK/Canada)*
	Route	Ross Sea (Cape Evans) – S. Pole
	Dates	3 Nov–11 Jan (70 days) **Distance** 1405 km
	Details	Party of 3, unsupported (except for meals from USARP camp), 160 kg sleds. Reached Antarctica by private vessel and overwintered 1985. Repeated Scott's route via Beardmore Glacier. 1st foot journey to S. Pole since 1912, longest Antarctic journey on foot to date without parasails. Planned exit by own aircraft, but flown out by US aircraft when support ship sank.

1988/89	**Name**	*Williams, et. al. Mountain Travel/ANI*
	Route	Hercules Inlet – S. Pole
	Dates	27 Nov–17 Jan (51 days) **Distance** 1000 km
	Details	Large party, commercially organised, plane and skidoo support. 1st commercial exp. to S. Pole. 1st women to ski overland to Pole – Shirley Metz, Victoria Murden.

1989/90	**Name**	*Fuchs/Messner/(Germany/Italy)*
	Route	Inland (82.08°S) – McMurdo via S. Pole
	Dates	13 Nov–12 Feb (92 days **Distance** 2800 km(?)
	Details	Arved Fuchs and Reinhold Messner. Began inland (unintended). Start 82°04.99'S, 71°58.46'W. 2 resupply drops, parasails. Longest Antarctic trek on foot until Ousland 1996–97. Not quite 3rd Antarctic crossing, 1st without machine power. Exited by Italian ship.
	Name	*Corr/Williams/McDowell (US)*
	Route	S. Pole – Ross Ice Shelf via Scott Gl
	Dates	**Distance** c. 500 km
	Details	Picked up by ANI plane from Ross Ice Shelf as planned.
	Name	*Steger/Étienne et. al. "International Transantarctic"*
	Route	Seal Nunataks (Larsen Ice Shelf) –Mirnyy via S. Pole
	Dates	27 July–3 March (220 days) **Distance** 6400 km

	Details	Party of 6: Co-leaders Will Steger (US-45) & Jean-Louis Etienne (France-43), plus Victor Boyarsky (USSR-43), Qin Dahe (China-43), Keizo Funatzu (Japan-33) & GeoffSomers (UK-40). Dogsled, air support. 3rd crossing of Antarctica and longest to date. Exited via Soviet aircraft.
1990/91	**Name**	*Mørdre, et. al. "Shackleton's Dream" (Norway)*
	Route	Berkner Island – Ross Island via S. Pole
	Dates	24 Oct–5 Feb (105 days) **Distance** 2930 km
	Details	Party of 5: Sjur Mørdre, Simen Mørdre, Hallgrim Ødergård, Ralph Høibakk, Herman Mehren. Start c. 78.25°S on west side Berkner. Pioneered route from Berkner Is via Pensacola Mtns. Dogsled (11 dogs) to Pole (14 Dec) with air support. Mørdre brothers & Ødergård continued to McMurdo unsupported from Pole via Axel Heiberg Gl., by parasail c.400 km. 4th crossing. Exited via cruise ship. Last major Antarctic dogsled journey.
1992/93	**Name**	*Erling Kagge (Norway)*
	Route	Berkner Island – S. Pole
	Dates	18 Nov–7 Jan (50 days) **Distance** c.1300 km
	Details	Solo, unsupported, no sail. Start 78°17'S, 49°26'W. 120 kg sled. 1st solo journey to S. Pole. Flown out by ANI.
	Name	*Ranulph Fiennes/Mike Stroud (UK)*
	Route	Berkner Island – Ross Ice Shelf via S. Pole
	Dates	9 Nov–11 Feb (95 days) **Distance** 2170 km
	Details	Unsupported, some parasail. Start 78°19'S. 220 kg sleds. Pole 16 Jan. Planned a complete crossing. Evacuated 82°52.5'S, 170°48.01W by ANI – illness, short of supplies. Longest unsupported sled journey at the time. 1st to cross geological continent on foot.
	Name	*Ann Bancroft, et.al. (US)*
	Route	Patriot Hills – S. Pole
	Dates	18 Nov–14 Jan (57 days) **Distance** c.1000 km
	Details	Party of 4: Bancroft, Sunniva Sorby, Sue Giller, Anne Dal Vera. Resupply flights. 90 kg sleds. Planned a complete crossing, flown out by ANI from Pole due to injury/weather delays and lack of funds. 1st all-women team to walk to S. Pole. Bancroft 1st woman to walk to both Poles.
	Name	*Kenji Yoshikawa, et. al. (Japan)*
	Route	Patriot Hills – S. Pole
	Dates	11 Nov–16 Jan (66 days) **Distance** c.1000 km
	Details	Party of 6. Flown out by ANI.
1993/94	**Name**	*Im-Gyung Go, et.al. (Korea)*
	Route	Ronne Ice Shelf – S. Pole
	Dates	**Distance** c.1100 km
	Details	Party of 5. Flown out by ANI.
	Name	*Monica Kristensen et. al. (Norway)*
	Route	Bay of Whales – Shackleton Mtns
	Dates	**Distance** c.1800 km (900 km each way)
	Details	Large expedition with dogteams, ground vehicles, own ship/air support. Planned return journey to Pole via Amundsen's 1911/12 route. Turned back after death of one person in crevasse and US govt assistance.

1994/95	**Name**	*Hauge, et. al. "Unarmed to the Pole" (Norway)*
	Route	Berkner Island – S. Pole
	Dates	4 Nov–27 Dec (55 days) **Distance** c.1300 km
	Details	Party of 3: Odd Harald Hauge (1956), Cato Zahl Pedersen (1959–physically disability), Lars Ebbersen (1954). Unsupported, no sails, 4 rest days, 120 kg sleds. Flown out by ANI.
	Name	*Liv Arneson (Norway)*
	Route	Hercules Inlet – S. Pole
	Dates	(50 days) **Distance** c.1000 km
	Details	Solo, unsupported, no sail. 1st woman solo to S. Pole. Flown out by ANI.
	Name	*Susumu Nakamura (Japan)*
	Route	Hercules Inlet – S. Pole
	Dates	**Distance** c.1000 km
	Details	Commercial, skidoo support. Flown out by ANI.
	Name	*Militar Espanola (Spain)*
	Route	Hercules Inlet – S. Pole
	Dates	**Distance** c.1000 km
	Details	Flown out by ANI.
1995/96	**Name**	*Marek Kaminski (Poland)*
	Route	Berkner Island – S. Pole
	Dates	5 Nov –27 Dec (53 days) **Distance** c.1300 km
	Details	Solo, unsupported, no sail. Start 78.146°S, 45.112°W. 120kg sled.. Flown out by ANI.
	Name	*Roger Mear (UK)*
	Route	Berkner Island – Polar Plateau
	Dates	3 Nov–16 Dec (42 days) **Distance** 753 km
	Details	Solo, unsupported, parasail. Planned a complete crossing. Evacuated 83.438°S, 55.358°W by ANI-sled problems
	Name	*Børge Ousland (Norway)*
	Route	Berkner Island – S. Pole
	Dates	15 Nov–29 Dec (44 days) **Distance** c.1350 km
	Details	Solo, unsupported, parasail. Planned complete crossing. Flown out by ANI just past Pole.
	Name	*Bernard Voyer (Canada)*
	Route	Berkner Island – S. Pole
	Dates	9 Nov–12 Jan (64 days) **Distance** c.1300 km
	Details	Solo, unsupported. Start 78.595°S, 49.294°W. Flown out by ANI.
	Name	*Fedor Konioukhov (Russia)*
	Route	Patriot Hills – S. Pole
	Dates	8 Nov–5 Jan (58 days) **Distance** c.1000 km
	Details	Solo, unsupported. Start 80°1.27'S, 80°11.21'W. Flown out by ANI.
	Name	*David Hempleman–Adams (UK)*
	Route	Hercules Inlet – S. Pole
	Dates	7 Nov–5 Jan (59 days) **Distance** c.1000 km
	Details	Solo, unsupported. Start 80.300°S. Flown out by ANI.

Name	*Escuela del Montaña del Ejercito (Chile)*	
Route	Patriot Hills – S. Pole	
Dates	19 Nov–4 Jan (46 days)	**Distance** c.1000 km
Details	Leader Sergio Flores Delgado. Start 80.342°S, 82.204°W. Flown out by ANI.	

1996/97

Name *Ranulph Fiennes (UK)*
Route Berkner Island – Polar Plateau
Dates 14 Nov–12 Dec (28 days)   **Distance** c.700 km
Details Solo, unsupported, parasail. 227 kg sled. Start 78.052°S, 49.694°W. Planned a complete crossing. Evacuated c. 83.5°S by ANI – kidney stones. Travelled 188 km in one day.

Name *Young Heo Ho et. al. (Korea)*
Route Ronne Ice Shelf – S. Pole
Dates –21 Jan   **Distance** c.1200 km
Details Party of 6, unsupported, no sail, began well south of 78°S. Flown out by ANI.

Name *Marek Kaminski (Poland)*
Route Berkner Island – S. Pole
Dates 15 Nov–13 Jan (50 days)   **Distance** c.1300 km
Details Solo, unsupported, parasail (200 km), 200 kg sled. Start 78.036°S, 49.974°W. Planned a complete crossing, abandoned just past Pole. Flown out by ANI.

Name *Børge Ousland (Norway)*
Route Berkner Island – McMurdo via S. Pole
Dates 15 Nov–19 Jan (64 days)   **Distance** 2845 km
Details Solo, unsupported, parasail. Start 78.23°S. 177 kg sled. S. Pole 19 Dec. Travelled 226 km in one day. Fifth crossing – 1st unsupported, 1st solo. Longest unsupported Antarctic journey to date. Flown out by US/NZ aircraft.

Name *Laurence de la Ferriere (France)*
Route Hercules Inlet – S. Pole
Dates –19 Jan   **Distance** c.1000 km
Details Solo, unsupported. Flown out by ANI.

Name *Swan/Day/Somers "One Step Beyond" (UK)*
Route S. Pole – Cape Zumberge (Ronne Ice Shelf)
Dates 12 Dec–18 Jan (38 days)   **Distance** 1657 km
Details Party of 3: Robert Swan, Crispin Day, Geoff Somers. Unsupported, parasail. Finish 76°33'3"S, 67°57'6"W. Swan finished Thiel Mtns. Travelled 164 km in one day (4 Jan). Flown out by ANI.

1997/98

Name *Helen Thayer (NZ/US)*
Route Hercules Inlet – 81.551°S
Dates 1 Nov–22 Nov (22 days)   **Distance** c.170 km
Details Solo, unsupported, no sail. Planned journey to Pole. Evacuated 81.551°S, 80.643°W by ANI – head injury.

Name *Haraldsson/'Olafsson/ Bjarnason (Iceland)*
Route Patriot Hills – S. Pole
Dates 12 Nov–1 Jan (51 days)   **Distance** c.1084 km
Details Party of 3: 'Olafur Örn Haraldsson (50), Haraldur Örn 'Olafsson (26), Ingthor Bjarnason (47). Unsupported, no sail. 1st father and son and youngest person at the time to walk to the South Pole. Flown out by ANI.

Name *Treseder/Williams/Brown (Australia)*
Route Berkner Island – S. Pole
Dates 2 Nov–31 Dec (59 days)   **Distance**   1317 km
Details Party of 3:Peter Treseder (40), Keith Williams (40), Ian Brown (43). Unsupported, no sail. Start 78.385°S, 45.754°W. Flown out by ANI.

Name *Hubert/Dansercoer (Belgium)*
Route Queen Maud Land (Roi Baudouin) – Scott Base via S. Pole
Dates Nov–10 Feb (97 days)   **Distance**   3499 km
Details Alain Hubert & Dixie Dansercoer. Limited support, parasails. Start 70.634°S, Finish 77.874°S. Pole on 3 Jan. Travelled 250.8 on one day (5 Jan). Sixth crossing – longest on foot at the time. Flown out by US/NZ aircraft.

1998/99

Name *Ola Skinnarmo (Sweden)*
Route Hercules Inlet – S. Pole
Dates 5 Nov–21 Dec (47 days)   **Distance**   c.1000 km
Details Solo, unsupported. Start 80.007°S. Youngest person (26) to walk to S. Pole. Flownout by ANI.

Name *Groupe de Haute Montagne (France)*
Route Berkner Island – S. Pole
Dates 21 Nov–9 Jan (49 days)   **Distance**   c.1300 km
Details Party of 5 – leader Capt Thierry Bolo. Start 78.311°S. Unsupported, no sails. Flown out by ANI.

Name *Ronald Naar/Coen Hofstede (Netherlands)*
Route Queen Maud Land (Blue 1) – S. Pole
Dates 16 Nov–11 Jan (56 days)   **Distance**   2249 km
Details (+ 40 km past Pole to 18 Jan) Ronald Naar & Coen Hofstede. Limited support, parasail. Start 71.924°S. Planned a complete crossing. Flown out by ANI.

Name *Phillips/Hillary/Muir (Australia/New Zealand)*
Route McMurdo – S. Pole
Dates 4 Nov–26 Jan (84 days)   **Distance**   c.1450 km
Details Party of 3 – Eric Phillips (Aust.), Jon Muir (Aust.), Peter Hillary (NZ). Planned return journey by laying depots on forward journey, aerial support, NZ/US Govt support, new route via Shackleton Glacier, parasails. Flown out on US/NZ aircraft.

Name *Mitsuro Ohba (Japan)*
Route Queen Maud Land (Blue 1) – Ellsworth Land via S. Pole
Dates 12 Nov–14 Feb (94 days)   **Distance**   3824 km
Details Solo (age 46), supported, parasail. Start 71.910°S, Finish 76.363 °S, 96.762°W. S eventh crossing – longest solo, longest on foot. Flown out by ANI.

NOTES:

1. The data included in this review and table have been obtained wherever possible from primary sources, such as expedition books, websites and participants. The author attempted to contact all expeditions for verification and further information, but this was not possible in every case, especially for non English speaking teams. Other knowledgable persons have checked the data. Special thanks to Colin Monteath and ANI.

2. Groups that cross through the South Pole, and hence the International Date Line, lose one day.

3. Total distances are usually calculated as the sum of each day's travel, measured camp to camp in a direct line. Actual distance across the ground may be significantly greater in rough terrain.

South Pole Book Selected References

Cherry-Garrard, A. *The Worst Journey in the World*. Picador, London, 1994.

Fiennes, R. *Mind Over Matter*. Mandarin, London, 1993.

Gildea, D. *The Antarctic Mountaineering Chronology*. D. Gildea, Goulburn, Australia, 1998.

Hall, L. *The Loneliest Mountain*. Simon and Schuster Australia, 1989.

Kagge, E. *Alone to the South Pole*. J.W. Cappelens Forlag a.s., Oslo, 1993.

Martin, S. *A History of Antarctica*. State Library of New South Wales Press, Sydney, 1996.

Mawson, D. *The Home of the Blizzard*. Wakefield Press, Kent Town, Australia, 1996.

Mear, R. and Swan, R. *In the Footsteps of Scott*. Jonathan Cape, London, 1987.

Messner, R. *Antarctica: Both Heaven and Hell*. The Mountaineers, Seattle, 1991.

Murphy, J. *South to the Pole by Ski*. Marlow Press, St Paul, Minnesota, 1989.

Ousland, B. *Alone Across Antarctica*. Borge Ousland, Norway, 1997.

Antarctica. Reader's Digest (Australia), Surry Hills, Australia, 1990.

Scott, K *The Australian Geographic Book of Antarctica*. Australian Geographic, Terrey Hills, Australia, 1993.

Scott, R. F.(N. D.). *Tragedy and Triumph: The Journals of Captain R. F. Scott's Last Polar Expedition*. Konecky and Konecky, New York.

In Thanks

Numerous individuals helped the expedition with advice, information and practical assistance. To all of you a great debt is owed – the expedition could not have succeeded without you. Apologies to anyone who may have been overlooked from this list.

Pam Allan; Ian Allanach; David Armstrong; Marianne Bate; George Bennett; Hilton Bloomfield; Kate Brown; Nick Buchner; Matt Burgess; Greg Buttle; Matthew Clegg; Alex Colley; Ian Connellan; Blossom Conway; Philippe Courrouyan; Colin Craig; Joanne Cross; Les Cupper; Steve Cuthbertson; Phil Daffy; Tracey Dare; Roger Daynes; Fiona Dennis; Michael Depalo; Allan Donnelly; Graham Erbacher; Hans Fah; Michael Fenely; Ranulph Fiennes; Bryan Fitzgerald; Gaston Florian; Jennifer Foreshew; Drew Gafney; Kenn Gardner; Jennie Garrett; Ian Gibson; Brian Gilligan; Lyn Goldsworthy; Robert Graham; Lincoln Hall; Marion Hetherington; Belinda Hickman; John Howard; Ross Ingram; Gary Justin; Marek Kaminsky; Johnny Kaw; Paul Kelly; Anne Kershaw; Kathryn Killingback; David Kinchin; Steve King; Anne Leece; David Leece; Robert Leece; Stuart Leece; Martin Long; Desmond Lugg; Geoff Luscombe; Troy Magennis; Roger Mear; Colin Monteath; Joann Morand; Sjur Mordre; Nona Morrison; Greg Mortimer; Geoff Moseley; Wendy O'Keefe; Guan Oon; Chris Ortlepp; Borge Ousland; Brian Paterson; Anna Permezel; Brian Pezzutti; Steve Pinfield; Margaret Raynor; Campbell Reid; Chris Roberts; Tracy Scrimmens; Catrina Sewell; Rachel Shephard; Will Silva; Dick Smith; Pip Smith; Faye Somerville; John Sutton; Peter Sutton; Steinar Sveen; Charles Swithinbank; Andrew Taylor; Jane Taylor; Les Taylor; Linn Taylor;Jerome F. Tolson Jnr; Beth Treseder; Howard Whelan; Barbara Williams; Leanne Williams; Bruce Wolpe; Doug Woods; Shane Woonton.

Index

Spirit of Australia South Pole Expedition 1997–1998

was sponsored by Australian Geographic

Major Sponsors of the Expedition

SCOUTS AUSTRALIA

Commonwealth Bank

 THE AUSTRALIAN

ARNOTT'S ADVENTURES